Reading Iris Murdoch's *Metaphysics as a Guide to Morals*

Nora Hämäläinen · Gillian Dooley
Editors

Reading Iris Murdoch's *Metaphysics as a Guide to Morals*

palgrave
macmillan

Editors
Nora Hämäläinen
University of Pardubice
Pardubice, Czech Republic

Gillian Dooley
Flinders University
Adelaide, SA, Australia

ISBN 978-3-030-18966-2   ISBN 978-3-030-18967-9   (eBook)
https://doi.org/10.1007/978-3-030-18967-9

This Palgrave Macmillan imprint is published by the registered company Springer Nature Switzerland AG
The registered company address is: Gewerbestrasse 11, 6330 Cham, Switzerland

To the memory of Kate Larson 1961–2018

ACKNOWLEDGEMENTS

This publication was supported within the project of Operational Programme Research, Development and Education (OP VVV/OP RDE), 'Centre for Ethics as Study in Human Value', registration No. CZ.02.1.01/0.0/0.0/15_003/0000425, co-financed by the European Regional Development Fund and the state budget of the Czech Republic.

CONTENTS

Notes on Contributors

Hannah Marije Altorf is Reader in Philosophy at St. Mary's University, Strawberry Hill, London. She has written on the philosophical and literary works of Iris Murdoch and on different forms of philosophical dialogue. She is the author of *Iris Murdoch and the Art of Imagining* (Continuum, 2008) and together with Mariëtte Willemsen she translated *The Sovereignty of Good* into Dutch (Boom, 2003).

Gary Browning is Professor of Political Philosophy at Oxford Brookes University and Associate Dean of Research in the Faculty of Humanities and Social Sciences. He has written a number of books including *Why Iris Murdoch Matters: Making Sense of Experience in Modern Times* (Bloomsbury, 2018), *A History of Modern Political Thought: The Question of Interpretation* (Oxford University Press, 2014), *Plato and Hegel: Two Modes of Philosophizing About Politics* (Routledge, 2012), and *Global Theory from Kant to Hardt and Negri* (Palgrave Macmillan, 2011).

Anne-Marie Søndergaard Christensen is Associate Professor in Philosophy at the University of Southern Denmark. She has published widely on the philosophy of Ludwig Wittgenstein and ethics, especially Wittgensteinian ethics and virtue ethics.

Christopher Cordner is Associate Professor of Philosophy at the University of Melbourne. His main area of philosophical interest is ethics, including its classical Greek and Judaeo-Christian heritage, and its overlap with art and aesthetics. He is currently writing a book on simple goodness.

Gillian Dooley is Honorary Senior Research Fellow at Flinders University in South Australia. She has published widely on Iris Murdoch, Jane Austen, V. S. Naipaul and J. M. Coetzee. She is the editor of *From a Tiny Corner in the House of Fiction: Conversations with Iris Murdoch* (2003) and *Never Mind About the Bourgeoisie: The Correspondence Between Iris Murdoch and Brian Medlin* (2014).

David J. Fine is Assistant Professor of English at the University of Dayton. His research explores secularisation and ethics in twentieth-century British literature, and he has published most recently on the fiction of Catholic converts.

Niklas Forsberg is Senior Researcher and Head of research at the Centre for Ethics at the University of Pardubice, Czech Republic, and the author of *Language Lost and Found: Iris Murdoch and the Limits of Philosophical Discourse* (Bloomsbury, 2013). He is currently working on a monograph on J. L. Austin's philosophy.

Andrew Gleeson has taught Philosophy at the University of Adelaide and the Flinders University of South Australia. His main interests are in moral philosophy and philosophy of religion. He is the author of *A Frightening Love: Recasting the Problem of Evil* (Palgrave Macmillan, 2012).

Nora Hämäläinen is Senior Researcher at the Centre for Ethics, University of Pardubice, Czech Republic and the author of *Literature and Moral Theory* (Bloomsbury, 2015) and *Descriptive Ethics: What Does Moral Philosophy Know About Morality* (Palgrave Macmillan, 2016).

Mark Hopwood is Assistant Professor of Philosophy at The University of the South, Sewanee, Tennessee. He has published papers on a range of topics in moral philosophy including love, beauty, narcissism, hypocrisy and the nature of moral reasoning.

Megan Jane Laverty is Associate Professor of Philosophy and Education at Teachers College, Columbia University and author of *Iris Murdoch's Ethics: A Consideration of Her Romantic Vision* (Bloomsbury, 2007).

David Robjant wrote: 'Who killed Arnold Baffin?: Iris Murdoch and philosophy by literature', in *Philosophy and Literature*; 'What use is literature to political philosophy? Or the funny thing about Socrates's nose' in *Philosophy and Literature*; 'The earthy realism of Plato's metaphysics, or: What shall we do with Iris Murdoch?' in *Philosophical Investigations*.

Craig Taylor is Associate Professor in Philosophy at Flinders University. He is the author of *Sympathy: A Philosophical Analysis* (Palgrave Macmillan, 2002) *Moralism: A Study of a Vice* (Routledge, 2012) and numerous scholarly articles in the area of moral philosophy. He is a co-editor of *Hume and the Enlightenment* (Pickering and Chatto, 2009), *A Sense for Humanity: The Ethical Thought of Raimond Gaita* (Monash Publishing, 2012) and *Morality in a Realistic Spirit: Essays for Cora Diamond* (Routledge, forthcoming, 2019).

Fiona Tomkinson is Associate Professor at the Graduate School of Humanities, Nagoya University (since 2017). She previously lectured at Yeditepe University (1997–2017). She holds a B.A. and M.A. in English Language and Literature from Oxford University and an M.A. and Ph.D. in Philosophy from Boğaziçi University. She has numerous publications in the fields of literature and philosophy, including many articles on Murdoch, such as 'Between violence and contemplation: Iris Murdoch's Coleridge' (*Poetica* Spring, 2016). She is currently researching Murdoch's use of Japanese literature and myth, and the influence of Buddhism, Shintoism and shamanism on the work of Murdoch, Lawrence Durrell and Ted Hughes.

Frances White is Visiting Research Fellow and Deputy Director of the Iris Murdoch Research Centre at the University of Chichester, editor of the *Iris Murdoch Review*, and Writer in Residence at Kingston University Writing School. She has published widely on Iris Murdoch; her *Becoming Iris Murdoch* (2014) won the Kingston University Press Short Biography Competition.

Mariëtte Willemsen is Head of Studies of the Humanities Department at Amsterdam University College and senior lecturer in Philosophy. She teaches courses in Ethics and Modern Philosophy, with a focus on Schopenhauer and Nietzsche. Together with Hannah Marije Altorf she translated Murdoch's *The Sovereignty of Good* into Dutch (*Over God en het Goede*. Amsterdam: Boom, 2003).

CHAPTER 1

Reading *Metaphysics as a Guide to Morals*: An Introduction

Nora Hämäläinen and Gillian Dooley

Metaphysics as a Guide to Morals (hereafter *MGM*) was Iris Murdoch's major philosophical testament and a highly original and ambitious attempt to talk about our time. Based on her Gifford Lectures in 1982, it was reworked over a ten-year period before its publication in 1992. Her manuscripts as well as her correspondence from the period attest that this was not an altogether easy process, as Frances White reveals in the second chapter of this book. Her ambition was to do serious philosophical work, and yet to speak in a way accessible to the ordinary educated person about the cultural and moral predicament of largely liberal modernity: perhaps a nearly impossible task in the academic and compartmentalised context of late twentieth-century anglophone philosophy.

It is perhaps precisely the broader ambition that gives *MGM* lasting philosophical relevance and opens up dimensions as yet unexplored. Murdoch's earlier work resonates with contemporary turns in ethics towards 'vision' rather than 'choice', to virtues, to love and other

N. Hämäläinen (✉)
University of Pardubice, Pardubice, Czech Republic

G. Dooley
Flinders University, Adelaide, SA, Australia

© The Author(s) 2019
N. Hämäläinen and G. Dooley (eds.),
Reading Iris Murdoch's Metaphysics as a Guide to Morals,
https://doi.org/10.1007/978-3-030-18967-9_1

emotions, to the relevance of literature and art for morality. These themes are also present, and further developed, in *MGM*, but are complemented by a profound exploration of our condition as spiritual creatures in a secular world and as creatures who cannot avoid holding metaphysical views even in a post-metaphysical age. The book makes distinctive contributions to questions of ethics, the possibility of metaphysics in the contemporary world, spiritual life without god, the nature and relevance of philosophy, questions of style and sensibility in intellectual work, and the nature of evil in a secular world, among other things.

Many of these topics in Murdoch's work have been discussed by scholars in the past 20 years, but the influence of *MGM* has been significantly smaller than that of her previous work, partly because many readers find the book difficult and messy. The nature of the difficulty is, however, hard to pin down. It has something to do with the scarcity of metatextual instructions for reading, and the unfinished and circling character of many of the chapters of the book. But it also has to do with the ways in which her take on its different subject matters, and indeed on philosophy overall, differs from what most readers expect her to deliver.

Stanley Cavell (1981, 10) notes that in some cases you must 'let the object or the work of your interest teach you how to consider it'. *MGM* is undoubtedly one of these works.

Though well received by theologians, who appreciate her sustained engagement with the question of faith in secular modernity, *MGM* has not been a great favourite among Murdoch's large readership of literary scholars and writers. The slighting attitude to the book sometimes gets what to a philosophical reader looks like a comic twist, as when Andrew Wilson, in his keynote talk at an Iris Murdoch conference at Chichester in 2017, aired the suspicion that the effort of writing of the book 'broke' Murdoch, that is, prevented her from developing as a literary writer in her last years; as if it were indeed obvious that more or stronger novels would have been preferable to *MGM*. Part of the difficulty is related to the form: chapters do not always open up as systematic arguments. But this should perhaps bother the philosophers more than the literary scholars; the latter's problems may rather be due to the difficulty of getting a good grasp of what she is up to, a difficulty they certainly share with many philosophical readers too. This is where the present volume comes in, offering paths through different topics and chapters in the book, in thoughtful company.

In this introductory essay we attend to a few themes that we believe will be useful for readers of *MGM* and this book: some central topics of *MGM*, the formal and textual aspects of her writing, and the continuing relevance of the book for contemporary philosophy as well as humanist and social scientific thought more widely. At the end, we provide a short tour through the essays included here.

PHILOSOPHICAL AMBITIONS

Murdoch's philosophical ambition in the book is nothing less than a comprehensive view of the human situation at the time of writing: a historical situation of gains and losses, distinctive matters of concern, things we can 'no longer believe in', things we take for granted, fundamental commitments, inspirational images, and root metaphors.

It shows deep commitment to the idea, shared by younger contemporaries like Charles Taylor, that a deep and complex, historically aware understanding of our present is a prerequisite for an intelligent normative conception of our moral lives. As she puts it at the end of *MGM*: 'We live in the present, this strange familiar yet mysterious continuum which is so difficult to describe. This is what is nearest and it matters what kind of place it is' (*MGM*, 495).

It matters, indeed, in more than one way. It does so for us as people: for our lives, for how the world of our present opens up for us, what it allows us to do or be, what options it gives for us in practical, moral, existential and spiritual terms. But it also matters for us as philosophers, scholars, social scientists, and theologians who try to get a more objective view of some contemporary phenomenon. In these capacities our challenge is double: to inhabit our present and yet also understand it as well as we can, *in medias res*, without the cooling benefit of hindsight.

In a letter to the French author Raymond Queneau in 1947 Murdoch writes, 'the question is, can I really exploit the *advantages* (instead of as hitherto simply suffer from the disadvantages) of having a mind on the borders of philosophy, literature and politics' (Horner and Rowe 2015, 99). The advantages of this mind lie in its capacity to read her own present, and the multiple pasts embedded in that present, without reducing experience to its historicity.

In the introductory chapter to *MGM* she talks about our thinking taking place against a horizon that goes back to the Greeks (or so we are taught), and about the claims made '(for instance by Nietzsche,

Heidegger and Derrida)' (*MGM*, 2) that this horizon has been sponged away. She does not quite buy the common story of a modern, disenchanted world, devoid of metaphysics. But she doesn't have a ready alternative account either: *MGM* is framed as an investigation of this situation.

Sometimes art is better and quicker than philosophy at picking up what is happening to us. As she puts it in the oft-cited interview with Bryan Magee: 'Our consciousness changes, and the change may appear in art before it receives its commentary in a theory, though the theory may also subsequently affect the art' (Murdoch 1997, 22). In *MGM* both literature and visual arts have a continuous strong presence in a variety of roles: as objects of contemplation, as sources of insight, sites of existential and phenomenological discovery, as clues to the historical formation of our conceptions of ourselves and our world.

What is also useful for a reader to appreciate, is how Murdoch's literary sensibility is at work in the book. It is not so much a matter of the 'literariness' of the text itself, but of her style of handling her plural subject matters. While writing something well recognisable as somewhat essayistic philosophical prose, she reads her present as a novelist, seeking out moods, modalities, metaphors and complexities. She is taking the pulse of her present as much as making claims about it. This exploratory emphasis may also be seen as a key to what is interestingly 'political' in her thought: not her normative political views (which changed over the course of her life), nor any normative political theory (she did not present one), but her critical interest in, and ways of looking at the interplay of worldviews, mythologies, forms of personhood, moralities and societal visions, in philosophy, art and society at large.

RELIGION

In his essay 'Iris Murdoch and moral philosophy', Taylor describes two transfers in Murdoch's philosophy: 'We were trapped in the corral of morality. Murdoch led us out not only to the broad fields of ethics but also beyond that again to the almost untracked forests of the unconditional' (Taylor 1996, 5).

Answering to a latent need in late twentieth-century anglophone moral philosophy, the move from the corral to the field, from morality (action and obligation) to ethics (the good life) has absorbed a large part of the philosophers' attention to Murdoch. Connecting the narrower issues of what we owe to each other to the Socratic question of 'how one ought to live', to what we find or should find worthy, important or beautiful; to the inflections of moral personhood, and so on, she served as an inspiration for thinkers like Bernard Williams, Alasdair MacIntyre, Cora Diamond, John McDowell, Raimond Gaita, and their students and followers, as well as for the boom of philosophical Murdoch scholarship in the twenty-first century.

The path to the forests of the unconditional, though central for *MGM*, has for the philosophers been less interesting, partly due to the secular tonality of contemporary philosophy and the lack of a relevant frame in which to place her thought on these issues. Though they are as convinced as Murdoch of the idea that 'God does not and cannot exist', they have been less concerned than she was with the spiritual needs and propensities of their contemporaries. For theologians like Hauerwas, Schweiker and Antonaccio the further move seems to be at the centre of their interest in Murdoch. Taylor thinks that she is genuinely out in the wilderness:

> The forest is virtually untracked. Or rather, there are old tracks; they appear on maps that have been handed down to us. But when you get in there, it is very hard to find them. So we need people to make new trails. That is, in effect what Iris Murdoch has done. (Taylor 1996, 18)

He points out two things that he finds particularly useful in Murdoch's contribution. The first is the way she addresses the shift from a theistic world to one where what we used to refer to as God appears lost or difficult to access. What she shows above all, is that 'the forest' is still there, and that we can and sometimes perhaps must enter it.

The other point has to do with plurality. 'Even in so-called ages of faith', people find different articulations of the higher useful, appealing and true. Especially those who have a strong calling to the spiritual life, are likely to make their own ways. This plurality, and the unity in or behind it, are central for Murdoch's engagement with 'the forest' (Taylor 1996, 19).

Faced with the spiritual flatness of modern secular moral and existential thought Murdoch insists that 'we need a theology which can continue without God' (*MGM*, 511). Stanley Hauerwas has expressed the belief that 'she wants to replace Christianity because she has a better alternative' (Hauerwas 1996, 196), a watered-down Buddhist

Christianity of some sort, based on a rejection of the dogmatic dimensions of the latter. But this may not quite capture the seriousness of her sense that God has slipped out of our world: it is not as if she could choose some form of 'ordinary' Christianity instead. In the face of what she sees as an impossibility of doctrinal faith, she searches out the Christian tradition, along with other forms of spiritual thought and experience. Not only have good and evil, *pace* Nietzsche, survived secularisation. Also, the concept of sin, prayer, the humility of selfless attention, and the affirmation of something higher in the ontological proof can, she believes, be retained, to enrich our understanding of ourselves as moral beings.

The effect of her ventures into the forest is not one of making ethics more absolute and categorical, but rather one of making it more complicated, giving it more psychological depth and social and historical resonances. In the midst of these, she develops the picture of the human being as directed toward a unifying idea of the Good.

This does not, however, quite amount to anything we would necessarily want to call a secular theology. Her thinking about the human being's striving for the Good is also helpfully read in a context of modern thought on perfectionist cultivation of the self and of philosophy as a transformative practice, as we find it in the work of Michel Foucault, Pierre Hadot, Alexander Nehamas, and Stanley Cavell among others.[1]

METAPHYSICS

The issue of metaphysics in *MGM* is far from exhausted by Murdoch's concern for the role of religion. The questions of God and the transcendent are surely a part of it, because how we deal with them has crucial implications for what we understand the world to be fundamentally like; what kinds of things we take to be real, and what kinds of things, correlatively, unreal; what we consider fundamental and derivative; what can be 'true' and what cannot, etc. But there is more.

Murdoch's big question about metaphysics and morals, at work from her early essays to *MGM*, is how our conceptions of 'the real' affect our moral orientation, and vice versa. Metaphysics thus does not enter with the concerns for a transcendent good. All thinking, even in a disenchanted world, and even in twentieth-century anti-metaphysical philosophy, rests on metaphysical assumptions. A naturalist metaphysics is a metaphysics too. Although such metaphysics, and a worldview based on it, has been widely considered morally neutral, it has moral and other evaluative commitments built in from the start. It is also, like any metaphysical view, contingent and arbitrary in relation to the experienced reality it conditions. It is far from the only way of making sense of a world where secular morality and natural science define much of our understanding of what there is.

Moreover, it is perhaps not even a good description the world in which most of us live. Like the 'modern settlement' that Bruno Latour (1993) talks about, which wrongly postulates an impermeable wall between nature and culture, the naturalist metaphysics which excludes the good as something real is in Murdoch's view based on a misunderstanding of 'where we are'. Latour seeks to show that we have never lived according to this modern settlement. Murdoch insists that the good, as something absolute, is very much a real part of the lived reality of ordinary people (*MGM*, 412), and that they are not mistaken in holding this view.

Heeding the central role of Kant for Murdoch in *MGM*, one might be led to think of her as concerned with universal conditions of possibility for human morality and knowledge. This is the interpretive line taken by Antonaccio (2000) in her pioneering work, and many others have, until recently, followed her cue.

We suggest a reading of *MGM* more in line with R.G. Collingwood's suggestion in *An essay on metaphysics*: 'Metaphysics has always been a historical science; but metaphysicians have not always been fully aware of the fact'. The 'absolute presuppositions' that metaphysical questions deal with are by necessity historical ones: what people in given times and places have taken for granted, relied on, in their understanding of the world (Collingwood 1998, 58, 60). Twentieth-century philosophers have in his view scorned metaphysics because they have mistaken it for something else: the postulation of universal structures. The metaphysics he considers fit for his time is a descriptive metaphysics or a metaphysics of experience, an inquiry into historically specific absolute presuppositions; our own or someone else's. This kind of descriptive work is also the core of the metaphysics of *MGM*.

Like Michel Foucault, as he lays it out in his 1984 essay 'What is enlightenment?', Murdoch is thus more concerned with historical *a prioris* than with allegedly universal ones. As observed by Gary Browning, 'Throughout her works, she engages with the historicity of the present and reflects upon the past from which it has emerged' (Browning 2018, 2).

The forms of our thought; its images, tensions, connections and lacunae, questions and answers, are all subject to time.

But the descriptive story is certainly not the whole story in Murdoch's case. She finds philosophy necessarily involved in both a descriptive and, in a broad sense, a normative endeavour. It does not only describe what is: through its choices of words and emphases, it makes positive suggestions as to how we could or perhaps should see things.

Murdoch's descriptive work in metaphysics is thus combined, not quite with a normative, but with a self-consciously constructive metaphysical effort. For her, this is not a matter of formulating a metaphysical system (she certainly thinks that kind of metaphysics is impossible for the modern thinker), but of giving an affirmative account of the human being as irreducibly placed between good and evil, striving for the good. This constructive metaphysics is to be seen as fundamentally and necessarily premised on a robust descriptive understanding of where we stand metaphysically, morally, existentially and epistemically. There is no point in postulating a God if we no longer can believe in him. But the world we can see—that makes sense to us—offers different, often metaphorical, options of articulation, and we need to work with these.

Both the descriptive and the constructive metaphysics is for Murdoch a thoroughly pictorial business: of discovering the metaphysical images we live by and making use of images that carry our understanding forward in helpful ways.

Many of Murdoch's engagements with other philosophers reflect this concern for the pictorial aspects of both philosophy and 'vernacular' thinking. Five of the 18 chapters of *MGM* are explicitly built around particular philosophers (in one case a pair) and many of those which do not, still have a particular philosopher's contribution as their central material. Her readings are engaged, personal and often troubled, much concerned with the directions and tendencies of the philosophers' pictorial and metaphorical thinking. There is her familiar suspicion that Wittgenstein, in spite of himself, is hostile to the 'inner life'; the idea that Derrida is locked in a cage of language; the warmth and stickiness of Buber's I-Thou. A familiar experience, expressed for example by Anne-Marie Søndergaard Christensen and Christopher Cordner in their essays, is that her readings can be unfair or off key, and yet, at the same time, interesting in how they pick up a tendency, a colouring, that is indeed there.

Borrowing from Frances White, who in her essay talks about Murdoch's 'subliminal language', meaning her casual but revelatory use of expressions such as 'of course', it might be helpful to think about Murdoch as, in many cases, a subliminal reader, reading only partly for argument, and as much for spirit, direction, mood, underlying beliefs and tendencies. This is another dimension of the literary sensibility we talked about before: at work in reading her contemporaries and predecessors as well as her present.

TEXTUAL FEATURES

The epigraph of *MGM* is from Paul Valéry, poet and intellectual: 'Une difficulté est une lumière. Une difficulté insurmontable est un soleil'. Confronting difficulty is thus Murdoch's abiding preoccupation in this work, and the nexus between difficulty and illumination is posed as central metaphor. She later, in the chapter on the Ontological Proof, glosses Valéry's image: 'Valéry speaks of the sunlight which rewards him who steadily contemplates the insuperable difficulty. What is awaited is an illuminating experience, a *presence*: a case of human consciousness at its most highly textured' (*MGM*, 419). The context here is a discussion of prayer, and of 'the artist who, rejecting easy false mediocre forms and hoping for the right thing, the best thing, *waits*', and of the broader application of this to 'work and human relations' (*MGM*, 418–419). The paradox inherent in the Valéry image, combining the ideas of insurmountability and illumination, seems to be resolved in Murdoch's formulation of a 'reward' for steady contemplation.

But one might also imagine that Valéry, writing in France in 1942, had in mind something less comforting: the light cast by unbearable and intractable circumstances which could be as much a torment as a reward. Pickering describes his approach:

> A slippery, eminently refractory discourse replaces time-honoured literary devices and genres. In their place Valéry proposes a view of the literary work as a field for experimentation and potentialization, the dwelling-place of the mind as it constantly strains towards the limits of its capacity. (Pickering 1988, 51)

Although Valéry's circumstances when writing *Mauvaises pensées* under the Vichy regime differed markedly from Murdoch's life in Oxford half a century later, and his epigrammatic, hard-edged style is quite different from hers, there is something in her method that echoes his, as Pickering describes it. While Murdoch's contemplation of the manifold difficulties of her subject in *MGM* is typically characterised by patience rather than torment, and could hardly be called 'slippery', the usual conventions of discursive writing—introductions, conclusions, topic sentences—without being totally absent, are de-emphasised. Her approach and style tend to be calm and undramatic, one substantial sentence following the last, forming solid paragraphs, rarely less than half a page long and usually considerably longer. Long quotations are inserted with the briefest of introductions, if any. Many of these features of *MGM* would be challenged by contemporary editors, who insist that authors shape their work for maximum readability.

However, in *MGM* the patient reader needs to look not for the excitements of a virtuosic or shapely prose style, but to appreciate the steady progress of an intelligent mind confronting difficult material, following the myriad pathways laid down by her predecessors and putting them into conversation with each other, allowing their difficulties to light her way forward through the maze: 'a mind straining towards the limits of its capacity', as Pickering writes. Instructively, Murdoch writes that

> Wittgenstein accuses Schopenhauer of evading what is 'deep'. Schopenhauer may thus 'give up', but he recognises his obstacle, rushes off at a tangent, tries to wander round it, talks, even chats, about it, and can instruct us in this way too. (An insuperable difficulty may or may not be a sun, but it gives some light.) (*MGM*, 251)

This passage appears well into in Chapter 8, the second on 'Consciousness and thought', and within a few pages Murdoch has referred not only to Schopenhauer and Wittgenstein and (obliquely) to Valéry, but to Plato, Arthur Koestler, Rilke, Simone Weil, Berkeley, Hume, Derrida, Zen Buddhism and more, bringing all these diverse thinkers and ways of thinking into dialogue with each other. Perhaps Wittgenstein would disapprove of her methodology too. But the attractions and virtues of *MGM* are inseparable from its questing, exploratory, conversational style, which insists only on the importance of trusting that which can be precarious, illusory and insurmountably difficult.

It is significant that this Valéry phrase is also quoted towards the end of Murdoch's 1987 novel *The Book and the Brotherhood*, when Gerard Hernshaw is contemplating 'the book that he had to write' in response to the book of the title, the work published by the sinister Marxist David

Crimond (Murdoch 1987, 574). Several contributors to this volume (White, Tomkinson, Browning) discuss the links between *MGM* and *The Book and the Brotherhood*, which Murdoch was working on concurrently. Gerard thinks,

> Well, more often no doubt an insuperable difficulty is an insuperable difficulty. ... Perhaps indeed all that awaited him was a long and final failure, a dreary fruitless toil, wasting his energy and his remaining time to produce something that was worthless. (Murdoch 1987, 575)

It is indeed difficult to avoid making the link between the book Gerard is contemplating, and the book Murdoch was writing. Gerard, although a fictional character embedded in a narrative situation, is engaged here in very much the same kind of debate which is often staged in *MGM*: 'Yes, I'll attempt the book, but it's a life sentence, and not only may it be no good, but I may never know whether it is or not' (Murdoch 1987, 584). It is clear from external sources that she approached the task in a similarly dogged and determined fashion: in May 1986, she wrote to her friend the Marxist philosopher Brian Medlin that she was 'writing some philosophy which may be hopelessly bad' (Dooley and Nerlich 2014, 7). Medlin, though he inevitably disagreed with much that she wrote, found *MGM* 'a marvellously exciting book' (Dooley and Nerlich 2014, 183), and its subsequent readers, while often expressing similar reservations, share his excitement and admiration.

MGM FOR THE NEXT CENTURY?

Among philosophers and philosophically oriented scholars who have written about Murdoch in the past few decades, there has been a strong consensus about the contemporary import and freshness of her work. When engaging her 1950s critique of modern anglophone moral philosophy, many have felt that what she says is in many ways as relevant for philosophy in the early twenty-first century. In spite of the emergence of virtue ethics and moral psychology, for which her friends Philippa Foot and Elizabeth Anscombe have been key figures; notwithstanding the renewed interest the interface between moral philosophy and literature; regardless of Murdoch's complex influence on the following generation, especially through *The sovereignty of good*, these philosophers have found themselves struggling against a moral philosophy too narrowly oriented to action, choice, rationality and overt principles. In this struggle Murdoch has been a most insightful ally and will most likely continue to be so.

But how about *MGM*? It is far less clear that her thinking in this late work has been or will be put to work for critical reconsiderations of moral philosophy. A closer look at its different topics and engagements will, in any case, place us in a better position to assess its affordances.

On the theme of religion our contemporaries are likely to find her both wrong and right. The 'impossibility' of theistic religion that seemed given in a setting of late twentieth-century European modernity, among Oxbridge dons and London intellectuals, may not appear quite as convincing any more. With a growing presence of Islam in the west; with a continued societal impact of Christian movements in America as well as in Europe; and with a deeper understanding of the plural faces of modernity in different parts of the world, we might have reason to think that modernity is after all not secular in the sense envisioned by Murdoch. People, also in our time, can believe many things, and make sense of the world in quite different ways.

The ambitious effort to speak about a whole 'age' in a single book is a hazardous one, always risking insipid simplification. Isaiah Berlin (2013), drawing on a Greek proverb from the poet Archilochus, makes the distinction between intellectual foxes (who know many small things) and hedgehogs (who know one big thing). Murdoch, in *MGM* more than ever, is very much a fox who likes dressing up as hedgehog, enjoying thus the benefits of both temperaments. This is never clearer than in *MGM* and makes the book more durable than any well-rounded, definite account of 'her times' would be.

The purpose of this volume is to invite old and new readers to follow her tracks. It is scholarly in the sense that it gathers researchers who are well conversant with her work and asks them to engage seriously with her text. But it is not a collection of regular research papers. To achieve its diplomatic mission of making *MGM* more easily approachable, we have given it a quite particular design. The book consists of chapters where different authors do relatively close readings of different chapters, themes or sets of chapters in *MGM*. Some of the book's central themes are easily approached by attention to individual chapters of *MGM*, while other themes, such as her interest in education and in Plato's Timaeus, are scattered throughout *MGM*. Thus, we have made room for chapters on individual chapters of *MGM* as well as on larger themes, complemented by chapters which attend to Murdoch's overall style. The chapters are written for a broad audience of scholars, students and intellectuals with an interest in Murdoch's work, including philosophers, theologians, literary scholars and social scientists.

In Chapter 2, Frances White traces the beginnings of *MGM* a decade earlier in the 1982 Edinburgh-based Gifford lecture series on Natural Theology. White also makes visible the rhetorical effect of expressions in Murdoch's prose style that are so characteristic and common as to be hidden in plain sight. These unconscious verbal habits reveal aspects of Murdoch's beliefs and her relationship both with her readers and with her subject matter.

Niklas Forsberg then continues with a discussion of the first chapter of *MGM*, elucidating how the for many readers puzzling opening of the book introduces its central topic: conceptions of unity and disunity in philosophy, art and life. Murdoch is here fuelled by the sense that philosophers often fail to understand the proper roles of unity and disunity in thinking, and that a better grasp, with important theoretical and metaphysical implications, can be obtained by looking at these themes in a broader perspective.

Chapter 4 also concerns Murdoch's first chapter on 'Conceptions of unity. Art'. Fiona Tomkinson draws connections between Murdoch's idea of the unity of the work of art in this chapter and her discussion of Japanese aesthetics and the thought of Katsuki Sekida in Chapter 8, 'Consciousness and thought II'.

Craig Taylor, in Chapter 5, tackles one of the most insuperable difficulties in Murdoch's work, one which she concentrates on in her second chapter, 'Fact and Value'. He explores how Murdoch, while dismissive of the philosophical tendency to exclude value from the natural world, also sees a more interesting and laudable motif in some philosophers' insistence on separating fact and value: the desire to keep value pure and untainted by contingent facts.

The next two chapters both concern Schopenhauer. First, Mariëtte Willemsen looks at Murdoch's sometimes apparently contradictory view of Schopenhauer's philosophy, concluding that she finds a way of reconciling his empiricism with his mysticism. Gillian Dooley then takes a literary approach to *MGM*, following on from Frances White's chapter by looking at the rhetorical features of Murdoch's prose and her depiction of philosophers as characters, in particular how her stylistic sympathy with Schopenhauer affects her reading of his work.

David Fine continues the focus on literature with a discussion of chapters 6 and 8, 'Consciousness and Thought' I and II, and chapter 7, 'Derrida and structuralism'. He discusses Murdoch's uneasy relationship with Derrida and her ideas about the nature and importance of literary criticism, connecting her work to the present day post-critical trend in literary studies.

In Chapter 9, Megan Laverty brings to the fore the many ways in which, without being the explicit subject of a chapter in *MGM*, Murdoch's concern with education permeates her philosophy, in her discussions of other philosophers as well as her moral vision for a life of continuous truth-seeking.

In Chapter 10, Anne-Marie Søndergaard Christensen tackles one of Murdoch's most important philosophical relationships, that with Wittgenstein, as it is expounded in Chapter 9 of *MGM*. She argues that Murdoch's misunderstanding of some aspects of Wittgenstein's approach to the inner life led to an ambivalent attitude which prevented her from realising certain similarities in their thinking.

Hannah Marije Altorf then looks at a central concern of Murdoch's philosophy: the importance of imagination, which appears as the subject of Chapter 11 of *MGM*. Altorf also considers formal aspects of the book and how they affect the reader's approach, placing the idea of imagination (and its troubling companion, fantasy) in the broader context of Murdoch's thought.

In Chapter 12, Gary Browning takes up the question of Murdoch as a political thinker, as she comes to the fore in Chapter 12 of *MGM*, 'Morals and politics'. He investigates her distinction between a perfectionist morality for the private sphere, and an anti-utopian morality for the public sphere, focused on practical negotiations and the protection of individual rights. Browning also looks beyond *MGM* to Murdoch's novels, such as *The Book and the Brotherhood*, to confirm his reading.

Andrew Gleeson's chapter concentrates on *MGM* Chapter 13, 'The ontological proof', a controversial and difficult philosophical topic that has occasioned much discussion over the centuries. Gleeson shows how Murdoch reinterprets the 'proof' for the purposes of secular morality but criticises her for representing moral goodness (in analogy with God) as unnecessarily distant and intangible.

Chapter 14 is concerned with *MGM* Chapter 15, 'Martin Buber and God'. In his discussion of Murdoch's disagreements with Buber's religious thought, Christopher Cordner includes a detailed consideration of Murdoch's pervasive and pivotal metaphor of vision and her defence of this imagery against Buber's preference for that of 'encounter and dialogue'.

In the next chapter, David Robjant critiques Murdoch's interpretation of Plato's *Timaeus* as it appears throughout *MGM* as well as in earlier philosophical works. He sees two contradictory strands in her discussion, one arising from an argument with Gilbert Ryle about the theory of forms, and the other an allegory of the demiurge as artist.

Mark Hopwood then takes on one of the shortest chapters in *MGM*, 'Axioms, duties and Eros'. He disputes the interpretation of many commentators who see Murdoch as a prescriptive moralist, arguing instead that she is primarily concerned with describing the nature of morality. This chapter underlines Murdoch's commitment to plural vocabularies for conceptualising our moral lives.

Finally, in Chapter 17, Nora Hämäläinen looks into the Void, another very short chapter which follows on from the discussion of axioms, duties and Eros in Chapter 17 of *MGM*. In this chapter, Murdoch confronts the darkest aspects of human experience. Hämäläinen shows how Simone Weil acts as her guide in this grim territory, and discusses the implications of the contrast between their worldviews, one secular and one religious.

This collection of themes reflects the interest of a specific group of writers and some special concerns of the editors. Many good chapters of *MGM* are here left without treatments of their own, and many overarching or dispersed topics of the book are left for future exploration. If anything, we hope that the reading of this book can inspire further writing and new dialogues with Murdoch's late work.

One text in particular is missing here: it was to be called 'The inverted sublime' and to take its cue from chapters 4, 'Comic and tragic' and 11, 'Imagination'. The Swedish novelist, philosopher and passionate Murdochian Kate Larson (b. 1961) who was about to write it died, much too young, in June 2018. We dedicate this book to her memory.

NOTE

1. For a discussion on Murdoch, Hadot, and Foucault, see Antonaccio (2012), for discussion of Murdoch and Cavell, see Forsberg (2017).

REFERENCES

Antonaccio, M. 2000. *Picturing the human: The moral thought of Iris Murdoch.* Oxford: Oxford University Press.

Antonaccio, M. 2012. *A philosophy to live by.* Oxford: Oxford University Press.

Berlin, I. 2013. *The hedgehog and the fox: An essay on Tolstoy's view of history,* 2nd ed. Princeton: Princeton University Press.

Browning, G. 2018. *Why Iris Murdoch matters.* New York: Bloomsbury.

Cavell, S. 1981. *Pursuits of happiness: The Hollywood comedy of remarriage.* Cambridge, MA: Harvard University Press.

Collingwood, R.G. 1998. *An essay on metaphysics.* Oxford: Oxford University Press.

Dooley, G., and G. Nerlich (eds.). 2014. *Never mind about the bourgeoisie: The correspondence between Iris Murdoch and Brian Medlin 1976–1995.* Newcastle upon Tyne: Cambridge Scholars.

Forsberg, N. 2017. M and D and me: Iris Murdoch and Stanley Cavell on perfectionism and self-transformation. *Iride: Philosophy and Public Discussion* 81 (2): 361–372.

Foucault, M. 1984. What is enlightenment? In *The Foucault reader,* ed. Paul Rabinow, 32–50. New York: Pantheon Books.

Hauerwas, S. 1996. Murdochian muddles: Can we get through them if God does not exist. In *Iris Murdoch and the search for human goodness,* ed. Maria Antonaccio and William Schweiker, 190–208. Chicago: University of Chicago Press.

Horner, A., and A. Rowe (eds.). 2015. *Living on paper: Letters from Iris Murdoch 1934–1995.* London: Chatto & Windus.

Latour, B. 1993. *We have never been modern.* Cambridge, MA: Harvard University Press.

Murdoch, Iris. 1987. *The book and the brotherhood.* London: Chatto & Windus.

Murdoch, Iris. 1992. *Metaphysics as a guide to morals* (Abbreviated *MGM*). London: Chatto & Windus.

Murdoch, Iris. 1997. *Existentialists and mystics: Writings on philosophy and literature,* ed. Peter Conradi. London: Chatto & Windus.

Pickering, R. 1988. Writing under Vichy: Valéry's *Mauvaises pensées et autres. Modern Language Review* 83 (1): 40–55.

Taylor, C. 1996. Iris Murdoch and moral philosophy. In *Iris Murdoch and the search for human goodness,* ed. Maria Antonaccio and William Schweiker, 3–28. Chicago: University of Chicago Press.

CHAPTER 2

The Gifford-Driven Genesis and Subliminal Stylistic Construction of *Metaphysics as a Guide to Morals*

Frances White

FROM THE GIFFORD LECTURES TO *METAPHYSICS AS A GUIDE TO MORALS*

Iris Murdoch's journal entry for 25 June 1978 reads flatly, 'Asked to give Gifford Lectures. Rain' (Murdoch Journals, KUAS202/1/13). One would think she would be thrilled to be in the illustrious company of Gabriel Marcel, who, she noted in a letter to Hal Lidderdale in late Spring 1948, 'is to give the Gifford Lectures' (Horner and Rowe 2015, 109), and of her own mentor Donald MacKinnon. But her journals and letters show no delight. Quite the reverse. Indeed, it would be fair to say that Murdoch and the Gifford Lectureship did not get on. An uneasy relationship is evident on both sides. The ordeal was worsened for her by being postponed from Spring 1982 to late autumn because John Bayley broke his ankle and she would not leave him. To Philippa Foot on 20th April 1982 she wrote: 'As to those Giffords I am very pessimistic, and also *pressed* about the whole thing. If it hadn't been for John's mishap,

F. White (✉)
University of Chichester, Chichester, UK

© The Author(s) 2019
N. Hämäläinen and G. Dooley (eds.),
Reading Iris Murdoch's Metaphysics as a Guide to Morals,
https://doi.org/10.1007/978-3-030-18967-9_2

17

the whole beastly thing would be over, I would have done it in a crazy impetuous way! Now I see, as I laboriously rewrite, how *hopelessly* bad, indeed partly *senseless* it is!' (Horner and Rowe 2015, 490). As the time approached Murdoch felt increasingly oppressed, writing to Brigid Brophy on 28th September, 'I go to Scotland about Oct 24. I dread the whole business', to Naomi Lebowitz in early October, 'I have to go to Edinburgh (to lecture) in two weeks and hate the idea – I just have to keep thinking that it will be a relief when it's over', and to Foot again on the 17th October, 'I go to Edinburgh next week, curse it, except that the sooner it starts the sooner it will be over'. When she returned she told Foot, 'I am still experiencing *relief* that the Gifford Lectures are over, and that I don't have to think about philosophy' (Horner and Rowe 2015, 494–497).

It was not a happy experience for her. Anne Rowe and Avril Horner note her 'bitter disappointment' as she 'found it difficult to articulate her philosophical thoughts. She did not perform well' (Horner and Rowe 2015, 469–470). Her biographer, Peter Conradi, remarks that Murdoch 'wrote and rewrote the Gifford Lectures repeatedly, but found it hard to bring her thoughts together, and the audience, partly of good ladies from Morningside, shrank during the fortnight it took to deliver them'; hence in 1982 'a letter praising her Gifford Lectures which had profoundly dispirited her, was "one she had hoped for"' (Conradi 2001, 565–566).

The gestation of the lectures can be glimpsed through Murdoch's journals. She habitually writes in the left-hand margin 'N' for an idea for a novel, 'Po' for a poem, and 'Pl' for a play: now 'G' begins to appear for thoughts which will feed into her Gifford Lectures. Examples are:

- G Good/bad cf noble/disgusting. Justice cuts across is an idea of another sort (9 July 1978).
- Giffords. How God Enters Philosophy? (22 July 1978).
- G Q of turning the wheel you can touch. Eg civil rights in China. Cf Plato's justice. Do your own job (8 October 1979). (Murdoch Journals, KUAS202/1/13)

And on 6 April 1982, despairingly, 'Giffords. It is so <u>difficult</u> to say <u>just</u> what one has thought and understood and <u>no more</u>' (Murdoch Journals, KUAS202/1/14).

One problematical aspect of the film *Iris* is that the intellectual life is not visible: just having Judi Dench writing at a desk fails to convey what thinking is like (Eyre 2001). But working in the archive offers a visual impact of the life of Murdoch's mind, pulsating, creating, furiously THINKING. Murdoch thought a great deal about thinking, as did Heidegger (*Wass heißt denken?*) and in her novels she demonstrates the difficulty of real thinking. Early on there is an amusing but sharp comment in *The Flight from the Enchanter*, '"I think it must be difficult to think," said Annette seriously. "Whenever I try to think I just day-dream"' (Murdoch 1956, 126). The late 'baggy-monsters', written contemporaneously with *Metaphysics as a Guide to Morals* (henceforth *MGM*), revolve around characters tormented by thinking. John Robert Rosanov in *The Philosopher's Pupil* 'could *feel* the billion electric circuits of his frenzied brain, and how his mind slipped and strained like a poor overloaded horse' (Murdoch 1983, 135), and Crimond in *The Book and the Brotherhood* (1987) says 'we must think – and that's what's such hell, philosophy is hell, it's contrary to nature, it hurts so much, one must make a shot at the whole thing and that means failing too, not really being able to connect, and not pretending that things fit when they don't – and keeping hold of the things that don't fit, keeping them whole and clear in their almost-fittingness – oh God, it's so hard –' (Murdoch 1987, 299–300), and, most succinctly, 'Thinking is agony' (Murdoch 1987, 294), whilst Gerard Hernshaw, having read Crimond's book tells Rose Curtland, 'I must write *my own book*. I can see how to do it now. It will mean a vast amount of reading, and *thinking* till one *screams* –' (Murdoch 1987, 566).

Murdoch experienced this mental strain personally: reading the lecture drafts is to watch her toiling. As with Murdoch's letters the left-hand margin is wide and gets wider as the lines go down the page forming a diagonal wedge-shape. In that margin she adds thoughts for later inclusion in the main text. In the margin beside this passage—'The active, even effortful, contemplation of a harmonising organised quasi-thing expressive of feeling and thought: an elegant summing up of something understood'—which is trying to find the words to explain what a work of art is and what it means to apprehend and appreciate it, Murdoch writes the comment, 'It is very familiar but not easy to describe'. She went over and over her work writing comments and instructions to herself. She evinces anxiety about repetition and accuracy and passages are hatched out, lines drawn through sentences, sometimes straight, sometimes in a zigzag. There are frequent exhortations to herself to 'CLARIFY!' Other such marginal instructions and exhortations to herself include:

- 'Curtail all this'
- 'my italics or N's italics'
- '/New para'
- 'ref and check for quotation'
- 'Def of Gnosis, check. DESCRIBE GNOSIS!'
- 'Add' and 'Check'
- 'Cut this stuff?' on page which has been totally hatched out
- 'Translation of Noesis?'
- 'put earlier'
- 'fuse with above'
- 'blend into'
- 'Notes for Plan: check all in'
- 'Is LW's "stoicism" explained/explored elsewhere inside Gifford lec area?'
- 'cd cut para'
- 'Expand'
- 'Improve'
- 'Is this argument ok?'
- 'Rewrite this bit – working out example more clearly.' 'Work in.'
- 'Check Greek for all quotes here'
- 'Cut some? Rewrite 541-544 CONDENSING & clarifying the points, leaving the queries clearer. Cut the colour case or explain it'
- 'CUT THIS PLATO STUFF?' (Murdoch Journals, KUAS202/6)

Reading both these drafts of the Gifford Lectures and the subsequent *MGM* is to see an intellect at work, wrestling with the expression of ideas.

As Murdoch's lectures metamorphose into the book, changes occur. 'See IM on M&D in Sovereignty of Good' is written in the draft. But she does not quote herself in the final text of *MGM*. The audience at the Gifford Lectures was composed of professional philosophers and theologians. When she comes to rewrite the material for publication Murdoch aims at a less specialist readership, the intelligent and educated but not professionally academic 'common reader'. She was again despondent about her work on it, telling Lebowitz 'I am ... trying to finish a version of some old mouldy philosophy lectures (*no good*)' (Horner and Rowe 2015, 564). The endings of the first two drafts are different from each other and the ending of *MGM* very different again from either, seemingly aimed at a different audience. The close of the first draft is defensive:

my argument such as it is, is coming to an end, and perhaps has not been really an argument at all, but just a development and criticism of certain images (metaphysics is after all a form of art) and a sense of interrelated considerations. And of course as one comes to the end, one cannot help feeling that there was, in all this travelling and in all these encircling movements, an objective, a quarry, which was certainly once there, but now seems somehow to have escaped. (Murdoch Journals, KUAS202/6)

This image also appears in *The Philosopher's Pupil*: 'He pursued quarries into thickets, into corners, into nets, and at the end found nothing there. Such were his own images of his terrible addictive trade' (Murdoch 1983, 135). The close of the second draft focuses on art:

We need free and various art, ubiquitous art, a free literature, poets, story-tellers and a general practice of lucid eloquent technical prose. Art is the creation of the idiosyncratic individual of whom it is the mirror and preserver and guarantor. (Murdoch Journals, KUAS202/6)

But choosing to close *MGM* with words from Psalm 139 places the focus on her neo-theology:

Whither shall I go from thy spirit, whither shall I flee from thy presence? If I ascend into heaven thou art there, if I make my bed in hell, behold thou art there. If I take the wings of the morning and dwell in the uttermost parts of the sea, even there shall thy hand lead me, and thy right hand shall hold me. (*MGM*, 512)

Conradi notes that 'the official historian of the Gifford Lectures wrote a sceptical report on Iris's performance' (Conradi 2001, 566) and Murdoch's somewhat adversarial relationship with the Gifford Lectureship was revived a decade later when *MGM* was published. Scottish academics attended seminars at St Andrews to discuss the work: Murdoch declined to attend or to comment on the papers subsequently published as a *Theology in Scotland*, Occasional Paper, *Iris Murdoch's Giffords: A Study of the 1982 Gifford Lectures*. Robert Gillies' Introduction has a querulous tone as Murdoch has clearly given offence: 'the book lacks many of the social decencies which usually grace published Gifford Lectures. There are no frontispiece acknowledgements to the Gifford Bequest, neither for host university courtesies nor yet for the honour of being invited to present the Lectures'. Yet he has the grace to admit the powerful impact of *MGM*, saying that the book 'is a testing read even for the most trained and acute mind. It contains a vast, expansive scholarship embracing art, literature, history, theology and of course, philosophy. No one in that St Andrews seminar series was unaffected by the experience of encounter with this majestic volume' (Gillies 1995, 5). Michael Partridge's Introductory Comments are discerning: 'The work is ... constantly fed by the perceptiveness, sensitivity and experience of the novelist, immersed in the details of our lives. The writing is lucid .... one has the impression of an elaborate dialogue' not only with philosophers but also 'with more ordinary anonymous people (who also have their experience and reflections). In representing these last, her long faithful work as a creative novelist is effectively drawn on' (Gillies 1995, 11). He identifies the change in tone from the Gifford drafts, which read like lectures, expounding, explaining, making statements, to *MGM* in which Murdoch conjures up the sympathetic reader rather than the critical lecture audience by an increase in the use of 'we', drawing us to her. This is evident immediately in the opening sentences: 'we see', 'we intuit', 'we seem to know', 'we grasp', 'we assume', 'we could not infer', 'we fear', 'we want to transform', 'what we cannot dominate', 'we are now being told', and 'us laymen' which places her alongside the reader.

'PERFECTLY PERSUASIVE':
IRIS MURDOCH'S SUBLIMINAL LEXICON

I turn now to Murdoch and words, to her choice and use of words. My interest in what I call Murdoch's 'subliminal lexicon' arose when, reading essays from *Existentialists and Mystics*, my eye was caught, and my mind arrested, by two passages. The first, from 'The idea of perfection' is this:

> I would suggest that, at the level of serious common sense and of an ordinary non-philosophical reflection about the nature of morals, it is perfectly obvious that goodness is connected with knowledge: not with impersonal quasi-scientific knowledge of the ordinary world ... but with a refined and honest perception of what is really the case, a patient and just discernment and exploration of what confronts one, which is the result not simply of opening one's eyes but of a perfectly familiar kind of moral discipline. (Murdoch 1997, 330)

And the second, from 'The sovereignty of good over other concepts' is this:

> How can we make ourselves better? is a question that moral philosophers should attempt to answer. ... the answer will come partly at least in the form of explanatory and persuasive metaphors. (Murdoch 1997, 364)

Two words in these passages jumped out of the page at me: 'perfectly', used twice in the first quotation, and 'persuasive' from the second. I found myself thinking how 'perfectly persuasive' she is, and then realised that these are two words you come across frequently in Murdoch's writing. My initial marginalia read: 'Watch out for tell-tale word "perfectly": it conveys Murdoch's impatience with "nonsense", theoretical/ abstract thinking'. And then:

> Note word 'persuasive' and cf. her use of 'perfectly': Murdoch is a rhetorician in style who cajoles and persuades by argument and passion, rather than convincing by solid factual logic. Her philosophy has an artist's rather than a scientist's turn of mind. She believes in the ultimate truth of her convictions and has a moral seriousness and urgency of tone.

This marginal note of mine is not a new thought but rather a truism of Murdoch criticism. But what I found myself wanting to know was how is it done? How does her rhetoric work? What are her habits of speech and tricks of style which convey this passion, this seriousness and urgency? So I started to look.

You do not have to look far. You can start almost anywhere in Murdoch's oeuvre and soon stumble upon the same vocabulary, the quintessential Murdochian lexicon. I am not here concerned with the 'big' obvious carefully selected words which give names to the concepts she believes to be important. Such words include good, truth, love, art, imagination, value, thought, consciousness, language, metaphor, imagery ... the list could go on—it is the common coinage of Murdoch's philosophy and is scrutinised by professional philosophers. Maria Antonaccio's *Picturing the Human* is an excellent example of this form of Murdoch studies. But what I am interested in here is the 'small' words, the 'in-between' words, which are part of the sentences which discuss and link these big words and concepts. I will investigate these small words and the work they do, but before that I want to unpack the phrase 'subliminal lexicon'. The *Oxford English Dictionary* (1979) defines 'subliminal' as 'Below the threshold of sensation or consciousness: said of states supposed to exist but not strong enough to be recognized'. I think the lexicon (word list) I want to focus attention on may be said to be 'subliminal' in two ways. First, although there is no doubt that Murdoch is a highly conscious wordsmith who thought carefully about words, I suspect that Murdoch herself was at least partially unconscious of these 'small' words and the extent to which she uses them. I think they lay below the threshold of *her* consciousness. The second way may simply mean that I am slow on the uptake. They seemed to lie below the threshold of this individual reader's consciousness, and it was not until I had read and reread (and, importantly, written out) so much of Murdoch's work that the impact of these small words rose above that threshold and became strong enough for me to recognise it. I will get to the particularity of these small words shortly, but I want to make a few other points first which feed into my sense of their importance. I am confining my observations to this single, though substantial, text, *MGM* for clarity's sake, but they are relevant to her entire oeuvre.

These are things which have been brought to the surface of my attention (that subliminal metaphor again) by other Murdoch readers and critics. Stephen Mulhall's illuminating review of Murdoch's *magnum opus*, 'Constructing a hall of reflection', mentions that 'the elements of its moral vision are ... endlessly reiterated' (Mulhall 1997, 219). Reiteration, repetition: that is one vital factor in the Murdoch effect. Peter Conradi remarks on 'the *voice* of this book [which] often feels like someone talking to us, or even thinking out loud' (Conradi 1992, 2). This second factor is the contrived informality, the private and personal musing tone which gives the sense of communion with the mind of the author. Conradi's comment also makes room for a sense that Murdoch is talking to herself as well as to her reader. We are made privy to the workings out of her thought. Maria Antonaccio and William Schweiker describe *MGM* as a 'brilliant, erudite but sprawling work that proceeds reflectively' and characterise it as 'a "guide" for a journey' (Antonaccio and Schweiker 1996, xv). One may be reminded of Murdoch's startling description of Plato's *Republic* as a 'spiritual guidebook' (*MGM*, 388). This 'spiritual' element is a third factor. Murdoch intuitively links the moral with the spiritual and says, 'The word "spiritual" ... seems to me to be at home in the moral sphere' (*MGM*, 495). She is concerned with 'the continuous daily moral work of the soul fighting its way' (*MGM*, 356)—not a common focus of philosophy in the twentieth century—and her writing has an exhortative and admonitory tone which crosses the border generally set between the cold dryness of the scholar and the warm passion of the preceptor. Murdoch views the 'border-line', 'this blurred edge' as 'often a good place to be' (*MGM*, 295), and like Schopenhauer, she 'dodges between metaphysics and common-sense' (*MGM*, 298). Border-crossing is a feature of her *sui generis* style as she uneasily acknowledges: 'In pursuing these reflections one ... find[s] oneself poised between uttering nonsense and laboriously saying the obvious' (*MGM*, 265). She is certainly afraid of neither and exhibits a rare freedom to speak her own mind. Murdoch is a moralist with a mission, a passionate belief in the existence and importance of a 'vast extra-linguistic reality' (*MGM*, 228), of 'value' and of the 'holy', concepts which she fears the loss of in contemporary thinking.

In 'The Preacher's Tone: Mentors and Moralists', Priscilla Martin highlights the indubitable element of instruction in Murdoch's philosophy, the headmistressy tone, found in such sentences as this: 'The persistence of these young persons is an example to us all' (*MGM*, 354). Martin notes Murdoch's admiration for her own headmistress at Badminton, the famous BMB (Beatrice Mary Baker) who was not afraid to tell people how to live. Nor is Murdoch. She has a natural certainty in the essential truth of what she is saying which brooks no argument. She desires to be absolute in her opinions and harks back on four occasions to the abrupt assurance and commonsensical approach of 'that excellent philosopher', Dr. Johnson, who declared that 'it just does' and 'there's an end on't', phrases which she quotes with wistful approval (*MGM*, 55, 233–234, and 274). Murdoch's likeness to Johnson is clear in the quality which leads Mark Patrick Hederman to describe her as a 'no-nonsense referee' in the world of 'muscular masculine thought' (Hederman 2001, 154) and her vocabulary, like Johnson's, is robust. There is evident patience in the way in which, in *MGM*, Murdoch describes and analyses the western philosophical tradition and grapples with the threat to all she holds dear which she sees as posed by contemporary developments in philosophy. But this patience in the structure of her book is underwritten by the subliminal lexicon which reveals her Johnsonian exasperation with 'nonsense'. This for Murdoch comes under various headings, signalled by such small words as 'romantic' (*MGM*, 76, 90, 121, 126, 129, 133, 290, 352, 354, 371, 443, and 499), 'authentic' (*MGM*, 200, 204, 352, 377 and 444), 'heroic' (*MGM*, 76, 159, 182, 186, 204, 268, 352, 377, 458, and 486) and, smallest of all, 'plausible' (*MGM*, 151, 185, and 227).

The big 'alarm' words are, of course, 'existentialism' 'deconstruction', 'structuralism', 'language games', and ... 'Derrida'!—her *bête noire* of *bêtes noires* in this book.

Before turning our attention to the 'perfectly persuasive' vocabulary Murdoch employs to engage readers with her thought and draw them into complicit agreement with her own values and opinions, we must look at the importance of word choice, and Murdoch's own awareness of this. Literary criticism of many kinds focuses on the particularity of individual words. Avril Horner's 'The "wondrous necessary man": Canetti, *The Unicorn* and *The Changeling*' considers a preoccupation with certain keywords in Murdoch's *The Unicorn* and Middleton's *The Changeling*, which alerts us to parallels between these two texts. Murdoch herself is acutely aware of the power of language, its use and misuse. She is opposed to 'jargon' (*MGM*, 167, 172, 291, and 296), fears the danger of slogans (*MGM*, 364–365) and wants to 'preserve and cherish a strong truth-bearing everyday language, not marred or corrupted by technical discourse or scientific codes' (*MGM*, 164). She highlights the words used by other writers: 'notice in the *Phaedrus* passage the four adjectives, perfect, simple, calm and happy' she tells us (*MGM*, 15) and it troubles her that Kant 'was not concerned with ... the *middle-range mediating moral vocabulary*' (*MGM*, 268, her italics) which is of such vital concern in her own moral philosophy. Words and morals are inextricably interlinked in Murdoch's view. She says that 'we develop an evaluative (moral) vocabulary which is in constant use' (*MGM*, 327) and 'we must protect the precision of ... secondary moral words, exercising them and keeping them fit' (*MGM*, 327). What we say affects what we think and how we act. The small words count as well as the big ones: 'Not only "true" and "good", but the *vast numbers of secondary* more specialised moral terms, are for us instruments of discrimination and mentors of desire' (*MGM*, 385). 'Stern words deserving respect', as Murdoch says of Don Cupitt's writing (*MGM*, 127).

Murdoch's subliminal lexicon aims (whether consciously or unconsciously) to teach the reader to discriminate, and it acts as a mentor of desire. It is time to lay out the lexicon which lies submerged in the text of *MGM*. What are these words which we can discern? They are perfectly ordinary familiar everyday words, like ... 'ordinary' (112 uses found in *MGM*), 'familiar' (29 uses) and 'everyday' (16 uses). If we take just the first of these words, it will become apparent why my original conception of this project was overambitious and naïve. Those 112 uses of 'ordinary' include the following concepts: ordinary 'being', ordinary 'life', ordinary 'value perception', ordinary 'sense of value', ordinary 'evaluative methods of thought', ordinary 'language' (this is used both as a philosophical term 'ordinary-language' as used by Ayer and others and as a simple description of common lay non-philosophical language), ordinary 'naïve attitudes', ordinary 'frailty', ordinary 'citizen', ordinary 'talk', ordinary 'simple compassion', ordinary 'people', ordinary 'usage', ordinary 'experienced world', ordinary 'unenlightened self', ordinary 'sense of a transcendent (extra-linguistic) real world', ordinary 'individuals', ordinary 'conceptions of ourselves', ordinary 'lay self-understanding', ordinary 'sophisticated observers', ordinary 'situation', ordinary 'egoistic consciousness', ordinary 'experience', ordinary 'failure of description', ordinary 'apprehension of' ordinary 'man', ordinary 'virtue', ordinary 'concept of truth', 'ordinary human beings', ordinary 'experience', ordinary 'distinction between true and false', ordinary 'moral motives' and so on and so on. Just a third of the way through my list of references I am forced to stop.

Some point to this exercise must be discerned. It might, notwithstanding Murdoch's displeasure, be a Derridean point. He specialised in investigating the persistent use of a word by writers, and in deconstructing texts by way of their subliminal vocabulary. But I do not think that Murdoch deliberately sets out to manipulate the minds of her readers through her use of language. She is open and simply truthful in what she says. Further, such overworking of a single word leads to an erosion of meaningfulness: when we gaze upon the list of 'ordinary' things above, it begins to seem that 'ordinary' is merely a 'tag' signifying approval ('ordinary concepts of truth' = concepts of truth upheld by Murdoch) or even just possession ('ordinary experience' = Murdoch's experience). Does 'ordinary' really *add* anything to the words it qualifies? I do not think Murdoch was always aware of using it, so is it no more than a stylistic tic, such as has been noted (and parodied) in her fictional writing (see Malcolm Bradbury on her use of 'sort of')? Similar charges might be levelled at her use of 'everyday'. All the following are given the tag 'everyday' at various point in *MGM*: everyday 'feeling for truth', everyday 'life', everyday 'experience', everyday 'awareness', everyday 'use of metaphor', everyday 'problem', everyday 'moral life', everyday 'advice', everyday 'moral activity', and everyday 'existence'. In this case, though, there is clearly a passionate philosophical stance being taken by Murdoch, which is anti-Heideggerian. (Late Heidegger is nearly as much of a *bête noire* as Derrida.) She recognises a Nietzschean tone of 'hubris' and 'hatred' in 'Heidegger's "heroic" contempt for *Alltäglichkeit* (everydayness)' (*MGM*, 182). And I think she is right in so doing. (Note the negative tag 'heroic' in that sentence.) Emphasis on the 'ordinary' and the 'everyday' is not just a stylistic tic in Murdoch's writing: it points to the locus of morality in her philosophy. These laden words appear in pairs and groupings. Murdoch speaks of '*ordinary everyday truth*' (*MGM*, 490, her italics), and of 'everyday language' (*MGM*, 459). Taken together, reiterated and repeated, paired and regrouped, they are knotted to form a patterned network throughout the text, of subliminally imprinted value and passion. (What I am trying to do here is to slip under her net.) When Murdoch instinctively uses these words she wants the reader to believe her, to follow her, to agree with her: she is aiming to *persuade*.

There are words that Murdoch uses as a sort of iconic mantra: 'calm' (18 appearances in *MGM*), and 'simple' (10) which derive from her mentor, Plato; 'lucid' (8), and 'space' (19) which are part of her construction of a 'huge hall of reflection' for her reader, 'full of light and space and fresh air, in which ideas and intuitions can be unsystematically nurtured' (*MGM*, 422). We could discuss her happy unselfconscious and unfashionable use of the imperative case: 'must' (16 uses), 'should' (7) and 'ought' (5). We could consider her consciously defiant use of 'better' (13): 'The pilgrim will not only produce a better series of acts, he will have (down to the last details) a better series of mental states. He can literally see better' (*MGM*, 177): 'A language is enlarged, *improved* (value judgement), by truthful utterance', she declares (*MGM*, 281). One could analyse her use of 'natural(ly)' and 'obvious(ly)', certain(ly)' and 'certainty', of 'recognise', 'know' and 'great'—Murdoch has no problem with the concept of a canon, her work is free with references to great art, great philosophers, great writers, great poets. It would be interesting to trace the shifts she makes between 'we', 'I' and 'one', sometimes with great self-awareness: 'It strikes one (me)' (*MGM*, 285) she admits at one point, and 'It is clearly (in my view)' (*MGM*, 383) she concedes at another. Her lack of embarrassment with the words 'instinct' and 'intuition' and 'experience' sets her apart from many other philosophers, felicitously in my opinion. And of course, we should explore the ubiquitous appearance in her writing of 'of course', which scores highly in the word lists I have made with a quite extraordinary 89 appearances. This is a habit of speech, but it also betokens both an impatience with those who wilfully refute the truth, and an earnestness of desire to carry conviction in her argument.

For Murdoch is not playing games in her moral philosophy as she accuses Derrida of doing to damaging effect. Truth, value, holiness, goodness, art, matter to her, indeed it matters to her that things matter—something she thinks has been lost with structuralism and its successors. She unashamedly believes in spiritual pilgrimage, 'unselfing', moral improvement. She includes in her philosophical lexicon theological terms, 'grace' (12 uses in *MGM*), redemption (8), salvation (35). She unfashionably retains the concept of the soul (16). She fears the 'loss' (36) of many things: 'confidence' (*MGM*, 194), 'sovereignty' (*MGM*, 210), 'concepts' (*MGM*, 364), 'ordinary everyday truth', the 'particular', the 'contingent' and the 'individual' (*MGM*, 490), 'discrimination' and the 'sense of value' (*MGM*, 503). She paradoxically grieves over the loss of 'God' (*MGM*, 448), and overtly over the decline of the *Book of Common Prayer* and the Authorised Version of the Bible (*MGM*, 460). She cleaves to the concepts of 'experience' and 'holiness', ending this ragbag of a book, an analogy of the 'ragbag mind' (Hegel's image, *MGM*, 237) which she both discusses and manifests in its pages, with an appeal to 'those matters of "ultimate concern", our experience of the unconditioned and our continued sense of what is holy' (*MGM*, 512). The final sentence, as we saw above, is intriguingly from Psalm 139.

Is all this counting-and-listing of words much used by Murdoch any more than a round-the-houses way of showing that there is in *MGM* what Bran Nicol has neatly termed a 'polemical impulse' (Nicol 2004, 159) and that in this book she reveals what Terry Eagleton identifies as 'her unconscious ideological prejudices'? (Eagleton 2003, 261). Maybe not. But I think there is rich material in this kind of linguistic dissection of the text which could feed into critical exegesis of Murdoch's philosophical and theological stances. Further, I believe it to be a significant element in the response she draws from her readers, something to which she was not indifferent. She writes of the differences in philosophical style between Schopenhauer and Wittgenstein:

> Schopenhauer's relationship to his reader is relaxed, amiable, confiding, that of a kindly teacher or fellow seeker. He tells stories and makes jokes. Wittgenstein does not relate to a reader, he passes by leaving a task behind. (*MGM*, 79–80)

'Here one is inclined to say (I am inclined to say)' (*MGM*, 69–70), to use her own words, that Murdoch does indeed leave a task behind, nothing less than 'the battle against natural egoism' (*MGM*, 260) which she calls 'unselfing', but she shares Schopenhauer's 'relaxed, amiable, confiding manner', a manner partially created by her casual use of words. Hilda Spear comments that Murdoch 'reaffirms', 'questions', 'offers' and is 'never dogmatic' toward her reader (Spear 2007, 112) and Hederman says: 'This book was written for everyone. It is ... generous and plain-spoken' (Hederman 2001, 78). Mulhall considers 'the book's lack of systematicity ... a function of its author's conception of her relation to her readers' (Mulhall 1997, 238). I want to suggest that the vocabulary employed in *MGM* performs a similar function.

Writing this account of Murdoch's lexicon puts me in a dilemma, because it is in danger of becoming something of a pastiche of *MGM*, making it seem as if I lack respect for Murdoch and for the academic endeavour of literary analysis. Neither is the case. Murdoch is for me, as for many others, as much a spiritual mentor as an object of study and I find *MGM* a great book full of charms. I particularly like the gradually built-up *vignettes* of Schopenhauer and Wittgenstein whom Murdoch loved in such different ways, and the marvellous image of the ratchet to describe the experience of thinking philosophically (*MGM*, 23). She is a powerful influence and I find myself perfectly persuaded of the truthfulness of her writing. Whatever her listeners did or did not make of the Gifford Lectures that cost her so much peace of mind, readers of the book they metamorphosed into over a decade of painfully hard work can reap much richness from this compendium of distilled reading, thinking, and ultimately, wisdom.

References

Antonaccio, M., and W. Schweiker (eds.). 1996. *Iris Murdoch and the search for human goodness*. Chicago and London: University of Chicago Press.

Conradi, P.J. 1992. A major new book of philosophy. *Iris Murdoch Newsletter* 6: 1–2.

Conradi, P.J. 2001. *Iris Murdoch: A life*. London: HarperCollins.

Eagleton, T. 2003. *Figures of dissent*. London and New York: Verso.

Eyre, R., dir. 2001. *Iris*. DVD, Miramax. UK.

Gillies, R.A. (ed.). 1995. *Iris Murdoch's Giffords: A study of the 1982 Gifford lectures—Theology in Scotland*. Occasional Paper No. 1.

Hederman, M.P. 2001. *The haunted inkwell*. Dublin: Columba Press.

Horner, A., and A. Rowe (eds.). 2015. *Living on paper: Letters from Iris Murdoch 1934–1995*. London: Chatto & Windus.

Mulhall, S. 1997. Constructing a hall of reflection: Perfectionist edification in Iris Murdoch's *Metaphysics as a guide to morals*. *Philosophy* 72 (280): 219–239.

Murdoch, I. 1956. *The flight from the enchanter*. London: Chatto & Windus.

Murdoch, I. 1983. *The philosopher's pupil*. London: Chatto & Windus.

Murdoch, I. 1987. *The book and the brotherhood*. London: Chatto & Windus.

Murdoch, I. 1992. *Metaphysics as a guide to morals* (Abbreviated *MGM*). London: Chatto & Windus.

Murdoch, I. 1997. *Existentialists and mystics*, ed. Peter J. Conradi. London: Chatto & Windus.

Murdoch, I. KUAS202. *Journals, poetry notebooks and other items*. London: Kingston University Archives and Special Collections.

Nicol, B. 2004. *Iris Murdoch: The retrospective fiction*. Basingstoke: Palgrave Macmillan.

Spear, H. 2007. *Iris Murdoch*. Basingstoke: Palgrave Macmillan.

CHAPTER 3

Unity and Art in a Mood of Scepticism (*MGM* Chapter 1)

Niklas Forsberg

METAPHYSICS AS A GUIDE TO MORALS NEEDS NO INTRODUCTION

Metaphysics as a Guide to Morals (henceforth *MGM*) begins in a peculiar way. There is no introduction. There is no explicit problem formulation, it does not present a clear thesis that the book is supposed to argue for, and there is not a single question mark in sight in its opening pages. It may even seem as if the book is lacking a clear introductory discussion that explains what will be discussed and in what order. There is no clear definition of either metaphysics or morals, even though the title tells us that the one is supposed to be a guide to the other. There is only a friendly nod to Elizabeth Anscombe and an elusive motto before it takes off. Iris Murdoch just begins—stating things, seemingly talking for all of us.

> The idea of a self-contained unity or limited whole is a fundamental instinctive concept. We see parts of things, we intuit whole things. We seem to know a great deal on the basis of very little. Oblivious of

N. Forsberg (✉)
University of Pardubice, Pardubice, Czech Republic

© The Author(s) 2019
N. Hämäläinen and G. Dooley (eds.),
Reading Iris Murdoch's Metaphysics as a Guide to Morals,
https://doi.org/10.1007/978-3-030-18967-9_3

> philosophical problems and paucity of evidence we grasp ourselves as unities, continuous bodies and continuous minds. We assume the continuity of space and time. (*MGM*, 1)

Murdoch gives the impression of saying something that we all should be familiar with, at least at some level. But are we? I assume that we rarely go about thinking about the 'idea of a self-contained unity or a limited whole', as if this was something we all are concerned with almost by instinct. ('Oh, what marvellous fur that puppy has! I wonder how to think about it in terms of a self-contained unity or a limited whole!') Similarly, it seems odd to say that we normally think of ourselves as seeing 'parts of things', but intuiting 'whole things'. Who, really, would *say*: 'Hey, there goes Edna, with her continuous body and her continuous mind, carrying her saxophone of which I only can see parts but that I nevertheless think of as a whole saxophone – and, amazingly, I *know* this (that I see this continuous body and continuous mind carrying the whole saxophone) based on so little evidence!' No one, I assume. No one, but an academic philosopher in an academic setting.

Murdoch's opening sentences move in a distinctively philosophical register, and they do so for a reason. The rhetoric of Murdoch's prose signals that the separations that she highlights (between parts and wholes, seeing and intuition), as well as the effort to establish of a bond between evidence and knowledge, are philosophical constructs of a peculiar kind. That is, Murdoch starts by implicitly showing that 'Philosophy is to some extent a foreign tongue' (*MGM*, 192). Of course, if a philosopher asks: 'Do you normally think of Edna as assemblages of body parts and mental events or as a whole?' it may seem very natural to respond by saying that I see/think of her as a whole. The naturalness with which one may be inclined to reach for that answer is similar to the sort of firm sense of merely stating the obvious that G. E. Moore gave voice to when he waved his hands and said:

> I can prove now, for instance, that two human hands exist. How? By holding up my two hands, and saying, as I make a certain gesture with the right hand, 'Here is one hand,' and adding, as I make a certain gesture with the left, 'and here is another.' (Moore, 145f.)

But Moore's hand-waving is an answer to a question posed in a distinctively philosophical setting; Moore is trying to show the hollowness of a specific understanding of certain forms of idealistic doctrines. Murdoch is trying to mark out how our ordinary forms of perception and cognition are distorted and misunderstood in philosophical discourse—and she aims to do that without downplaying what is real and true in the philosophical temptation (to think that unity is only real if we can solidify it theoretically) itself.

Thus, it is not *false* to say that we intuit unities; they are parts of our ordinary non-philosophical understanding. So, of course we can say we do without speaking nonsense. But Murdoch wants to take us back from assemblages of body parts and mental events to Edna herself, while at the same time investigating the philosophical impulse to split her up into parts and that impulse's supposed naturalness, as well as the following effort to glue her together again theoretically. That is why she says that unity and limited wholes are clear to us when we are '[o]blivious of philosophical problems' (*MGM*, 1). So philosophical problems seem to arise as forms of departures from a lived form of intelligibility—and the real kind of unity can only be found where its philosophically problematic formulation is no longer present. But it may require a great deal of philosophical work to get there.

Thus, when Murdoch—a few lines further down—says, 'The urge to prove that where we intuit unity there really is unity is a deep emotional motive to philosophy, to art, to thinking itself. Intellect is naturally one-making' (*MGM*, 1), she is not saying that the task of this book is to present a philosophical theory or system that explains how we can go from parts to wholes in a philosophically abstract manner. Rather, she is suggesting that we need to take this specifically philosophical impulse as seriously as we possibly can, *without* taking the separations and epistemological views that underpin the impulse for granted. She wants to investigate the motive itself, not present yet another doctrinal response to it. Indeed, for her, it is quite clear that the philosophical effort to 'evaluate, understand, classify, place in order of merit' and to unearth a 'wider unified system' (*MGM*, 1), is an urge that should be scrutinised rather than taken for granted. In an oft-quoted passage, Murdoch says that 'There is a two-way movement in philosophy, a movement towards the building of theories, and a move back again towards the consideration of simple and obvious facts' (Murdoch 1999, 299). The first is a move away from reality, a move that is rooted in a well-motivated fear of 'plurality, diffusion, senseless accident, chaos' (*MGM*, 1). This is thus the particularly philosophical effort to find ways to overcome various forms of plurality, particularity, and contextuality by means of abstraction and generalisation—that is, in an effort to raise above *life itself*. The other movement is the homecoming where we return to the ground, to the 'muddle', to use a Murdochian turn of phrase (see e.g. *MGM*, 8), to life itself. It is immensely important to realise that Murdoch claims that 'both these aspects of philosophy are necessary to it' (Murdoch 1999, 299; see also *MGM*, 197, 211). The theoretical and systematising effort is merely the first step, but good philosophising requires the second movement too, the move *back*.

It is true that many people and most philosophers think of the first of the aforementioned movements—that of theory construction and generalising endeavours—as *the* philosophical movement. It is equally clear that most contemporary philosophers think that 'metaphysics' just is the 'one-making' endeavour that aims to lay down requirements for what the *really real is*, systematically and in the abstract, and this is something that belongs exclusively to one of the two movements of philosophy that Murdoch describes. Therefore, one may be led to think a book whose title makes evident that we are now venturing upon an inquiry into metaphysics, and how that metaphysics guides morals, must be a book that aims to lead us *from* the particular, historical, social and contextual *to* the general by means of a kind of theorising that in some way brings forth *the* one-making principle. That would constitute a fundamental misunderstanding of *MGM*.

In fact, what the first pages of the book really tell us is almost the reverse: we fear plurality and diffusion, with good reason, and the philosophical one-making impulse comes in as a response to that fear. This impulse is not to be taken lightly. But the philosophical aspiration easily leads us to think that general distinctions such as particular/general, temporary/eternal, parts/wholes (and to add one more that will become really important later on in the book: fact/value), are always applicable and hence to be overcome by metaphysical and theoretical speculation. To accept such divisions as given would be to try to domesticate the ways in which the 'intellect is naturally one-making' (*MGM*, 1), and to fall back into a blind reliance on distinctions and epistemological assumptions that she aims to contest. That '*intellect* is naturally one-making' does not mean that *philosophy* is the *only* one-making endeavour—and one of Murdoch's main concerns is that philosophy, in particular, tends to misunderstand what real, functional, one-making efforts are like.

What Is Metaphysics?

How, then, are we to think about the terms 'metaphysics' and 'morals' here, if the idea of abstract generalising, over-historical principles and a-temporal ideals are *not* what Murdoch means by 'metaphysics'? And what, then, could 'morals' mean if we are to refrain from any such principles and ideals? What notion of *guidance* are we to insert between these two concepts? And if Murdoch is so critical of the idea that philosophy can 'prove that where we intuit unity there really is unity' (*MGM*, 1), then why does she embark on this over-500-page journey into the ways in which metaphysics is a guide to morals?

As Murdoch sees it, our present intellectual culture seems to have resigned from the task of thinking clearly about unity and generality. Now, she says, we seem to live in a time in which a 'mood of scepticism' (*MGM*, 7) is predominant, which is characterised by 'the "pluralisation" or "demythologisation" of history, art, religion, science' (*MGM*, 2). The predominant sceptical mood that Murdoch discerns can be seen as a form of backlash to, or the flipside of the coin of, misguided systematic and scientific efforts to lay down the true fundamentals of all one-making efforts. 'Since one cannot find one overarching principle of unity, there is none to be found!'; 'If one cannot pinpoint *the* meaning of concepts, there is only an endless multitude of linguistic possibilities to immerse oneself in'. This 'either/or' structure is itself, Murdoch suggests, too easy to employ, and on many occasions not true to the facts. One central reason why this is a false dilemma is a fundamental neglect of historicity. That unities exist does not mean that they are eternal. That historical changes occur does not mean that there are no unities. Of course, we misunderstand historicity too, if we think of that as yet another 'either/or': either unity is ahistorical, or there are only historically conditioned temporary resting points.

> Philosophy and science and theology have always been to some degree iconoclastic; and the 'everyday outlook' or 'natural standpoint' undergoes historical change. How much it changes many voices now tell us, how little it changes can be learnt from reading Homer. (*MGM*, 2)

Murdoch's emphasis on the historical means to suggest that all our beliefs are formed from within a horizon, and that such horizons change. But this does not mean that our beliefs are ungrounded or merely temporary hypotheses (i.e. a limited set of beliefs that we hold for a limited number or reasons). Horizons are broad and in the background, and change slowly in hardly perceptible ways. The scepticism that characterises our times is one in which the understanding and appreciation of a shared (yet often hardly perceptible) horizon has been 'sponged away', as Murdoch describes it, quoting Jacques Derrida (*MGM*, 2). In particular, the dominant mood of scepticism that Murdoch thinks that we now live in is one in which the idea that there is nothing beyond us, beyond our language, thrives.

On the kind of traditional view of what metaphysics is, which Murdoch contests, philosophical explorations can be performed in a somewhat detached manner. It is often assumed that the philosopher can stand back from the world and observe it, more or less neutrally, ponder the facts of it calmly, and then retreat to his or her desk and construct a manual for how to proceed in thinking and acting at a second stage. That would be one way in which one may think about how metaphysics guides morals. We may call this form of thinking about how metaphysics may guide morals 'top-down'.

Murdoch, however, does not think that there is such an ideal vantage point and underlines, in contrast, the ways in which our perceptions of our world always already are coloured. Murdoch claims that 'morality is and ought to be connected with our whole being' (*MGM*, 495). This means that morality is practically everywhere, always, to a higher or lower degree of course, and that 'moral life is not intermittent or specialized, it is not a peculiar separate area of our existence' (*MGM*, 495). And in a very famous and oft-quoted parenthetical passage—written in a style that is characteristic of Murdoch that sometimes lends itself to slogan-like one-liners, which in turn often invite simplification and misunderstanding—Murdoch asks and answers: '("But are you saying that every single second has a moral tag?" Yes, roughly)' (*MGM*, 495). The qualification 'Yes, roughly' is important, for it would be an immense simplification to say that everything, always is a moral concern. What is true is that there is no separate sphere of morality and no morality-free zone, which means that morality and clarity about moral issues are to be sought for pretty much everywhere (see *MGM*, 26).

To formulate Murdoch's understanding of how metaphysics guides morals, one may say that her view is not that philosophy should forge, or construct, a metaphysics that we can employ as a guide. Rather, she is urging us to unearth the metaphysics that already guides us, even if we are unaware of this guidance.[1] We must begin by trying to make clear who and what we are, and how we have become who and what we are. We must dig where we stand. The direction of thought must be 'ground-up'. 'Who and what we are' is a rather large thing, not possible to discern by means of looking only at minute details of concrete situations. One thing that Murdoch's view of how metaphysics guides morals entails is that we will misunderstand morality fundamentally if we focus too much on concrete moral acts and their relation to ideals or virtues whose sense we have determined beforehand.

> Of course virtue is good habit and dutiful action. But the background condition of such habit and such action, in human beings, is a just mode of vision and a good quality of consciousness. It is a *task* to come to see the world as it is. A philosophy which leaves duty without context and exalts the idea of freedom and power as a separate top level value ignores this task and obscures the relation between virtue and reality. We act rightly 'when the time comes' not out of strength of will but out of the quality of our usual attachments and the kind of energy and discernment which we have available. And to this the whole activity of our consciousness is relevant. (Murdoch 1999, 375)

Murdoch's view is that we are always guided by metaphysics in the sense that it constitutes the horizon within which all our claims—moral, factual—make sense and carry the kinds of weights they do.

At this point, one must acknowledge how immensely complex Murdoch's relation to virtue and virtue ethics is. Of course, to the extent that 'virtue ethics' is merely an overarching broad characterisation of all kinds of philosophies that put emphasis on the development of character, Murdoch could be said to belong to that group. However, as soon as one tries to invest that emphasis on character development with a more substantial view of what the virtues are and of how they are supposed to be action guiding, Murdoch parts way with that tradition (at least in its contemporary neo-Aristotelean dispensation).[2] To the extent that virtue ethics tries to narrow down morality to a single principle, Murdoch's view is diametrically opposed. And to the extent that virtue ethics seeks to establish and explicate *the* sense of the supposedly relevant virtues, Murdoch will have some serious reservations: 'I don't think that the moral life can in this sense be reduced to a unity. On the other hand I do not think it can be satisfactorily characterised by an enumeration of varying "goods" and virtues' (*MGM*, 492).

Now, Murdoch's prioritising of vision over choice and worldview over action does not mean that hers is a view according to which we are, as it were, *victims* of our situatedness, thrown into a world that is not ours, destined and determined to follow the linguistic structure that conditions our meaningful thought and each of our individual uses of language. Such a view is rather one of the positions that Murdoch feels the pressure of (that is, feels that there's *something* to it), but which she nevertheless finds deeply problematic. The view of language (where it is presented as 'a cage') is one that she attributes to Derrida and to Wittgenstein, through readings of their respective views which are, to be fair, contestable. But, even if one finds Murdoch's readings of Derrida and Wittgenstein problematic, one should keep in mind that her aim is not to do exegesis but to point out and reflect over trends of thought that are formative and capture something essential of 'the spirit of our times', the *Zeitgeist*—that is, exactly the ways in which certain ideas gain currency and tend to inform us, and guide us, more or less unconsciously.

The idea that we are preconditioned by our linguistic belonging is itself a philosophical, metaphysical idea, and it becomes important to Murdoch, not (merely or even primarily) because it is a well-argued philosophical claim that deserves to have its pros and cons scrutinised, but because it partakes in forming our self-understanding. It presents a unified image of the human being and her condition.

This means that thinking seriously about 'metaphysics', as Murdoch conceives it, does not merely mean thinking about how various images inform us and make possible various thoughts, actions, habits. Pictures of who and what we are, are also, constantly, created. And it is equally important to bring into view the ways in which we partake in forming various images of unity: 'The world is not given to us on a plate, it is given to us as a creative task' (*MGM*, 215). Thus, Murdoch is required to look at, and reflect upon, explicit metaphysical systems put forth by traditional philosophers, historians, psychological theories, anthropology, religion, sociology, and indeed, everyday lives of ordinary people. It is, perhaps, no surprise then, that art (and perhaps literature especially) plays a central role here, since 'art does register or picture, sometimes prophetically, the movement of the *Zeitgeist*. The way we grasp the world changes, and the artist knows first, like the animals whose behaviour foretells an earthquake' (*MGM*, 4).

If morality is everywhere and if metaphysics is everywhere; and if metaphysical imageries are both forming us (by having formed the kind of *Zeitgeist* we happen to be thrown into) *and* are formed by us (by the kinds of views and theories and images of ourselves that we form), then a study of how metaphysics guides morals will necessarily have a very complex structure (if it is to remain true to the facts); necessarily criss-crossing between different fields of discourse and different locations on our history's axis. And if this is the book's subject, it follows that it demands a specific form. For this reason, I think Stephen Mulhall is right to say that the apparently disorganised structure of the book is well-motivated and true to the themes under discussion. If the book challenges top-down approaches to metaphysics and ideas of unity, it cannot assume that form itself. The work needs to 'take on exactly the appearance of disorganization or disunity ..., in order to contest the legitimacy of the ideal of organization or unity that generates this appearance' (Mulhall, 221).

IMAGES OF ART

Since we now know that Murdoch wants to elucidate how images of ourselves have shaped, shape, and might come to shape us and our world, it is no wonder that the concept of art plays a crucial role. This is so, not only because art itself (often) is a form of image making; which means that studying the concept of art must entail an enrichment of one's own understanding of how images are made and how they may guide us. Neither does art become important solely because it sometimes 'foretells an earthquake'. Inquiring into our different concepts of the artwork also unearths various forms of understandings of what unity is. In Murdoch's view, 'the traditional concept' (*MGM*, 2) of the artwork builds on the idea that an artwork only becomes an artwork by presenting a unified picture. Traditional art, as Murdoch conceives it, 'involves the idea of a sustained *experienced* mental synthesis' (*MGM*, 2).

The idea of unity is here presented in a somewhat phenomenological register. It is not so—not merely anyway—that the artwork itself, physically as it were, brings things together. Unity is also formed by our experience of it, by *how* we perceive it. Seeing (or hearing, or reading) an artwork, is experiencing a limited unified whole. Again, this is grounded in ordinary experience. When we hear a symphony, we do not hear a great number of notes played simultaneously, creating sound waves that are in accordance with our musical habits and expectations (or challenge them); we hear a symphony. Unity is what we hear. When we view a painting, we do not see a number of colours arranged so as to form a recognisable pattern; we see a landscape or a bowl of fruit or a woman with a saxophone. Unity is what we see. At this phenomenological, experiential, level, synthesis is natural, whereas the separation of that unity into dispersed atoms whose relations to each other need to be explained is unnatural. It requires a specific attitude (philosophical for example) to break up the unity into parts and claim that the separate entities are what the thing itself *really* is made of. That form of philosophical analysis—of breaking unities apart to their constituent members—is thus a very theoretical form of metaphysics, which builds on a specific (moral) stance where we detach ourselves from natural forms of perception, understanding and engagement. We may come to learn and understand why somebody may feel inclined to perform such acts of dissembling; but that would only be to follow the first of philosophy's two movements mentioned above. The return is not performed. In philosophical analysis, we may struggle to see parts. In real life (that to which Murdoch aims to return us), we see wholes. This minute reflection on how we experience an artwork also sheds light on what an *experience* is and what *attending* to an object is 'in ordinary life, unshadowed by philosophy' (*MGM*, 3). Thus, Murdoch contends: 'This ability to sustain and *experience* imagined syntheses has importance in other areas where we make use of analogous or related conceptions of authoritative limited wholes' (*MGM*, 3).

Of course, Murdoch's talk about 'the traditional concept' of the artwork is way too simplistic. There are, after all, many such concepts. But Murdoch is intentionally painting with broad brush strokes, trying to shed light on a specific idea of unity that has been pervasive in most of them—at least up until quite recently. One may describe Murdoch's strategy here as one of bringing into view two seemingly opposing views of the work of art that had reigned up until the rise of esoteric varieties of modernism. One is a concept of art that we loosely might label 'Platonic' since it is organised around the concept of *mimesis*. The other can be called 'Kantian' since its organising principle is the idea of the artwork as an autonomous whole, not to be judged by virtue of how it corresponds to the world out of frame.

Central to the Platonic conception is the idea of mimesis. The difficult aspect of this notion is, obviously, its representational character. Art is supposed to be measured by determining how well it represents, or captures, our reality. This is one of the reasons why Plato had to down-grade poetry. Art, he claimed, is a 'third remove from truth'—where each step taken in the chain '*idea*→ *thing*→ *image*' is a representation, and thus a step away from the really real (the idea). Art is this reduced to a representation of a representation (Plato, the *Republic*, Book X, see *MGM*, 12f.). The idea of mimesis, as here understood, entails that there is a 'transcendent reality' (*MGM*, 6) beyond all representational spheres that all representations aim for. Even though Murdoch is quite adamant when it comes to holding on to the idea that a work of art is *about* some-thing outside itself, a transcendent reality, she is nevertheless critical of Plato, arguing that he goes wrong by contrasting *mimesis* with *anamne-sis* (recollection, anamnesis—'"memory" of what we did not know we knew', Murdoch 1999, 12), and for thinking that art has nothing to do with *anamnesis*. Plato is thereby led to believe that art always is less real than what it represents and that it 'caters for the lowest part of the soul', or 'the bad unconscious' (*MGM*, 12). Plato thus has two reservations against art which are tied together in intricate ways. One is epistemolog-ical, one moral. Even though Murdoch thinks Plato's epistemological rea-son is unfair to the facts, she still holds on to parts of the moral reason. Murdoch, just like Plato, recognises art's ability to corrupt our thinking, for precisely the same reasons that Plato warns us. Art is, in Murdoch's view too, a powerful thing, and precisely because it is a powerful thing it may lead us away from clear thinking and unreserved appreciation for what feels right. We may become, as she says, 'lazy spectators' (*MGM*, 13).

> Art is most pernicious when it poses as a spiritual achievement and inhibits serious reflection and self-criticism. Enjoyment of art is soothing, and may persuade us that we 'understand' (life, people, morality) and need to make no further efforts. The great artists always make us feel that we have arrived; we are home. We feel that we are already wise and good. (*MGM*, 13)

One can discern this Platonic inheritance in Murdoch most obviously in her somewhat comical disdain for television, and her worry about how creativity is threatened by new inventions such as the word processor (see e.g. *MGM*, 13, 19f., 210). But it also comes into view in a much more profound way when Murdoch distinguishes good art from bad, and imagination from fantasy. In her view, bad art feeds our fantasies and our egoistic desires precisely by leading us to assume that we already know what the good is, that our own understanding of the world and our others is correct, and which thereby leaves out the absolutely central call for self-critical examination.

In Murdoch's reading, 'Plato's attack on art must be seen in the context of his whole moral philosophy' (*MGM*, 14). For even though Plato claims that art appeals to the lower part of the soul, by presenting ready-made images of goodness or evil that prevent us from thinking things through for ourselves, and even though he claims that art is lacking in epistemological closeness to truth, he nevertheless presents us with an image of the magnetism of truth; a truth that imagery guides us towards. Love (Eros) and beauty are central here. We are pulled towards the truth by unified images. Always. Crucially, however, there is no final point here. Ideas of the good are like the sun. They shine a light, but we cannot stare into it without going blind, and the whole idea of 'going there' is bluntly absurd since we would burn long before we get there. This is why there is no knowledge of 'the good'. This is why images of virtue may guide us, even though there is little sense in believing that virtue has been realised. All we have are images that shine light on our world. There's no room, in Murdoch's work, for what one might call a 'real idea(l)'. Rather:

> The good life is thus a process of clarification, a movement towards selfless lucidity, guided by ideas of perfection which are objects of *love*. Platonic morality is not coldly intellectual, it involves the whole man and attaches value to the most 'concrete' of everyday preoccupations and acts. (*MGM*, 14)

An ideal image shines light on our own words, concepts and conceptions, and we thereby can scrutinise them and see more clearly. If we are faithful enough to this task, and selfless enough to be honest in it, then improvement will come to be by means of acknowledgments of one's own imperfections, a reorientation of one's vision. And, since differences in moral vision are conceptual differences (Murdoch 1999, 84; see also Forsberg 2018), moral progress includes, centrally, a willingness to test, expand, and reconsider the concepts one lives by. Thus, there is no idea to be realised, and the value of art is not to be found in how well it represents the world in the photographic sense of one-to-one correspondence. Art and love are two concepts that are extremely close to each other in Murdoch.

Incidentally, these brief reflections on Murdoch's inheritance of Plato already give us a central clue about how to understand how Murdoch's novels relate to her philosophy. Given that she often lets her characters 'speak philosophically' using sentences and images that bear some resemblance to her own philosophical thoughts, one might become tempted to think that she uses the novels as vehicles for her own philosophy. Nothing could be more wrong.[3] Her novels, like all good art (assuming that she struggled to write good art, not necessarily claiming that she succeeded, or that *she* thought that she had succeeded in doing so) present unified wholes that are about our world in the sense that they portray what our life is (or may be) like. And by doing so, they give clear images of various lives, ideals and concepts. That's it. All (good) novels do this. But at no point do they make claims of this sort:

Think like this!

Act like this!

Here's a colourful image of my philosophy – go imitate it!

If they succeeded in doing things like these, they would be a poor form of literature by Murdoch's own standards: blocking the central task of self-examination, feeding our egos by making us believe that we have the real world framed, betraying the idea that the Good is always beyond our reach and that virtue is not something that can be explicated and then copied. The images that art present should put us to work, not rest. Art is neither a copy, nor a proxy. Thus, learning from literature is not a matter of imitating it, but a matter of being called to think.

> The notion of copying the model itself would be a 'category mistake', since the model is not a particular thing, like a particular command or picture; *imitatio Christi* does not work by simply suggesting that everyone should give away his money, or wondering how Christ would vote. (*MGM*, 11)

Whereas the Platonic concept of art placed mimesis at its centre, leading Plato to discredit its representational value, the Kantian image of art is precisely driven by disconnecting the artwork from stale questions about representation. The artwork now becomes autonomous and the question about representation or reference simply falls out of play. For Kant, the artwork must be understood in terms of 'independence, of self-containedness' (Murdoch 1999, 219) and this is one point that clearly appeals to Murdoch—even though she will need to part ways with Kant too at some point.

As Kant seeks to lay bare the conditions of possibility of knowledge in general, the central discovery he makes is that 'intuitions without concepts are blind; concepts without intuitions are empty' (Kant, A51/ B75). We may speak of intuition (or experience) and concepts (or understanding) as two independent 'things' in some sense, and so as two independent *sources* of knowledge. A judgement (a conceptualisation) is of something else (the thing that we experience). But if there is to be anything worth calling 'knowledge' these two must be in harmony with each other. In Kant's view, empiricism and rationalism are two sceptical varieties of a failure to see this. A judgement (a conceptualisation) is of something else (the thing that we experience).

Art holds a special place in Kant's thought precisely because of its 'self-containedness'. An artwork is what it is about, is about what it is. It is its own idea. Therefore, it does not point outside itself to any empirical objects, and it is not to be measured by means of how well it mimics the real world. It creates its own. To put it as simply as possible: an artwork is a work where the word is its own concept, the expression is its own content, and there is no distinction to be drawn between ideality and exemplarity. A beautiful work of art is one that realises its own idea well. A failed work of art does not. So the beauty of the artwork is not at all to be measured by means of how well it represents something else (or if it 'looks appealing' or not).

One can easily see what Murdoch finds attractive here, for Kant offers a way to explicate the unity of a work of art in terms that circumvent the Platonic worry of art being merely a representation of a representation. Murdoch, however, is worried that the Kantian idea of the autonomous work of art will entail that the true connection between the work of art and the world is lost entirely. That the work of art is about us and our world and has 'conceptual content' are ideas that Murdoch will never let go of, even if she countersigns the Kantian idea of the work of art as self-contained and not to be measured by means of simplistic representational standards.

Murdoch's brief investigations into the two dominating trends of thought regarding the concept of the artwork can now be unpacked rather easily. An artwork is a limited whole; it presents a unified image of who and what we are that is to be measured as a self-contained whole (and not in terms of naïve photographic images of 'aboutness' as strict reference or representation). Art does not function as images of the good or the bad, the virtues or the sins, that we should mimic (or distance ourselves from), but as images that should make us think and rethink ourselves and our concepts. By forcing us to do that, artworks are also, necessarily, about us and our world. And this is why Murdoch finds such a close link between love and art as she does: they are individualities that pull us up, unified wholes that force us to pay attention to a world outside ourselves and which thereby call us to engage in self-criticism (see *MGM*, 16f. and Murdoch 1999). They are unified wholes that make claims about how things hang together, and ask if we can see the unity they present. If they truly were cut off from the world—that is, if they really were internal affairs without any connections to the everyday lives and struggles of ordinary people—the threat is not merely esotericism. Truth itself is threatened.

ART IN A MOOD OF SCEPTICISM

This is exactly the threat that she discerns in the contemporary sceptical mood. Murdoch thinks that the traditional idea of a 'work of art' is 'under attack', as she says (*MGM*, 2), from ways of thinking influenced by the contemporary sceptical mood in which art is 'demythologised' (*MGM*, 17). At bottom, the demythologisation of art that really worries Murdoch is the thought that language is a form of play in which signs are not in touch with either us or the world, and that language truly refers to nothing else than language.

> Structuralism may also be seen in its more popular manifestations as a new sensibility in art, an attack on traditional art forms, where it operates both as an exercise in, and an image of, demythologisation, the removal of the transcendent: a removal which analyses (deconstructs) the familiar concepts of individual object, individual person, individual meaning, those old and cherished 'limited wholes'. (*MGM*, 5)

What is truly worrying in the mood of scepticism for Murdoch is thus not merely that we will end up with artworks that are only about other artworks, or works of art that question their own concept of what an artwork is, but that we will stop seeing artworks as openings to 'an imagined world which is both like and unlike the "real" world, but which relates to it intimately' (*MGM*, 205). What we risk here is not merely a diminished sense of the importance of works of art. Rather, 'the fundamental value which is lost, made obscure, made not to be, by structuralist theory, is truth, language as truthful, where "truthful" means faithful to, engaging intelligently and responsibly with, a reality which is beyond us' (*MGM*, 214). When Murdoch is speaking about 'what is beyond us' here, she is indeed speaking about metaphysics. That is, 'the transcendental network, the border, wherein the interests and passions which unite us to the world are progressively woven into illusion or reality, a continuous working of consciousness' (*MGM*, 215). Thus, Murdoch's worry is that a metaphysical image of language is seeping into public consciousness in a way that will partake in forming who and what we are; and this metaphysical image will render the idea that we are responsible to a world outside us empty. Metaphysicians are destroying metaphysics by misunderstanding metaphysics.

In a way, the problem with 'structuralism' (as Murdoch understands it) is precisely that metaphysical requirements are laid down 'top-down'—while the real structures that guide us are made obscure. The theoretical failure to 'prove that where we intuit unity there really is unity' (*MGM*, 1) does not show that there is no unity at all. 'We must check philosophical theories against what we know of human nature (and hold on to that phrase too) and feed philosophy with our ordinary (non-theorised, non-jargoned) views of it' (*MGM*, 216). If we fail this task, the journey home is still to be done, and thinking has only just begun.

Acknowledgements My thanks to the editors for helpful and valuable comments. This publication was supported within the project of Operational Programme Research, Development and Education (OP VVV/OP RDE), 'Centre for Ethics as Study in Human Value', Registration No. CZ.02.1.01/0. 0/0.0/15_003/0000425, co-financed by the European Regional Development Fund and the state budget of the Czech Republic.

NOTES

1. For a helpful and clarifying discussion of how Murdoch's conception of metaphysics differs from more traditional and theoretical variations, see Hämäläinen (2013).
2. This is a point well-argued both in Robjant (2012) and in McLean (2000).
3. I have argued so more extensively in Forsberg (2013).

REFERENCES

Forsberg, N. 2013. *Language lost and found: On Iris Murdoch and the limits of philosophical discourse.* New York: Bloomsbury.

Forsberg, N. 2018. Taking the linguistic method seriously: On Iris Murdoch on language and linguistic philosophy. In *Murdoch on truth and love*, ed. Gary Browning, 109–132. London: Palgrave Macmillan.

Hämäläinen, N. 2013. What is metaphysics in *Metaphysics as a guide to morals? SATS: Northern European Journal of Philosophy* 14 (1): 1–20.

Kant, I. 2007 [1781, 1787]. *Critique of pure reason*, trans. Norman Kemp Smith, 2nd ed. Houndmills: Palgrave Macmillan.

McLean, M. 2000. On muffling Murdoch. *Ratio* 13: 191–198.

Moore, G.E. 1959. *Philosophical papers.* London: Allen & Unwin.

Mulhall, S. 1997. Constructing a hall of reflection: Perfectionist edification in Iris Murdoch's *Metaphysics as a guide to morals. Philosophy* 72: 219–239.

Murdoch, I. 1999. *Existentialists and mystics: Writings on philosophy and literature*, ed. Peter Conradi. New York: Penguin.

Murdoch, I. 2003. *Metaphysics as a guide to morals* (Abbreviated *MGM*). London: Vintage.

Robjant, D. 2012. Review of *Iris Murdoch, philosopher*, ed. Justin Broackes. *European Journal of Philosophy* 20 (4): 621–635.

Murdoch's Question of the Work of Art: The Dialogue Between Western and Japanese Conceptions of Unity (*MGM* Chapters 1 and 8)

Fiona Tomkinson

INTRODUCTION

In *Metaphysics as a Guide to Morals* (Murdoch 2003, henceforth *MGM*), Murdoch returns again and again to the question of art—in its widest sense—and to its relationship to life and to ethics. This question is not one which can be neatly compartmentalised or marginalised. It is not a mere footnote either to metaphysics or to morals, but is an integral part of the philosophical project which she undertakes in the work. Nor is her consideration of art solely concerned with its impact on our conceptions of morality, or with the likelihood of putting our moral theories into practice.

This article is part of a study 'The influence of Eastern religion on selected British authors' which has received grants from the JSPS KAKENHI Grant-in-aid for Scientific Research (C) Grant no. 19K00416.

F. Tomkinson (✉)
Nagoya University, Nagoya, Japan

She does, indeed, make her contribution to the age-old debate as to the way in which, say, our reading of literature, our response to music, or our contemplation of visual art, can impact on our moral and spiritual life, but her engagement with the question of art does not end there. I hope to show how she goes beyond this by analysing the relationship between art and her conception of the Good. For Murdoch, art and our creation or perception of it are not merely instantiations of the good; rather her discussion of these questions is the key to her account of what actually constitutes the Good. It impacts not only on how we see and experience meaning and value in life, but on the meaning and value which we assign to life as a whole.

I shall not attempt here to discuss her comments on aesthetics and the artwork in their entirety, but shall focus on two related aspects of her exploration of the relationship between art and philosophy. The first is the 'fictional genesis' of *MGM* itself in her 1987 novel, *The Book and the Brotherhood*, in a passage which, I shall argue, expresses the experience of a vision of artistic unity. This 'fictional genesis' is not a genesis in the chronological sense, since the project of *MGM* was conceived before the composition of *The Book and the Brotherhood*, and was already being put into execution in the 1982 Gifford Lectures (as Frances White's chapter in this volume shows), but a genesis in the sense of her providing us with a fictional moment which symbolises her first recognition of her own philosophical task. The second aspect is the theoretical treatment of the question of the unity of the artwork within the text itself. I shall discuss this mainly with reference to two passages: the explicit discussion of the question in Chapter 1 (*MGM*, 1–25), 'The unity of the artwork', and the subsection of Chapter 8 (*MGM*, 235–246) in which she implicitly resumes her consideration of the question through her discussion of Japanese aesthetics and philosophy, in particular through her engagement with the concept of pure cognition in the thought of the Zen master, Katsuki Sekida.

Murdoch's reading of Sekida is a crucial step—more so than she herself makes explicit—in her confrontation of the attacks by contemporary philosophical discourse on the meaning of the artwork and the recognition of the human individual. She begins her book with a meditation on artistic unity within the Western tradition and upon the threats posed to it by recent critical and artistic movements which promote an aesthetics of fragmentation and erode traditional certainties concerning the status of the artwork. She does not immediately present us with a solution to this problem, but her solution will emerge both through her re-examination of Western metaphysics and through her rediscovery of a lost sense of unity through her engagement with Eastern thought. The implicit dialogue which she sets up between Western and Eastern conceptions of artistic unity sheds further light on the major philosophical issues with which she grapples in the work; indeed, her position is a synthesis of Sekida's thought with her reinterpretation of the Western tradition. Her understanding of what Sekida calls pure cognition connects with what her ethical vision takes from Plato and from Anselm, more specifically, with the way in which she understands participation in the Platonic Form of the Good and the way in which she turns Anselm's ontological argument for the existence of God into an argument for the existence of the Good.

THE 'FICTIONAL GENESIS' OF *METAPHYSICS AS A GUIDE TO MORALS* IN *THE BOOK AND THE BROTHERHOOD*

It is well-known that Murdoch liked to insist on the complete separation between her novels and her philosophical work (notably in her 1978 BBC interview on 'Philosophy and literature' with Bryan Magee [reprinted in Murdoch 1997]), but nevertheless the novels frequently reference her philosophical preoccupations and show characters grappling with them as they attempt to make sense of their lives. In the case of *The Book and the Brotherhood*, the link is especially close. One of the hints that she was conscious of dealing with the same issues in both works is the repetition in *MGM* of a quotation from Heraclitus referenced in *The Book and the Brotherhood*, where the saintly schoolmaster Jenkin Riderhood, in response to his friend Gerard Hernshaw's comment 'I hate God', remarks, '"He who alone is wise wants and does not want to be called Zeus." Heraclitus wasn't altogether a disaster, you know' (Murdoch 1987, 127–128). In Chapter Two of *MGM*, the full significance of this fragment is spelled out, and the attentive reader can also pick up on the fact that Jenkin's misquotation is being corrected:

> Heraclitus tells us that 'The One who alone is wise does not want and wants to be called Zeus' (Fr. 32). This is indeed the problem. We yearn for the transcendent, for God, for something divine and good and pure, but in picturing the transcendent we transform it into idols which we then realise to be just contingent particulars, just things among other things here below. If we destroy these idols in order to reach something untainted and pure, what we really need, the thing itself, we render the Divine ineffable, and as such in danger of being judged non-existent. Then the sense of the divine vanishes in the attempt to preserve it. No wonder 'that which alone is wise' is in two minds about how to proceed. (The order of the wishes

may be significant; fundamentally it does not want, but is forced by the
frailties of human nature into wanting.) (*MGM*, 56)

The question of how to strike the balance here—of how to retain 'religion' and ethics without traditional concepts of God, indeed without
the concept of God at all, is at the heart of *MGM*, and also recurs again
and again in Murdoch's novels. In *The Book and the Brotherhood*, this
question is tied up more closely than usual with the political. The plot
centres around the question of whether a group of liberal middle-class
friends in the grip of mid-life crises can be justified in retaining the values
which they hold dear. Jenkin quotes W. H. Auden to Gerard as a summary of their dilemma: 'What by nature and by training we have loved,
has little strength remaining, though we would gladly give the Oxford
Colleges, Big Ben, and all the birds in Wicken Fen, it has no wish to
live' (Murdoch 1987, 127). Though Gerard rejects this idea and claims
that Jenkin himself does not really subscribe to it, it can be considered
to constitute the underlying mood of the novel. It is against this background of a crisis in values that the 'book' of the novel's title is composed. We are never given any extract from the book or summary of its
contents, but we are given to understand that it is a work intended to
refute most of the humanist values cherished by bourgeois liberals. It is
written by the maverick nihilist-Marxist, David Crimond, a charismatic
and sinister character, described by Gerard as a 'terrorist' (Murdoch
1987, 126). Crimond, after being funded in his writing for years by 'the
Brotherhood', a group of well-meaning former socialist friends (that is,
both former friends and former socialists) from his Oxford University
days, returns the favour by seducing, and then years later, re-seducing
Jean Cambus, a member of the group and wife of another of its members, and, to crown it all, when his book is finally completed, lures her
into a suicide pact in which they will drive their cars towards a fatal crash
along a Roman road. Jean fortunately escapes by choosing to swerve at
the last moment; Crimond then abandons her, makes an unsuccessful
attempt to seduce her best friend, Rose, and goes on to challenge her
husband, Duncan, to a duel in the process of which he will inadvertently
bring about the death of the innocent Jenkin.

Crimond's intellectual position is never described in full, but it is
referred to as 'a fashionable amalgam, senseless but dangerous – a
kind of Taoism with a dash of modern physics, then labelled Marxism'
(Murdoch 1987, 26) We may deduce from this that his tenets include

a critique of conceptions of unity—the dash of modern physics probably means to emphasise a reductionist view which sees the universe in
terms of the interaction of small particles, whilst the Taoism emphasises
the non-discrete nature of the human personality and the non-existence
of anything corresponding to the traditional Western concept of soul. We
also know that he holds the view that society is doomed. It is somewhat
unclear what, if any, solution for the future of humanity is proposed as an
alternative. Indeed, Crimond is represented in terms of pure negation:
he is identified with the Second person of the Hindu Trinity, Shiva, and
this suggests that the role of Vishnu, renewer and preserver, should fall
to someone else. Throughout the plot, the themes of the Marxist critique of liberal humanist values are intertwined with themes of suicide
and abortion, each constituting an attack on humanist life-affirming values from a different angle and presenting the misery of the planet as a
challenge both to the desire to continue or perpetuate human life, and to
the defence of ethical absolutes. That this intertwining is not accidental
can be seen from a passage in *MGM*, which in the context of an analysis
of popular structuralism and deconstruction and its tendency to replace
authors, characters and narratives with their linguistic components,
deplores how quasi-scientific terminology and technology may take the
place of human beings:

> We, who still in spite of everything live in a Greek light, have yet to see
> how far science and its satellite theories can actually alter our human
> world. Intelligent tyrants reflect on this; and Marxism, for all its utilitarian
> virtues, carried this hypothesis, unclarified and semi-conscious within itself.
> Could it seem before long *naive* to believe in the value and being of indi-
> vidual consciousness, even in that which is oneself? (*MGM*, 159)

The task of negating the negation by refuting Crimond—the role of
Vishnu—falls to Gerard, a character who, like his creator, has long been
devoted to a quasi-Platonic idealism, and at the end of the penultimate
chapter, he dedicates himself to this task. Gerard has also had his fill of
human suffering, despite his relatively comfortable middle-class background. He has suffered a number of bereavements, including the recent
losses of his father and Jenkin, and that of Sinclair, the homosexual love
of his student days, but his first traumatic loss, and possibly the one
which marked him the most deeply, is the loss of his childhood pet, a
parrot called Grey, who was got rid of by his family when he was away at

school. It is the thought of Grey which gives rise to the epiphanic vision of the book which he is to write:

> The thought that Grey might have starved to death was so terrible to Gerard that he suddenly sat bolt upright, and there flowed into him, as into a clear vessel, a sudden sense of all the agony and helpless suffering of created things.
>
> He fell asleep and dreamt that he was standing on that mountainside holding an open book upon whose pages was written *Dominus Illuminatio mea* – and from far far above an angel was descending in the form of a great grey parrot with clever loving eyes and the parrot perched upon the book and spread out its grey and scarlet wings and the parrot was the book. (Murdoch 1987, 585)

The book is also, I think, *MGM*—thus presented as a book written *contra* Crimond, *contra* Marxism and linguistic idealism, but also written in response to the predicament of suffering and as a consequence of trauma—and, finally, as the use of the motto of the University of Oxford suggests, it is presented as something which seeks to mysteriously combine scholarly learning and divine illumination, the word and the world. We are also given a number of hints from Gerard's characterisation as a kind of Platonist, that Plato will be a major presence in the work. The discussion of Japanese aesthetics in *MGM* is also prefigured by the presence in Gerard's house of 'nineteenth-century Japanese paintings, shadowy exquisite things with sparse smudgy lines and dashes of colour, representing birds, dogs, insects, trees, frogs, tortoises, monkeys, frail girls, casual men, mountains, rivers, the moon' (Murdoch 1987, 193).

What, then, is the essence of this book?

PLATO, ANSELM AND MURDOCH'S PHILOSOPHICAL PROJECT

To summarise Murdoch's project as briefly as possible, it is an attempt to speak of meaning and of goodness without recourse to traditional religious faith in a personal deity or an afterlife, and to assert the need for a theology which can continue without God—she anticipates the question as to why we do not content ourselves with calling this an ethics, by saying that one may do so if one wishes, but it should be an ethics which should treat of 'our continued sense of what is holy' (*MGM*, 512) which we find in that which is beyond ourselves (nature, great art, other human beings) and with which we strive to bring ourselves into a correct relation. In practical terms, this translates into a belief in a revival of Aristotelian virtue ethics, an advocacy of practical participation in goodness through small acts of attentiveness and mindfulness, through resistance to tyranny, through the creation of art and through love. She is well aware that erotic love can be blind and selfish, and that saintliness can degenerate into masochism. Indeed, the novels document numerous cases of the complications of love and of the spiritual quest which can also be read as a litany of the demonic and egotistical qualities of Eros. As she remarks in Chapter Ten of *MGM*, 'Eros is a great artist, not a pure being' (*MGM*, 343). She confronts the question of the void and of suffering, and yet nevertheless defends the value of a purified Eros and a belief in an absolute Form of Good in the sense of Plato.

It might be a common initial response of the layperson to ask whether metaphysics is really doing anything here? What exactly is this mystical parrot of Gerard's dream-vision, which like Hegel's owl of Athena takes flight in the dusk? For those of us familiar with the tradition of British television comedy, might it not resemble the parrot in a famous *Monty Python* sketch, in which a man played by John Cleese comes into a pet shop with a dead parrot, which the man behind the counter assures him is only sleeping, when in fact, it is deceased, it has ceased to exist? Do we really have the right to use the term metaphysics when we have given up applying it to the study of supernatural beings? Is not Murdoch, in defending the practice of a metaphysics redefined as a study of the essence or essences of reality in the context of belief in a purely physical world, performing the function of the pet-shop owner who nails the dead parrot to its perch? And what, might it be asked, in practical terms do we get out of all this? To reference *Monty Python* once more, do Murdoch's moral injunctions amount to much more than the answer to the question of 'The Meaning of Life' handed out in an envelope in the 1983 film of the same name? That is: 'Try and be nice to people, avoid eating fat, read a good book every now and then, get some walking in, and try and live together in peace and harmony with people of all creeds and nations' (Jones 1983). Do we really need to wade through over five hundred pages of metaphysical or quasi-metaphysical discussion to get to this point? Should we not rather say with the Louis MacNeice (2007) of 'London Rain', that we need no metaphysics to sanction what we do?

In response to these imagined objections, I would like to focus on what I see as both the crux and the culmination of Murdoch's argument as stated towards the conclusion of the work, where she states that she wishes 'to use Plato's images as a sort of Ontological Proof of the necessity of Good' (*MGM*, 511).

The phrase 'the necessity of Good' implies not only an injunction to be good, but an acknowledgment that there is good in life and that life can be seen as a good. But how are we to understand her bringing in of the ontological proof? What she seems to suggest is that the existence of the Idea of Good in the mind proves the existence of the Good as something which transcends the mind—a move which many people might well find problematic regardless of their personal belief concerning the existence of goodness. The Kantian and Humean objections to the ontological proof of God's existence apply equally to the demonstration of the existence of anything outside the mind by the fact that it can be thought of. Murdoch was well aware of these objections, which she references in Chapter 13 of the work. (*MGM*, 391–430) She also remarks upon the circularity of the argument at the end of Chapter 2, saying of the concept of God that 'unless you have it in the picture at the start you cannot get it in later by extraneous means' (*MGM*, 57). Why then does she adopt the argument, which might be thought of as the deadest of all dead parrots in the metaphysical tradition—and what exactly does she mean by a *sort of* ontological proof here? This might seem a desperately vague term to use in a philosophical text. She clearly does not mean a new *version* of the ontological argument as we might refer to Anselm's version or to Gödel's, since she makes no attempt to advance one. My claim is that her meaning only becomes clear in the context of her discussion of aesthetics. The first part of this discussion in Chapter 1 gives us a clearer awareness of what she means by *Plato's images*, and the second, the discussion of Japanese aesthetics in Chapter 8, will, I shall argue, clarify what she means by the *sort of ontological proof.*

In Chapter 1, 'Conceptions of Unity', Murdoch argues that the idea of self-contained unity is 'a fundamental instinctive concept'; that we fear 'plurality, diffusion, senseless accident, chaos' (*MGM*, 1), but as philosophical idealism is replaced with the hermeneutics of suspicion (to use a phrase of Ricoeur's not adopted by Murdoch herself) we are now faced with a pluralisation or demythologisation of art and the 'sponging away', in Nietzsche's phrase, of a horizon within which we have dwelt since the time of the ancient Greeks. The result is deconstructive approaches to literary criticism and cults of the ephemeral or incomplete.

Freudian theory in particular is to be held responsible, since despite the fact that, on the level of therapy, it aims for a reintegration of the personality, on the level of metaphysics, it is iconoclastic in its reductionist 'explanation by sex' and its dismissal of religion as illusion. Moreover, art, for Freud, is a kind of 'fore-pleasure' which suggest that all art aspires to the condition of pornography. Murdoch asks, 'What now becomes of the dignity and innocence of the work of art?' (*MGM*, 21). Yet she finds a ray of hope in the point at which Plato and Freud coincide, in Freud's identification of the concept of the libido with Plato's Eros—she believes that the Platonic distinction between high and low Eros can be rediscovered in Freud's concept of the redeployment of energy—a transformation which she sees as our life-problem. She then takes the connection further in seeing in Plato's theory of recollection or *anamnesis* the ancestor of the Freudian unconscious, even though the memory of pure Forms of goodness and beauty, put forward in the *Meno* to account for the origin of virtue, are, she confesses, very different from anything that we find in Freud's 'glimpses of infantile sexuality' (*MGM*, 23). She also sees a demythologised concept of *anamnesis* in the concept of 'live remembrance' in Plato's Seventh Letter and in the Kantian solitary moral private agent 'continually doing it all, over and over, for himself' (*MGM*, 23). She concludes the chapter with a description of the moral life in the Platonic understanding as an orientation of Eros towards the Form of the Good in which the artist as virtuous truth-seeker may also participate, a movement:

> not, by an occasional leap, into an external (empty) space of freedom, but patiently and continuously a change of one's whole being in all its contingent detail ... There are innumerable points at which we have to detach ourselves, to change our orientation, to redirect our desire and refresh and purify our energy, to keep on looking in the right direction: to attend upon the grace that comes through faith. (*MGM*, 25)

Although 'grace' and 'faith' sound like—and in a sense still are—Christian concepts, we are still very much in an ancient Greek light at the end of this chapter, though her original point of departure, the concept of the unity of the artwork itself, has disappeared from view. Art can be redeemed within Plato's system, if not in Plato's opinion, but it is redeemed as a kind of *techne*, as virtuous practice.

In her following discussion of Japanese aesthetics, not only is the concept of virtuous practice elaborated upon, but the concept of unity is reintroduced in a different guise. Murdoch takes as her point of departure Katsuki Sekida's critique of the phenomenologist Edmund Husserl's eidetic reduction, or rather his insistence on its distinction from the pure consciousness sought after in Zen practice. For Husserl, the ego is suspended as an intellectual exercise allowing us to attain the pure phenomenon. (Thus, we come to understand, for example, that the essence of a triangle is not being blue or pink, but having three sides.) Sekida remarks that this is done in the head without too much difficulty, whereas for the Zen practitioner, the suspending of the personal ego involves the discipline of *zazen*, which is not a simple change of mental attitude, but a discipline of body and mind—we root out the emotionally and intellectually habituated consciousness so that a pure state of cognition may emerge (*MGM*, 240). As a pointer in the direction of what is meant by a pure cognition, Murdoch gives us a quotation used by Sekida from what she calls a Japanese poem by Nansen, a poem which was perhaps in her mind when she wrote of the mountains and rivers in Gerard's Japanese paintings:

> Hearing, seeing, touching and knowing are not one and one;
> Mountains and rivers should not be viewed in the mirror.
> The frosty sky, the setting moon – at midnight
> With whom will the serene waters of the lake reflect the shadows in the cold? (*MGM*, 242)

Murdoch presents Sekida's position here briefly as follows: in pure cognition there is no separation of the subject and object—subjectivity and objectivity only arise in the second stage of the recognition of pure cognition; we should not say as the idealist does that the external world is nothing but the projection of the subjective mirror of our mind.

If we turn to the work of Sekida quoted, *Zen Training*, we find that the poem is not, in fact, by Nansen: Murdoch probably made this error by skimming the relevant passage in Chapter 14 when she returned to reference it. The poem is actually given as a work by Setcho, the author of the Hekigan Roku (or Blue Cliff Record), commenting on the story 'Nansen Views the Flower'. In this story, the high government official Rikko Taifu, speaking with the Zen master Nansen Osho, says, 'Jo Hoshi said, "Heaven and earth and I are of the same root. All things and I are of the same substance." Isn't that fantastic!' (Sekida 2005, 173). Nansen responds by asking Rikko if, like the Tathagata, he can see Buddha nature with his naked eyes, and when Rikko confesses that he can only see a peony, Nansen replies by pointing to a flower and saying, 'People of these days see this flower as though they were in a dream' (Sekida 2005, 175). For Sekida, seeing the Buddha nature in a flower is equivalent to the state of *kensho* in which the freshness of perception is renewed as the practitioner returns from deep meditation, from the state of absolute *samadhi* in which consciousness almost disappears. Reading a little further in Sekida, we also see that the explication of the poem is grounded in the theory of mind underlying Zen practice. He divides the action of consciousness into the activity of three *nen*, the first corresponding to what Husserl calls 'perception', the second to the reflecting action of consciousness and the third to a further step in self-consciousness involving recollection and memory. Pure cognition comes from the meeting of the first *nen* and the object (Sekida 2005, 170). However, the activity of the first *nen* is suppressed by and needs to be liberated from the third *nen* (Sekida 2005, 190). In absolute *samadhi*, all three *nen* disappear, but the first *nen* is the last to disappear and the first to return as we emerge from this state, so that stimuli rush in all their unlimited profusion: 'In the kensho experience it is this strength of impressions that brings before you the objects of the external world with fresh and inspiring originality' (Sekida 2005, 179).

We can assume that Murdoch was bearing in mind the background in Zen thinking given by Sekida as she composed this chapter, but it is significant that she chooses to emphasise not the Zen phenomenology of mind per se, but the link between pure cognition and the Japanese aesthetic: for her, the throw-away simplicity and pointless 'thereness' of Zen art makes comprehensible the notion of achieving a pure cognitive state (*MGM*, 245) and the haiku points at some aspect of the visible world in such a way as to suggest that inner and outer are one, without losing or subjectivising the world:

> Emphasis is laid by Zen, partly in its instruction through art, upon the small contingent details of ordinary life and the natural world. Buddhism teaches love and respect for all things ... The enlightened man returns to, that is, *discovers*, the world. He begins by thinking that rivers are merely rivers and mountains are merely mountains, proceeds to the view that rivers are not rivers and mountains are not mountains, and later achieves the

deep understanding that rivers are really rivers and mountains are really mountains. (*MGM*, 244)

Murdoch then goes on to give an account of the unselfing achieved in pure cognition as a place where morality and aesthetics meet—and illustrates this process with examples from Adorno, Rilke and Simone Weil. One quotation from Rilke in particular comes close to Sekida's concept of pure cognition. Rilke describes a self-portrait by Cézanne as being made 'with the credulity and extrinsic interest of a dog which sees itself in the mirror and thinks: there is another dog' (*MGM*, 246).

How, then, does this relate to the preoccupations of Murdoch with aesthetic unity in Chapter 1? I believe that we are given a significant clue in the comparison she makes between Sekida and Plato in Chapter Six of *MGM*, where Sekida's critique of Husserl is said to have the characteristics of a double movement, which we also find in Plato, away from the private and personal and then back again (*MGM*, 174). In Sekida, we have first pure cognition and then the recognition of pure cognition (a kind of return to the personal); in Plato, as with the other ancient Greek philosophers, we have the world, not the Cartesian *cogito*, as starting point (the first stage of the movement), but his insistence on the fundamental importance of the speaking individual, shown by his distrust of writing in the *Phaedrus*, and his concern with personal salvation 'as personal vision and change of being' (*MGM*, 174) in the *Phaedrus* and the *Symposium* bring us back to the individual again.

READING PLATO AND ANSELM THROUGH SEKIDA

I would like to take this one stage further—to think the unthought or perhaps the incompletely explicated—of Murdoch by applying the back-and-forth movement which we see in Sekida to the Platonic forms and to the ontological proof. For Murdoch, ethics can only begin by taking the existence of the Good as a starting point. In the terms of Platonic philosophy, this ultimately amounts to a participation (*methexis*) in the Form of the Good, in the sense not merely of *mimesis* (copying) but of *parousia* (presence)—the good itself must be actually present. Indeed, in a certain sense, there can be in this case no *mimesis* without *parousia*. A copy of the good is not like a copy of a chair in a painting. (Faking goodness is something else.) If we really have made a copy of the good, then the good is present.

But there is a way in which we can have an abstract idea of the good within us, in the same way that an atheist might have an idea of God simply as an imagined entity considered to be non-existent (and whose existence might be desired, or not desired, or to the existence of which he or she might even be indifferent). Good would then be something of which we might be aware as a hypothetical entity, but which we feel we have not tasted, as when someone says, 'I have never tasted happiness in all my life', though in order to say so they must have at least some faint notion of what happiness is. This brings to mind Sekida's quotation of the mountains which should not be viewed in the mirror. Such an abstract conception of goodness can function as a starting point, as a felt lack which might transmute itself into its opposite, but it is insufficient. The mountains are in the mirror. But perhaps it is also not enough to experience goodness as immanence without feeling that it is also transcendent. (This brings to mind Merleau-Ponty's critique of the bracketing of the question of existence in Husserl; our eidetic reduction of something considered real can never be the same as something considered to be non-existent/imaginary [Merleau-Ponty 1960].) We can experience the Good, but believe it is confined to our own mind. The mountains are still in the mirror. It is only the awareness of goodness as *participation* in something which is *transcendent* that brings the mountains out of the mirror, though the mirror is not shattered, and we may in fact continue to see the mountains reflected in multiple mirrors.

How does this movement relate to the ontological proof? Just as Anselm begins by believing rather than by understanding, and so has already within himself a concept of God which includes the belief in His Existence, so the Form of the Good must be initially *experienced* as something *transcendent* in a move which involves something like Sekida's pure cognition. (We have here the restoration of both a pure interiority and a pure exteriority—both of which have been under threat by linguistic idealism and deconstruction.) Reflection on the concept only comes as a second stage. There is a circularity here, but it is a hermeneutic, not a vicious circularity.

How the initial step towards participation in the Form of the Good/the first stage of the ontological argument can be made is a different question, to which I do not here propose to give a definitive answer, but I would suggest that there are a number of paths, some of which Murdoch has marked out for us in her discussion of the deployment of Eros. Sometimes it may be less a question of stepping than of finding ourselves thrown into this sense of participation in the transcendent, like Murdoch's character Effingham in *The Unicorn* (Murdoch, 1963), whose near-death experience results in an automatic experience of love for the universe beyond the self and a vision of something which seems to correspond to the Platonic Form of the Good. Although these feelings cannot be sustained at the same level, they can, Murdoch suggests, permeate the life which follows. This roughly corresponds to the tenth stage of Zen training described by Sekida, which he calls 'In town with helping hands' (Sekida 2005, 230–231). Once the initial step has been taken, what may follow is a living in a faith in the existence of Good, not in the sense of adherence to a particular religious dogma, but in a manner somewhat akin to Merleau-Ponty's description of perceptual faith—our belief in the reality of the visual world—as that in which we necessarily live despite our familiarity with all the arguments of scepticism. We see the mountains outside the mirror and reach out to touch them.

It is such a moment which, I believe, Murdoch, perhaps basing the description on a personal experience of her own, is attributing to Gerard Hernshaw in the visionary dream-state in which parrot and book, representing the living world and the written word which mirrors it, merge. Despite the apparently abstract and theoretical nature of *MGM*, it is a work which calls on the reader to take a similar step as a precondition for embarking on the life of virtue: to come out of the cave—our own version of the cave of Plato's *Republic* Book X where we depend on reflections—and to access the Form of the Good and the 'sort of ontological proof' through pure cognition.

Going a little further than Murdoch, I would claim that in so doing, we shall also, in each moment, create a unified artwork at the intersection of exteriority and interiority. Also going a little further than what is explicitly stated, I would conclude that in *MGM*, if it is the philosophers of the Western tradition (Plato, Anselm and Kant) who point the way towards virtue, it is the Zen master who leads us there by the hand.

References

Jones, T., Dir. 1983. *Monty Python's the meaning of life*. New York, UK: Universal Pictures.

MacNeice, L. 2007. *Collected poems*, ed. Peter McDonald. London: Faber & Faber.

Merleau-Ponty, M. 1960. Le philosophe et son ombre. In *Signes*, 201–228. Paris: Gallimard.

Murdoch, I. 1987. *The book and the brotherhood*. London: Vintage Classics.

Murdoch, I. 1997. *Existentialists and mystics*, ed. Peter J. Conradi. London: Chatto & Windus.

Murdoch, I. 2003. *Metaphysics as a guide to morals* (Abbreviated *MGM*). London: Vintage Classics.

Sekida, K. 2005. *Zen training methods and philosophy*. Boston and London: Shambala Classics.

CHAPTER 5

Fact and Value (*MGM* Chapter 2)

Craig Taylor

Followers of debates in contemporary moral philosophy about whether moral judgements can be true are likely to be surprised, even disappointed, with the discussion of fact and value offered here.[1] This chapter is not in any sense a contribution to recent debate about whether there are any moral, or more generally evaluative, facts. While Murdoch holds in *Metaphysics as a Guide to Morals* (Murdoch 1992, henceforth *MGM*) that one cannot derive values from facts, so long as we understand facts as simply empirical facts and the province of science, she is quick to add that the 'concept of "fact" is complex', by which she means to point to how 'values pervade and *colour* what we take to be the reality of our world' (*MGM*, 26, her italics).[2] For Murdoch the place of value in our lives and in our understanding of the world is ubiquitous; as she says, 'forms of evaluation haunt our simplest decisions' (*MGM*, 26). More to the point, Murdoch's discussion of the distinction between fact and value, including her insistence that value cannot be derived from facts, is grounded in the idea that value is supremely important in our lives. As Murdoch sees it, those that have thought hardest about the distinction between fact and value have been concerned as she puts it 'to keep [value] pure and untainted, not derived from or mixed with empirical facts' (*MGM*, 25).

C. Taylor (✉)
Flinders University, Adelaide, SA, Australia

© The Author(s) 2019
N. Hämäläinen and G. Dooley (eds.),
Reading Iris Murdoch's Metaphysics as a Guide to Morals,
https://doi.org/10.1007/978-3-030-18967-9_5

Two philosophers she focuses on here are Immanuel Kant and Ludwig Wittgenstein (influenced Murdoch thinks by Arthur Schopenhauer).

Our problem, as Murdoch sees it, is that in the segregation of (empirical) fact from value, particularly given the advance and success of science, value can appear to be a rather small and insignificant thing, even nothing at all. Some people, or at least some of those philosophers participating in current debates about fact and value, might be quite happy to accept that last conclusion. What, they may ask, is the problem?[3] Murdoch, though, is addressing herself to those who see that there is a problem here, and a very fundamental one at that, going to the heart of our understanding of ourselves and the world. Those familiar with Kant and the Wittgenstein of the *Tractatus* might immediately understand why Murdoch should focus on them.

To start with Wittgenstein, in the *Tractatus* ethics is placed outside the world. To understand this idea, we need to consider Wittgenstein's so-called 'picture theory' of meaning. According to this theory, '*The Limits of My Language* mean the Limits of My World', where 'the world is the totality of facts not of things', and 'the totality of propositions is language' (Wittgenstein 1961, §5.6, §1.1, §4.001). Propositions indicate ways in which the world could be, in Wittgenstein's terms, 'the existence and non-existences of states of affairs' (Wittgenstein 1961, §4.1), but in our talk about ethics we refer to no possible states of affairs, there is nothing that such utterances might picture in the way that propositions provide a (possible) picture of the world, a way in which the world, as I just noted, could be. In other worlds, with respect to our ethical utterances there is nothing in the world that they refer to, they are, again in Wittgenstein's terms, nonsense; they have no sense so are not genuine propositions. As Wittgenstein says there are no 'propositions of ethics' (Wittgenstein 1961, §6.42).

However, that is not an end to the matter. As Wittgenstein immediately adds 'propositions can express nothing that is higher'. Noting that Wittgenstein's remarks here at the end of the *Tractatus* concerning ethics have often 'been treated as an arcane idiosyncratic tailpiece',[4] Murdoch suggests they are in fact of crucial importance for Wittgenstein. Here Murdoch refers to a letter from Wittgenstein to Ludwig Fricker where he explains that he had wanted to add a sentence in the preface to the *Tractatus* to the effect that the book's point is an ethical one, that there are two parts to the work, the one written and the other not, where 'this second part is the important one' (qtd. in Waismann 1979,

68). That while what others have said about ethics is 'just gassing', he, Wittgenstein, has 'put everything in its place by being silent about it' (cited *MGM*, 29). But isn't that to admit that ethics, the whole realm of value, really is nothing? Not quite, as Wittgenstein also says 'There are indeed things that cannot be put into words. *They Make Themselves Manifest*. They are what is mystical' (Wittgenstein 1961, §6.522). It is only that value does not enter into the world so as to in any sense change the facts. Value, as Murdoch puts it in this picture 'resides rather in an *attitude or style* in one's acceptance of all the facts' (*MGM*, 28). To explain Wittgenstein's point here I need first to turn to Kant.

Kant, too, wants to remove value from the world, or at least what was for him the phenomenal world. However, he would have rejected the moral stoicism, as Murdoch puts it, indicated above by Wittgenstein. Crucial for Kant is the distinction between the noumenal and phenomenal worlds: the world as it is in itself, the real, and the world as it appears to us, respectively. While value is for Kant no part of the phenomenal or empirical world (that world is determined purely by cause and effect), value, that which is higher, does enter that world, in Murdoch's wonderful image, as a 'laser beam' with practical reason, our sense of duty and the moral law understood as a universal principle of practical reason (Kant's categorical imperative). Somehow our will as rational beings, Kant's 'good will', does bring about change in the world, though as Murdoch notes how all this works is never made very clear by Kant. The important point for us is just to notice that there has clearly been some break between Kant and Wittgenstein—and for Murdoch it seems we can attribute this to Schopenhauer and his influence on the young Wittgenstein, the Wittgenstein of the *Tractatus*.

Key here is the notion of the will, or the problem of the will. Schopenhauer accepts Kant's distinction between the phenomenal and noumenal worlds. But our wills are for Schopenhauer a manifestation of what he calls the 'Will to Live', which is, as Murdoch puts it, 'the fundamental reality and basis of our world as a ruthless powerful cosmic force'. We experience the world 'as objectivised ideas of the Will. The Will to Live, to *exist*, takes care of the continuation of the species and general ordering of entities' (*MGM*, 32). The result is that our most basic motive is that of egoism, so that each pursues his own interest heedless of others to the mutual misery of all—or at least for the most part; Schopenhauer does posit the further—rarer, weaker—motive of compassion according to which '*another's* weal and woe ... become directly my motive'

(Schopenhauer 1965, 146). But more generally, according to this rather dismal picture, escape from suffering and evil depends, as Murdoch says, on the 'total denial of the Will' (*MGM*, 32)—something Schopenhauer was pessimistic about our achieving but that Wittgenstein can entertain, as we have noted, as a stoical acceptance of the world. So the will, then, for Wittgenstein, becomes just an attitude of acceptance of all the facts which one cannot, by any act of will, change. What changes is just the world as a whole; it, as Wittgenstein says, 'waxes and wanes as a whole. The world of the happy man is a different one from the world of the unhappy man' (Wittgenstein 1961, §6.43).

Crucial for Murdoch in these remarks by Wittgenstein is his 'image of the limited whole', and the importance of this imagery in 'metaphysical and religious thinking' (*MGM*, 37). By the idea of a limited whole Wittgenstein suggests our contemplation of particular things, for example Wittgenstein says a stove, 'in such a way as they have the whole world as a background'; not our contemplation of an object, as one thing among other things, but rather 'contemplating the stove [such that] *it* was my world and everything else colourless by contrast with it' (Wittgenstein 1979, 83e). For Wittgenstein a work of art or a good life are limited wholes in this sense; there is a way recognising them as not one thing within the world but a world unto themselves.

The image of a limited whole is, as Murdoch goes on to suggest, deployed in the 'quest for satisfying sovereign imagery which is to indicate a very, or absolutely, important reality'. But, as she adds and as I have observed before, 'philosophers divide between those that do, and those who do not, think morality is such a reality' (*MGM*, 37). I started by noting Murdoch's suggestion that those who have thought hardest about the distinction between fact and value have done so out of a sense of the absolute importance of the reality of value and a corresponding desire to keep value pure and untainted by empirical facts. However, it does not follow that if a philosopher distinguishes between fact and value he or she will *necessarily* think that morality is such an important reality. Thus, as Murdoch notes, David Hume separates fact from value, although he, unlike Kant or Wittgenstein, 'portrays morality in a way that is important, but not supremely so' (*MGM*, 37).[5] With Hume Murdoch places A. J. Ayer. Ayer, according to Murdoch, misreads Wittgenstein's silence about value, taking this silence and the distinction about fact and value it indicates so as to 'remove value' from the realm of the real (*MGM*, 43).

Ayer's mistake with respect to Wittgenstein is, in Murdoch's view, of a piece with that of many other thinkers with respect to Plato and his explanatory myths. In being silent about value, by placing it somehow outside the world, Wittgenstein is not saying that value is nothing. In a similar manner, Plato's myths and allegories are not just useful fictions; yes, they are myths and allegories, but they indicate or point to something real. As Murdoch puts it, for Wittgenstein as with Plato, 'the "picturesque" structure indicates something beyond it; it is not to be taken literally' (*MGM*, 43). (Value, the Good, is not literally a myth, that is to say, unreal.) As against someone like Ayer, the philosophers that most occupy Murdoch in this chapter take seriously the problem that the dichotomy between fact and value tends to undermine our sense of value as something not only real but supremely important. Murdoch sees these philosophers as aware of the way both the unreality and reality of value are dependent on metaphysical pictures. Value needs to be in the picture of the real from the start: it cannot be 'put in' later, for example as an empirical discovery. As Murdoch says here, and this remark seems key to understanding her account of fact and value, 'That is in the nature (or magic) of metaphysics' (*MGM*, 43); it is the nature of metaphysics to present pictures of what we take to be an important reality beyond the empirical facts.

In different ways, however, Murdoch thinks all these pictures fail to satisfy us, do not meet the deep human need, as she puts it, on account of which we turn to them. Thus, against Wittgenstein for example, 'we want to be comforted by our thoughts [about morality] and are reluctant to admit that we can say nothing about it' (*MGM*, 44). Or as Murdoch says against G. E. Moore, he was right to argue that we cannot define good naturalistically in terms of empirical properties, but in defining the good instead in terms of some simply non-natural property 'he diminished his concept of good' (*MGM*, 46).[6] Or turning to the later Wittgenstein of the *Philosophical Investigations*, where the 'metaphysical, pictorial, method of the *Tractatus*' has been abandoned, Murdoch experiences a sense of loss with the way Wittgenstein there deals with questions concerning 'meaning and "mental contents"', like sensations (*MGM*, 49). Why for Murdoch this sense of loss? Concerning mental contents like sensations Wittgenstein claims only to 'reject the grammar that tries to force itself on us here' (Wittgenstein 1968, §304), such that 'if we construe the grammar of the expression of sensation on the model of "object and designation" the object [the sensation] drops out of consideration as irrelevant' (Wittgenstein 1968, §293). But we still lose, Murdoch suggests, 'some sort of inner thing' (*MGM*, 49). The passages in the *Investigations* to which Murdoch is rather too obliquely referring to here raise difficult philosophical problems and concerns that I cannot clarify in this chapter.[7] But what readers of Murdoch's other philosophical works, particularly *The Sovereignty of Good*, may recognise here, once again, is her insistence that we are able to justify a sense of an inner life—and change within that inner life and the (moral) vision of the world that goes with it (think here of Murdoch's famous example of M and her daughter in law D [Murdoch 1985])—as something real and distinct from outward action.

A related motive for the separation of fact and value that Murdoch discusses and I have touched upon, but which deserves further elucidation, is the desire, felt by the philosophers she has been most concerned with, to liberate the will as 'the carrier of value … from the ordinary factual world' (*MGM*, 52). Kant, as we have seen, achieves this by setting the real, noumenal will free from the apparent, phenomenal, world where our actions are causally determined. Wittgenstein, on the other hand, and again as we have seen, removes will from the factual world by counting it as an attitude to the whole world, ideally an attitude of acceptance of all the facts. It is in terms of this attitude that we can recognise that the world changes as a whole; as Wittgenstein says, 'The world of the happy man is a different one to the unhappy man'. This later view of the will has a certain attraction for Murdoch, which is evident in various of her philosophical writings, particularly where she discusses certain ideas of Simone Weil, notably Weil's idea of 'attention' understood by Murdoch as 'a just and loving gaze directed upon a particular reality' (Murdoch 1985, 34). As Murdoch states in this chapter,

> Weil says that will does not lead to moral improvement, but should be connected only with strict obligations. Moral change comes from an attention to the world whose natural result is a decrease in egoism through an increased sense of the reality of … other people … but also things. (*MGM*, 52)

But as Murdoch goes on, while Weil connects the will with duty in this way, for Wittgenstein and for Schopenhauer before him the will as far as the individual agent is concerned may seem 'a kind of fiction' (*MGM*, 53).

Murdoch's remarks are here again very compressed. Crucial is her reference to Schopenhauer's explanation of compassion which I mentioned earlier. Schopenhauer's problem is to explain how 'it is possible for *another's* weal and woe to move my will immediately, that is to say, in exactly the same way in which it is usually moved only by my own weal and woe?' For this to be the case, Schopenhauer thinks, I must 'feel his woe just as I ordinarily feel my own', which in turn 'requires that I am in some way *identified with him* ... that this entire *difference* between me and everyone else, which is the basis of my egoism, is eliminated, to a certain extent at least' (Schopenhauer 1965, 143–144). Duty as we understand it with Kant—which appears as an element of our phenomenal, empirical lives—has no place then in Schopenhauer's account of morality; as he says, the 'conception that underlies egoism [as the sole source of human motivation] is *empirically* considered strictly justified' (Schopenhauer 1965, 205). But this denial of the will cannot be right, Murdoch contends, since it denies our everyday experience of morality; as she says 'a realistic view of morality cannot dispense with [duty]; duty is for most people the most obvious form of moral experience'. Thus, we approach another divide in morality such that 'the good life becomes increasingly selfless through increased awareness ... of the world beyond self. But meanwhile requirements and claims [duty] ... demand to be met' (*MGM*, 53). As Murdoch adds, the concept of duty does not necessarily require the will here—with many duties she notes Hume's idea of habit and custom are enough—nevertheless, with those duties that 'are abstract in relation to our nature', so that 'we do not identify with them ... there may be a place for the concept of the will as a name for the *strain* which is then felt' (*MGM*, 53).

Murdoch's interest in the fact–value distinction in this chapter is not, as I said, in the difficulty of defending the idea that there are any moral facts as that is usually understood in contemporary analytic philosophy. Rather, it has to do with defending morality as something deep, fundamental to human nature, the most important thing' (*MGM*, 54) in a world where the realm of fact is increasingly given over to science. Solutions to this problem, Murdoch suggests, involve the notion that 'if we reflect about moral value, we cannot properly avoid certain pictures of the world' (*MGM*, 55). This indicates for Murdoch one aspect of the turn of philosophers to metaphysics; the pictures she has in mind here serve to meet our need that morality be provided with deep foundations, foundations certainly deeper than the pronouncements of science. Here again Kant is instructive. Kant said that Hume woke him from his 'dogmatic slumber', as Murdoch goes on to suggest, really to defend science from the 'vague (sloppy) psychological accounts' of both science and morality that Hume offered (*MGM*, 40). But, of course, in placing science on the first side of the phenomena–noumena distinction Kant provides the kind of system, the kind of foundation, in which ethics (grounded in our noumenal selves, rational, free) is safe *from* science. What Kant is really doing here is an example of what Murdoch means when she says concerning such pictures, such foundations, that 'it is often felt, there is something essential; and this essential thing must be built into the explanation from the start, or else it tends to fly away and become problematic and remote and extremely difficult to integrate' (*MGM*, 55).

But the problem then is, as she immediately adds, that 'if it is built in at the start, the thinker may be accused of an unwarrantable act of faith or intuition' (*MGM*, 55). So continuing with Kant, he 'finds it perfectly clear and primary that we all recognise the absolute call of duty' (*MGM*, 56), *that* according to him is our freedom. Yet what greater act of faith could there be? In the end, Kant recognised this act of faith. As Murdoch, like many others, have noted, when Kant attempts in his *Groundwork of the metaphysic of morals* 'to establish these ideas on a more profound basis he admits the circularity of the argument' (*MGM*, 56). So as Kant says in the *Groundwork*,

> In this we must frankly admit there is shown a kind of circle, from which, as it seems, there is no way of escape. In the order of efficient causes, we take ourselves to be free so that we may conceive of ourselves to be under moral laws in the order of ends; and we then proceed to think of ourselves as subject to moral laws on the grounds that we have described the will as free. (Kant 1964, 118)

In conclusion, for Murdoch the problems with, or tensions within, different versions of the fact–value dichotomy—understood in her terms as attempts to present a convincing picture of the world in which value is registered as something real and of fundamental importance—corresponds to deep human need, one that is fundamental to our nature. Noting how close here philosophy and theology can come to each other, Murdoch sums up our problem with a final picture, which is also a religious one. I quote Murdoch at some length,

Heraclitus tells us that 'The One who alone is wise does not want and does want to be called by the name of Zeus.' This is indeed the problem. We yearn for the transcendent, for God, for something divine and good and pure, but picturing the transcendent we transform it into idols which we then realise to be contingent particulars, just things among others here below. If we destroy these idols in order to reach something untainted and pure, what we really need, the thing itself, we render the Divine ineffable, and as such in peril of being judged non-existent. (*MGM*, 56)

While Murdoch focuses in this chapter mostly on Kant and Wittgenstein, hovering in the background is of course Plato. As I noted earlier, for Murdoch 'values pervade and *colour* what we take to be the reality of our world'. And for Plato, to see the world as it really is *just is* to see it in the light of the Good, as the allegory of the Cave indicates. Which will perhaps seem to many again an extreme act of faith.

So, is that all one can say on the dichotomy between fact and value? I think not, and at this point I want to return to Wittgenstein; not the Wittgenstein of the *Tractatus*, but of the *Investigations*. While Wittgenstein did not himself write in a substantial and extended way on morality or value more generally, the distinctly non-metaphysical approach to philosophical questions and problems in the *Investigations*, along with other of his later writings, has been applied very fruitfully to morality by others.[8] In particular some have seen in the *Investigations*, in a distinctly non-metaphysical way, the articulation of a conception of human life and of what it is to be human that is conditioned by a sense of our participation in a shared form of life that is already partly constituted by moral ideas or concepts. It is perhaps in this way that value—as Murdoch has argued from her early papers such as 'Vision and choice in morality' (Murdoch 1956) all the way to *MGM*—*pervades* our understanding of the world.

One philosopher who has shone particular light on the above idea is Cora Diamond. In discussing fact and value in relation to Murdoch, Diamond explains what she takes to be Murdoch's view here in terms of a two-stage argument. Stage one is to note that 'Value [for Murdoch] is not the object of some branch of thought or discourse'. For any given branch of thought—Diamond's example is historical understanding—it must be the case that 'there … be some practice or practices of coming to understand facts belonging to the particular subject matter'. Value is, by contrast, ubiquitous: in so far as morality has no particular subject matter in this sense 'morals ... are not facts' (Diamond 1996, 106–107). But this is not to concede that value is nothing, that it is unreal. In stage two of the argument Diamond turns to the particular, moralised, form of visual attention that Murdoch, as we have seen, takes from Weil. As Diamond says,

> if we consider the taking in of the visual world with a kind of wonder and freshness of perception ... which can simply marvel at a shade of blue or at the twistedness of a tree trunk, which can take in the goodness and beauty of the world, then we do indeed have a model of moral awareness of reality. (Diamond 1996, 108)

Morality is ubiquitous in that with human experience of any situation whatsoever it 'can shape our vision of what the situation is' (Diamond 1996, 108). Here is, in Diamond's reading of Murdoch, a kind of distinction between fact and value, but one that does not foreclose our experience of value as real. Though now one might ask: is this really so far from the Wittgenstein of the *Tractatus*, who could write, 'The world of the happy man is a different one from the world of the unhappy man'? There is I suspect much more one could say, but only at much greater length, on the influence of Wittgenstein in particular on Murdoch's thinking. As it is, Murdoch's argument in 'Fact and Value' traverses both a wide and difficult philosophical territory and I have only been able to draw out, and hopefully illuminate, some of that territory in this chapter.

Notes

1. As an example of such debates see Hooker (1996).
2. By '*colour*' here Murdoch does not mean to suggest, cf. David Hume, that value is merely projected by us onto the world. I will return to this point at the end.
3. At the same time though, some such philosophers might think there are certain practical problems with eliminating morality, say, related to morality's value in motivating cooperative behaviour. See for example Garner and Joyce (2019).
4. Though not always. See here for example what have become known as resolute (or therapeutic) readings of the *Tractatus* by among others Cora Diamond and James Conant. For example, see Diamond's 'Throwing Away the Ladder: How to Read Wittgenstein's *Tractatus*', in Diamond (1995).

5. Given my account of Murdoch here, it appears that she must have thought that Hume did not in the end think very hard about this distinction.

6. What Murdoch is referring to here is Moore's *naturalistic fallacy*. Moore asks us to consider any simple analysable natural property that we might wish to identify with 'good'; take, he suggests, with utilitarianism in his sights, 'pleasurable'. Moore suggests that it is 'an open question' whether anything that possess that property is good, from which he concludes that the word 'good' cannot simply mean 'pleasurable', and Moore's point is then that this result holds for any simple natural property. Nevertheless, as we understand the word 'good', this must, Moore thinks, refer to some property, which he concludes must be a simple non-natural property which we perceive through moral intuition, which is a mode of recognition apart from empirical modes of perception.

7. I should add though that I am not sure Murdoch herself ever came to terms with, or to a thorough understanding of, Wittgenstein's treatment of mental contents in those passages in the *Investigations*.

8. To give just a few recent examples: Diamond (1995), Gaita (2004), and Crary (2007, 2016).

References

Crary, A. 2007. *Beyond moral judgment*. Cambridge, MA: Harvard University Press.

Crary, A. 2016. *Inside ethics: On the demands of moral thought*. Cambridge, MA: Harvard University Press.

Diamond, C. 1995. *The realistic spirit: Wittgenstein, philosophy and the mind*. Cambridge, MA: MIT Press.

Diamond, C. 1996. 'We are perpetually moralists': Iris Murdoch, fact, and value. In *Iris Murdoch and the search for human goodness*, ed. Maria Antonaccio and William Schweiker. Chicago: University of Chicago Press.

Gaita, R. 2004. *Good and evil: An absolute conception*, 2nd ed. London: Routledge.

Garner, E., and R. Joyce, eds. 2019. *The end of morality: Taking moral abolitionism seriously*. London: Routledge.

Hooker, B. (ed.). 1996. *Truth in ethics*. Oxford: Blackwell.

Kant, I. 1964. *Groundwork of the metaphysic of morals*, trans. H.J. Paton. New York: Harper & Row.

Murdoch, I. 1956. Vision and choice in morality. *Proceedings of the Aristotelian Society, Supplementary* 30: 32–58.

Murdoch, I. 1985. *The sovereignty of good*. London: Routledge & Kegan Paul.

Murdoch, I. 1992. *Metaphysics as a guide to morals* (Abbreviated *MGM*). London: Chatto & Windus.

Schopenhauer, A. 1965. *On the basis of morality,* trans. E.F.J. Payne. Indianapolis: Bobbs Merill.

Waismann, F. 1979. *Wittgenstein and the Vienna Circle.* Oxford: Basil Blackwell.

Wittgenstein, L. 1961. *Tractatus logico-philosopicus.* London: Routledge & Kegan Paul.

Wittgenstein, L. 1968. *Philosophical investigations,* trans. G.E.M. Anscombe. Oxford: Basil Blackwell.

Wittgenstein, L. 1979. *Notebooks 1914–1916,* 2nd ed., trans. G.E.M. Anscombe and ed. G.H. von Wright and G.E.M. Anscombe. Chicago: University of Chicago Press.

CHAPTER 6

Schopenhauer and the Mystical Solution of the Riddle (*MGM* Chapter 3)

Mariëtte Willemsen

INTRODUCTION

Arthur Schopenhauer is one of the philosophical heroes in *Metaphysics as a Guide to Morals* (henceforth *MGM*). It is especially in the third chapter of the book that Murdoch converses with him, developing her own stance in dialogue with this nineteenth-century German philosopher whose main work, *Die Welt als Wille und Vorstellung*, she read in the 1909 translation from Haldane and Kemp, *The World as Will and Idea*.[1] While the third chapter includes the lengthiest reflection on Schopenhauer's philosophy, there are many other passages in which she refers to him, often adding characterisations that reveal both her admiration and her critique.

A first thing to note is that Murdoch distances herself from the tradition that considers Schopenhauer an outright pessimistic thinker: 'People call Schopenhauer pessimistic. Not at all. He is as cheerful as Hume whom he admires and in some ways resembles' (*MGM*, 123). On the other hand, she acknowledges his grim side, thus nuancing the

M. Willemsen (✉)
Amsterdam University College, Amsterdam, The Netherlands

© The Author(s) 2019
N. Hämäläinen and G. Dooley (eds.),
Reading Iris Murdoch's Metaphysics as a Guide to Morals,
https://doi.org/10.1007/978-3-030-18967-9_6

'not at all', when she writes that his 'empiricist gaiety is in tension with his nihilistic hatred of the ordinary world' (*MGM*, 70). In a different context, she characterises him as 'muddled and relaxed'. She calls him a 'great empiricist' with an 'omnivorous' mind and an 'eye for detail' (*MGM*, 69, 73, 252, 255). Early in *MGM* she talks about the 'outrageous simplicity' of Schopenhauer's picture of the world (*MGM*, 32). Related to this, she agrees with Wittgenstein, though not wholeheartedly, that Schopenhauer lacks depth (*MGM*, 252, 255). She is amused by Schopenhauer's 'awkward (valuable) frankness', finds him somewhat blunt, and sees it as a merit 'that he is prepared to exhibit his puzzlement and to ramble' (*MGM*, 250–251). The pithiest passage on Schopenhauer, and one that could be read as a synthesis of all the previous characterisations is offered in the tenth chapter, 'Notes on duty and will'. Here she describes him 'as an example of empiricist know-all, confused metaphysician, and simple-hearted moralist', and a couple of lines later she completes this description by calling him a 'cheerful pessimist' (*MGM*, 297–298).

This blend of esteem and reservation is certainly helpful to introduce Murdoch's evaluation of Schopenhauer. However, to understand the influence of the cheerful pessimist's thought on Murdoch's own philosophy a careful analysis of the more substantial passages on Schopenhauer is needed. They can be found in the second, third, eighth, and tenth chapters of *MGM*, with the third chapter fully dedicated to his philosophy. In this chapter, Murdoch offers a multi-faceted exploration of Schopenhauer's philosophical theory. She not only relates to both volumes of *The World as Will and Idea* but also to the 1840 essay *On the Basis of Morality*, manifesting a thorough knowledge of Schopenhauer's metaphysics, and more specifically of his ethical stance.

Murdoch's treatise on Schopenhauer is complicated by her allusions to many other philosophers who seem only loosely connected to the overall discussion. It is understandable that Murdoch weaves in Plato and Kant, since Schopenhauer himself is heavily influenced by these philosophers. It is more difficult to comprehend the role of Wittgenstein in the chapter, and even more so to grasp the references to Nietzsche, Heidegger, and Derrida.

One of the most interesting ideas in the chapter is that Murdoch considers *The World as Will and Idea* a religious, mystical book. She explains this in the second half of the Schopenhauer chapter, in which she mentions Buddhism, Hinduism, and Christianity, Plato, Schopenhauer, and

Wittgenstein, and Julian of Norwich, and Eckhart in an attempt to clarify the notion of the mystical. In my view, these episodes provide the key to a deeper understanding of the chapter's structure and content. Based on a close reading of both these two passages and of 'A note on the riddle', the short section that is appended to the Schopenhauer chapter, I will argue that the concept of the *mystical* is central to Murdoch's reading of Schopenhauer and to her critical affinity with Schopenhauer's notion of compassion. Of course, an elucidation of the concept of the mystical will be part of the investigation. It is my aim to show that examining the concept of the mystical will not only help to understand connections between Schopenhauer's philosophy and the early Wittgenstein, but will also contribute to an insight into Murdoch's own solution of the riddle of the world.

I will start off with a summary of Murdoch's introduction to Schopenhauer in the second chapter of *MGM*. Next, I will outline the first half of the third chapter, 'Schopenhauer', highlighting crucial paragraphs and sentences, and on occasion turning to Chapter 10, 'Notes on will and duty', for more explanation. Then, in section "Mystic Freedom", I will focus on the mystical. For a deeper understanding of the concept of the mystical references to Chapter 8, 'Consciousness and thought II' will prove helpful. Also in section "Mystic Freedom", Murdoch's note on Wittgenstein's famous riddle will be related to Schopenhauer's mysticism. Finally, in the conclusion, I will return to Murdoch's portrayal of Schopenhauer as cheerful empiricist wiseacre, wondering how, in light of Murdoch's enquiry, his apparently shallow empiricism can be attuned to his seemingly deep mysticism.

'A Brief Account'

Murdoch introduces the philosophy of Schopenhauer in the chapter on Fact and Value, in the context of an examination of (the early) Wittgenstein. In this 'brief account' she sketches the distinction that pervades Schopenhauer's philosophy: the cosmic Will versus the world as we perceive it. She sketches how, in Schopenhauer's philosophy, 'the horrors of the human scene result from the selfish wills of individuals as manifestations of the Will to Live'. According to Schopenhauer, she explains, the will rules the world, and human individual wills are 'necessarily selfish'. There are, nevertheless, escape routes. We can overcome selfishness, at least temporarily, via the contemplation of works of art, or through moments of compassion. A permanent liberation from pain and suffering is reserved for 'exceptional individuals', who through 'extreme ascetism' may reach a denial of the will. In her description of this final, exceptional stage, Murdoch brings in the concept of the mystical: 'This "dying to the world" is, according to Schopenhauer, a *mystical* spiritual condition which cannot be described' (*MGM*, 32–33, italics mine). Apparently Murdoch is referring to §68 of the first volume of *WWI*, since it is here, near the end of the fourth and final, ethical part of the book, that Schopenhauer talks about the denial of the will and the 'Christian Saints and Mystics' (Schopenhauer 2011, 499), notably Meister Eckhart. The concept of the mystical is almost absent from the first three books of *WWI*, in which Schopenhauer, respectively, unfolds his epistemology, ontology and aesthetics.[2] It is only after Schopenhauer's explanation of the value and the limits of compassion (in §67), in the fourth ethical part of *WWI*, that the mystical can enter the scene as the final way to reach permanent liberation. Although the concept is not explicitly addressed in the first three books of *WWI*, it will be argued below, in section "Mystic Freedom", that one can recognise degrees of the mystic in Schopenhauer's thought, parallel to what Murdoch will call 'a gradation of ... awareness' (*MGM*, 251); one can mount from a kind of intuitive perception, through contemplation, and via compassion to mystical experience in the strict sense of the word.

After her indeed brief account Murdoch explains how the early Wittgenstein was influenced by Schopenhauer. In a very dense passage she hints at what she sees as connections between the two thinkers: they both have a concept of the mystical; they both reject Kant's Categorical Imperative and his concept of duty; they both postulate a world of facts; they both embrace some sort of determinism. The passage leads to an intriguing sentence, that can be seen as a helpful stepping stone to the full chapter on Schopenhauer: 'The segregation of the factual world allows in both cases a stoical morality which verges towards mysticism' (*MGM*, 33). This sentence triggers many questions. How separate are Schopenhauer's two worlds really? And is the distinction between Will and Idea comparable to the one between value and fact, as Murdoch seems to suggest? To what extent can Schopenhauer be seen as a stoical thinker, given his critique of Stoicism especially in §16 of *WWI*, where he accuses the Stoa of an über-rational type of ethics? And how does a stoical attitude border a mystical approach?

Murdoch's introduction of Schopenhauer, embedded and entangled in a treatise on Wittgenstein and the distinction between fact and value, paves the way for the full chapter on Schopenhauer. Here she will return to the notions addressed in her brief account, especially contemplation, compassion, duty, stoicism and mysticism. And again (the early) Wittgenstein will play a major role in Murdoch's investigation.

Nasty Determinism

In the first paragraph of the chapter on Schopenhauer Murdoch lists the three central notions of *WWI*: 'Will', 'Idea' (translation Haldane and Kemp) or '(Re)presentation' (newer translations), and 'Platonic Idea' (Haldane and Kemp), or 'Idea' (newer translations).[3] Murdoch uses the Haldane and Kemp translation, although she is aware of the fact that their translation of two of the three keywords is confusing. However, I will use the term 'Representation' for the German 'Vorstellung' and 'Idea' for 'Idee', because Schopenhauer's 'Idee', though borrowed from Plato, is not a Platonic Idea, since it is not a transcendent Form but a kind of glue between Will and Representation. Murdoch explains how in Schopenhauer's system the undivided, cosmic Will to live objectifies itself in the world of Representations, the world as we perceive it, with the Ideas as an intermediate stage. These ideas are 'universal concepts or models of which particular [representations] are instantiations' (*MGM*, 58). The status of Schopenhauer's ideas is a topic of heated debate in Schopenhauer studies.[4] Murdoch too questions the position of ideas in Schopenhauer's system, asking how they relate to the particular representations. And more in general she is critical of Schopenhauer, already this early in the chapter, because she finds the metaphysical structure he offers incoherent (*MGM*, 58). Still, there are many things in Schopenhauer's system that Murdoch finds attractive, as can be read from the paragraphs that follow.

The chapter on Schopenhauer is dense in content, and freely, associatively structured. Before focusing on the pivotal passage on the mystical let's see if we can get a sense of the structure of the chapter. What are the main ideas Murdoch presents in conversation with Schopenhauer? And how does she develop her argument? Are there specific claims and, if so, how does she support them?

If I am counting correctly, the twenty pages of this chapter include sixteen longish paragraphs before the two-page note on the riddle.[5] In this section, the first nine paragraphs will be summarised and discussed. This synopsis will lead up to an analysis of the mystical, related to the second half of the chapter on Schopenhauer.

After the opening paragraph, discussed above, Murdoch first pays attention to Schopenhauer's theory of art, as one of the routes to escape from the nasty will with its 'perpetual struggle'. She explains how, according to Schopenhauer, through contemplation of art 'the walls of the ego fall'. Artists see beyond the particular and go beyond their self-ishness: they have access to ideas, to what is universal. Murdoch comments that this contemplative theory of art may give insight into certain forms of visual art, but that quite often art is engaged in 'the busy contingent rather than the still icon'. She furthermore explains that in Schopenhauer's aesthetics music has a special status, because it doesn't relate to ideas but immediately to the will and its emotions, with the melody finding satisfaction in its return to the keynote. And also here she adds that this theory doesn't apply to all kinds of music, especially not to modern music (*MGM*, 59–60).

Then follows a paragraph in which she starts to offer more fundamental critique. A first point of critique is that Schopenhauer doesn't seem to allow moral progress. We find some temporary relief through art, but this doesn't help us to reach a higher stage. A second point of critique is that one could wonder why we would need art at all to move away from the ego. As to these points of critique Murdoch sides with Plato, who is, according to Murdoch, a believer in (moral) progress and who is critical about the role of aesthetics. Furthermore, it seems that in Schopenhauer's system, unlike Kant's philosophy, freedom is not available. The determinism of the will is pervasive, whereas in Kant's philosophy there is a realm of freedom co-existent with a realm of necessity: 'Schopenhauer's Will is, with Nietzsche's, and that of the later Heidegger, one of the nastiest' (*MGM*, 60–61).[6] These critical notes imply that Murdoch is even more of a disciple of Plato and Kant than Schopenhauer himself.

In the fourth paragraph of the chapter, Murdoch moves from a discussion of Schopenhauer's view on temporary liberation to that on a complete escape from selfishness. She describes how Schopenhauer proposes radical asceticism: 'a salvation by dying to the world'. This is a stage beyond virtue, and thus beyond morality—and again Murdoch prefers Plato, since Plato suggests a return to the world of the cave and the appearances, whereas the 'extreme ascetic' gives up his existence, for (literally) *nothing*. Although Murdoch seems to be intrigued by the ascetic 'completely selfless person', she asks herself 'must we live with so austere a picture, as if we are to be utterly damned or utterly saved?' (*MGM*, 61–62).

One might think that Schopenhauer's dualism of Will and Representation is similar to Plato's distinction between reality and appearance. Murdoch challenges this similarity in the fifth paragraph of the chapter. In Plato we do not find a 'blind, merciless Will'. Instead we find the form of the Good, 'whose magnetic influence', says Murdoch, 'reaches to all' (*MGM*, 63). This is an important point for Murdoch. Unlike Plato, and also unlike Kant, says Murdoch, Schopenhauer doesn't describe morality as something that is central in human life. This should be understood in the following way. 'Dying to the world' is an act via which the ascetic withdraws from life. Thus the ascetic can and will no longer play any moral role in existence. If asceticism is, as it seems, the highest possible thing or no-thing to do, then the role of morality is of subordinate importance.

It seems that Schopenhauer himself is aware of the disputable place of morality in the system he unfolds in *WWI*. In a later essay, *The Basis of Morality*, to which Murdoch turns in the second half of the fifth paragraph, he offers a moral theory more to her liking, based on a simple slogan: 'Hurt no one, rather help everyone as much as you can'. Here, says Murdoch, we recognise the two cardinal virtues of justice and compassion, of which the latter is the more fundamental one.[7] According to Schopenhauer compassion is grounded in nature: we tend to sympathise with other beings, and to participate in their suffering. This is a phenomenon that cannot be explained any further, it is a metaphysical given, and thus not in itself a problem of ethics. Schopenhauer contrasts his notion of compassion with the Kantian concepts of duty and conscience, which he rejects because they are dogmatic and dependent on religious commandments (*MGM*, 63–64).

Schopenhauer's endorsement of compassion goes hand in hand with a rejection of duty. Although Murdoch finds Schopenhauer's notion of compassion attractive, she does not agree with his accompanying dislike of Kant's ethics. In a strong passage in Chapter 10 of *MGM* she explains why we cannot dispense of duty. She explains that we need certain rules, supported by explanations, especially early in our lives: 'Do not lie, do no steal, be helpful, be kind'. But also later on, she continues, we sometimes find ourselves in situations where we hear a voice saying 'Don't do it', comparable to Socrates' daemon, who told him what not to do. Murdoch beautifully talks about the 'quiet pressure of duty' and concludes that this concept 'is *indispensable*, though it cannot stand alone' (*MGM*, 302–303). In terms of ethical normative theories, it could be argued that Murdoch defends a combination of virtue-ethics (compassion) and Kantian deontology (duty).

In the sixth, seventh, and eighth paragraphs Murdoch continues comparing Schopenhauer to Plato and Kant, and repeats many of the things said earlier. It is especially Schopenhauer's concept of the Will and its determinism that is attacked. Murdoch finds Schopenhauer's resulting view that 'guilt and merit lie in what we are, not in what we do' confused, and his idea that 'freedom is simply the recognition of necessity' not persuasive. Again, she prefers the Kantian approach, in which there is the possibility of rising above determinism, over this *amor fati*, stoical type of attitude. Nevertheless, it seems that even in Schopenhauer's philosophy we can sometimes 'move a little against the Will', through acts of compassion, including kind acts towards animals (*MGM*, 65–67).

Finally, before transitioning to the concept of the mystical, Murdoch describes the role of sexual love in Schopenhauer's philosophy. She explains how, according to Schopenhauer, both non-human and human animals are driven by the egoistic Will, for the benefit of the species.

To recapitulate, Murdoch makes several related claims in her discussion of Schopenhauer. Firstly, ethics needs to make room for moral progress. Secondly, an ascetic withdrawal from the world, different from returning to the cave, puts an end to morality. Thirdly, not all the moral work can be done by compassion; the concept of duty is indispensable. We will now have to see if and how these three claims are connected to the concept of the mystical.

Mystic Freedom

In the second half of the chapter on Schopenhauer, Murdoch revisits the last sections of *WWI*, already discussed earlier. How should we understand the final stage of nothingness, the 'dying to the world'? It seems that we 'lack concepts with which to express or describe this state', although we do know that we are nearing liberation: 'Any "release" must be thought of in terms of mysticism' (*MGM*, 68–69). The question is, of course, what mysticism is. Murdoch herself gives a definition: 'a mystic is a good person whose knowledge of the divine and practice of the selfless life has transcended the level of idols and images' (*MGM*, 73). She arrives at this definition after an intense and sometimes difficult to follow, almost stammering exploration of religious and mystical ideas. As a starting point, she refers to what Buddha said to his disciples: 'throw everything away and become beggars'.[8] It is here that she adds that Wittgenstein actually obeyed this imperative, whereas Schopenhauer could not live up to these ascetic standards. She also quotes how Schopenhauer refers to Meister Eckhart's mysticism and his appeal to 'seek not God outside himself'.[9] This appeal, says Murdoch, is on the one hand a warning 'against idolatry'. On the other hand, if we withdraw into the self, we run the risk of reinforcing our egoism (*MGM*, 69–70). The latter remark can be read as a restatement of Murdoch's problems with a 'dying to the world' that does not go hand in hand with moral responsibility towards the world, or, with the platonic imagery so often used by Murdoch, with a return to the cave.

Now, how are we supposed to understand Schopenhauer's mysticism? And to what extent does Murdoch embrace this? It seems there is a certain sympathy from Murdoch, when she talks about Schopenhauer's 'on-the-way-mysticism', praising his tenderness for animals and love of nature (*MGM*, 70). This 'on-the-way-mysticism', I would say, is in fact the same as compassion. In *On the Basis of Morality* we can read that Schopenhauer sees compassion as 'a piece of mysticism put into practice' (*MGM*, 278).[10] We could even go one step further in this direction, moving back from absolute mysticism, via practical compassion, through contemplation to perception. There is a wonderful section near the end of the first, epistemological book of *WWI I* in which Schopenhauer explains, via a visual 'proof' of the proposition of Pythagoras, that perception is 'the primary source of all evidence' (Schopenhauer 2011, §15). A long, logical Euclidean proof may be possible, but without visual, direct insight, Schopenhauer claims, there is no real understanding of the theorem. Like the mystic and like the artist or the compassionate person, a perceiving being has immediate awareness of the object of his attention, without the intervention of concepts.

To my knowledge Murdoch does not refer to §15 of *The World as Will and Idea*. In Chapter 8 of *MGM*, 'Consciousness and Thought II', she does, however, quote a long passage from *WWI I* §9, a related section, in which Schopenhauer explains how, in language, we depend on concepts: 'It is reason which speaks to reason, keeping within its own province' (*MGM*, 252). Although Schopenhauer himself, and any author for that matter, depends on language and on concepts, one of the main aims of his philosophical project is to explain, be it in concepts, the importance of perception, of direct awareness. In this sense he is, indeed, a 'great empiricist' (*MGM*, 252). His 'eye for detail' is consistent with his hunger to be in immediate perceptual touch with the world (*MGM*, 69).

It is a small step from this type of mystical empiricism to Wittgenstein's famous riddle, mentioned near the end of the *Tractatus* (Wittgenstein 1961, 6.4312; 6.5). Murdoch cleverly connects Wittgenstein to Schopenhauer, referring to a passage in the appendix to Volume 1 of *WWI*, where Schopenhauer writes: 'The world and our existence presents itself necessarily as a riddle' (qtd. in *MGM*, 78), and of course thinking of Wittgenstein's notes on the mystical and the ineffable (*Tractatus* 6.44; 7). Murdoch's point here is, that Schopenhauer and Wittgenstein are talking about the same riddle. According to Schopenhauer, this riddle—the meaning of our existence, the metaphysical truth—can only be solved 'through the proper connection of outer with inner experience' (*MGM*, 79). This unification is a mystical solution, comparable to the silence of Wittgenstein's last words in the Tractatus.[11]

CONCLUSION

At the end of her chapter on Schopenhauer Murdoch writes: 'In spite of his metaphysics and his mysticism, Schopenhauer may in general appear as a genial empiricist' (*MGM*, 77). There are good reasons to replace the 'in spite of' by 'in line with', since it can be argued that Schopenhauer's mysticism is grounded in his empiricism. In this sense, Schopenhauer's solution to the riddle of the world is down to earth, or indeed 'cheerful' and 'simple', in the way some mystical thinkers were joyful and unpretentious. One could think of Julian of Norwich, mentioned by Murdoch, and her simple Christian dictum 'All shall be well, and all shall be well'.[12]

If we think back to Murdoch's three claims, summarised at the end of the third section of this essay, we can conclude that Murdoch is closer to Schopenhauer than one might think at first sight. Indeed, as already quoted, Schopenhauer 'moves a little against the Will' (*MGM*, 65), or even more than a little, by means of his practical mysticism, such as his kindness to animals and his embracing of compassion. There is thus room for moral progress after all, and in this sense Schopenhauer's determinism is de-nastified. Furthermore, although *WWI* ends in Nirvana, the general message of the book seems to be in tune with an attitude of empiricist openness to the world. However, in Murdoch's moral philosophy the concept of duty, at least as an educational tool or as a Socratic daemon, should be part of the picture, whereas Schopenhauer's philosophy rigidly rejects any commandments.

NOTES

1. To avoid confusion, I will be using the same translation as Murdoch. I will refer to the two volumes of *The World as Will and Idea* as *WWI I and WWI II*. The first volume was originally published in 1818. Schopenhauer added a second volume, with supplements to the first volume, in 1844.

2. There is a reference to the 'great Mystic Angelus Silesius' in §25, the second book of *WWI I*, the section in which Schopenhauer introduces the Platonic Idea, preparing his aesthetic theory, and to Anacreon and, again, to Silesius in §51, near the end of the third book of *WWI I*, in relation to poetry. The other eight uses of 'mystic' and 'mystics' can be found in book 4 of *WWI I*, all but one in §68.

3. Both the 1957 (Dover) translation by Payne and the 2010 (Cambridge) translation by Norman and Welchman opt for *The World as Will and Representation,* whereas Carus and Aquila (Longman, 2011) go for *The World as Will and Presentation.*

4. See White (2016) for an explanation and critique of Schopenhauer's concept of ideas, including a list of sources that express 'surprise or puzzlement' in regard to ideas (145).

5. Each new paragraph is indented, even after a quote, arguably with the exception of the paragraph beginning with 'So, is it all a game and a jest?' on p. 71, and the one beginning with 'Elsewhere ... Heidegger connects ...' on p. 73.

6. It goes beyond the scope of this article to analyse the paragraphs on Nietzsche and Heidegger near the end of the chapter on Schopenhauer (Murdoch 1993, 74–77). Suffice it to say that Murdoch explains the nastiness of the will in their respective philosophies.

7. The German original is 'Mitleid'. This term could be translated with 'pity'. However, there are good reasons to opt for 'compassion', to avoid the negative connotations of pity. See Cartwright (2016, 257).

8. Murdoch does not always clearly refer to her sources. The passage on Buddha can be found in *WWI II*, section 48 (Schopenhauer 2012, 447). This chapter correlates to §68 of *WWI I*.
9. Schopenhauer (2012, section 48, 421).
10. See Steven Neely (2016, 112–116) for an insightful exploration of Schopenhauer's mysticism. Neely underlines the importance of intuitive perception in Schopenhauer's philosophy and mentions his 'practical mysticism' (115).
11. Schroeder (2016), in his article on Schopenhauer's influence on Wittgenstein, argues that Wittgenstein's notes on the riddle and the mystical are 'of little philosophical value'. He points, however, to interesting connections between the two thinkers, especially concerning idealism and solipsism. There is, as can be seen from Schroeder's article, discussion about the exact influence of Schopenhauer on Wittgenstein. However, for the current article it suffices to say that Murdoch sees clear connections between the two thinkers, especially concerning the 'riddle'.
12. Murdoch refers to this fourteenth-century English mystical thinker several times in *MGM*, and more extensively and approvingly on pp. 463 and 486.

REFERENCES

Cartwright, D.E. 2016. Schopenhauer on the value of compassion. In *A companion to Schopenhauer*, ed. Bart Vandenabeele, 249–265. Maldon, MA: Wiley-Blackwell.

Murdoch, I. 1993. *Metaphysics as a guide to morals* (Abbreviated *MGM*). Harmondsworth: Penguin Books.

Neely, S.G. 2016. The consistency of Schopenhauer's metaphysics. In *A companion to Schopenhauer*, ed. Bart Vandenabeele, 105–119. Maldon, MA: Wiley-Blackwell.

Schopenhauer, A. 2011. *The world as will and idea (Volume 1 of 3)*, trans., Haldane and Kemp, 1909. Urbana, IL: Project Gutenberg. https://www.gutenberg.org/files/38427/38427-pdf.pdf. Accessed December 31, 2018.

Schopenhauer, A. 2012. *The world as will and idea (Volume 3 of 3)*, trans., Haldane and Kemp, 1909. Urbana, IL: Project Gutenberg. http://www.gutenberg.org/files/40868/40868-pdf.pdf. Accessed December 31, 2018.

Schopenhauer, A. 2014. *The basis of morality*, trans., Arthur Brodrick Bullock, 1903. Urbana, IL: Project Gutenberg. http://www.gutenberg.org/files/44929/44929-h/44929-h.htm. Accessed December 31, 2018.

Schroeder, S. 2016. Schopenhauer's influence on Wittgenstein. In *A companion to Schopenhauer*, ed. Bart Vandenabeele, 367–384. Maldon, MA: Wiley-Blackwell.

White, Frank C. 2016. Schopenhauer and Platonic ideas. In *A companion to Schopenhauer*, ed. Bart Vandenabeele, 133–146. Maldon, MA: Wiley-Blackwell.

Wittgenstein, L. 1961. *Tractatus logico-philosophicus*, trans. D.F. Pears and B.F. McGuinness. London: Routledge & Kegan Paul.

CHAPTER 7

Metaphysics as a Guide to Morals: The Debate Between Literature and Philosophy

Gillian Dooley

Iris Murdoch, in *Metaphysics as a Guide to Morals* (henceforth *MGM*), writes about art, and specifically literature, as a consumer or reader, rather than a novelist. Apart from one passing reference to 'my first novel, *Under the Net*' (*MGM*, 187), a reader who (improbably) knows nothing about her career as a novelist would be none the wiser from reading this book. She talks in the third person plural about 'fiction writers' wrestling with the difficulties of representation, while 'we the readers appreciate and judge their solution' (*MGM*, 146); and invites us 'to look at what novelists do … They have constantly to invent methods of conveying states of mind … Artists are famous for not knowing how it is done, or for perhaps rightly feeling that at their best they do not know what they are up to' (*MGM*, 169). She speaks as an informed reader, one who has thought seriously, and probably read, about the creation of fiction, but except on that one occasion she never speaks as a novelist in her own right.

The reason she gives for pausing at this point in her philosophical argument to contemplate the process of writing fiction is the possibility

G. Dooley (✉)
Flinders University, Adelaide, SA, Australia

© The Author(s) 2019

N. Hämäläinen and G. Dooley (eds.),
Reading Iris Murdoch's Metaphysics as a Guide to Morals,
https://doi.org/10.1007/978-3-030-18967-9_7

that 'the best model for all thought is the creative imagination' (*MGM*, 169). If this were true, would this place the creation of works of philosophy, such as *MGM*, on a lower plane than the great novels? Where would that leave the reader of *MGM*? Is it an invitation to abandon this book, leaving the subsequent 340 pages unread, because one's time would be better spent reading Tolstoy and Austen or even Murdoch's own novels? Or could one profit by directing a novel-reader's appreciation and judgement towards the creative imagination on display in works of philosophy like this and assessing their success at exhibiting 'personal morality in a non-abstract manner as the stuff of consciousness' (*MGM*, 169)?

To try and understand the attitude Murdoch herself would have to such an enterprise, I look to Murdoch's (1977) discussion of literature and philosophy with Bryan Magee. In this interview, he challenges her to explain, as a practitioner of both types of writing, exactly where the differences (and similarities) lie. She draws a clear distinction between them, seeing them as different on a very basic level: 'Literature is (mostly) "works of art". Works of philosophy are quite different things. Very occasionally a work of philosophy may also be a work of art, such as the *Symposium*, but these are exceptional cases' (Murdoch 1997, 5). Furthermore, while

> philosophers often construct huge schemes involving a lot of complicated imagery, [a] philosopher is likely to be suspicious of aesthetic motives in himself and critical of the instinctive side of his imagination. Whereas any artist must be at least half in love with his unconscious mind, which after all provides his motive force and does a great deal of his work. (Murdoch 1997, 7)

The ambiguity and playfulness inherent in a work of art must be suppressed in philosophical writing, she says: unlike the novelist or poet, the philosopher must leave no 'space for his reader to play in' (Murdoch 1997, 5). Her austere description of a philosopher's craft—or perhaps it is an injunction to philosophers to 'avoid rhetoric and idle decoration' (Murdoch 1997, 4)—is a severe challenge to a literary critic, who is trained to read with an appreciation of decoration, even sometimes 'idle' decoration, and certainly with an ear for rhetoric. For such readers, rhetoric has no negative connotations: brought up on Wayne Booth's *The Rhetoric of Fiction* (1961), we find it difficult to accept that any writing consisting of more than the baldest labelling *can* avoid rhetoric. Niklas Forsberg writes,

> The philosophical significance of literature is certainly not its capacity to illustrate or exemplify philosophy; its strength is that it is the other of philosophy: a contrast fluid. Of course, there is philosophy 'in' it, in all literature. But then again, philosophy is everywhere. (Forsberg 2013, 12)

I agree, but I would add that literature, and its companion vehicle, rhetoric, is also everywhere. As Forsberg says, 'literature and (good) philosophy both speak the same language: *ours*' (Forsberg 2013, 13). Anthony J. Cascardi, further, writes that 'the issues of greatest concern in the sometimes vexed relations between literature and philosophy are rarely ones that can be settled by defining them as wholly different kinds of writing' (Cascardi 2014, 2). Murdoch herself had conceded, in *The Fire and the Sun*, that 'although aesthetic form has essential elements of trickery and magic, yet form in art, as form in philosophy, is designed to communicate and reveal' (Murdoch 1977, 78).

Is it possible that my difficulty is merely with Murdoch's use of the term? Chris Baldick, in his 1990 dictionary of literary terms, defines rhetoric as 'the deliberate exploitation of eloquence for the most persuasive effect in public speaking or in writing'. He goes on to say that 'the usual modern sense of the term implies empty and ineffectual grandness in public speech', while 'modern critics sometimes refer to the rhetorical dimensions of a literary work, meaning those aspects of the work that persuade or otherwise guide the responses of readers' (Baldick 1990, 189). No doubt her objection to rhetoric in philosophy would be to the use of deliberate persuasiveness. However, she certainly uses rhetoric in Baldick's first sense in her philosophical writing. I open *MGM* at random and find her 'shadowy sketch' of the 'structuralist Utopia', in which she talks about 'an old tired tradition, heavy with unavailing thoughts … an exasperated weariness with the old metaphysical world … and its grand self-conscious conceited art' (*MGM*, 214). And so it proceeds, a lively, one might almost say *playful*, caricature of a movement with which Murdoch clearly has little sympathy, freely using all the rhetorical means at her disposal to 'guide the responses of readers'. Does this make *MGM*, or this passage and others like it, bad philosophy?[1] Is it an allowable exception to the 'certain cold clear recognisable voice' in which a philosopher should usually speak? (Murdoch 1997, 5). Or is it inherent in the nature even of philosophical writing that what is consciously suppressed should sometimes escape and show itself? Murdoch herself writes, 'a metaphysic or *Weltanschauung* may be felt to omit something which then peripherally and disturbingly haunts it, or else disappears to be rediscovered later' (*MGM*, 84). Could this be true not only of the kind of concepts with which she is concerned here, such as 'a detailed picture of virtue' or 'a view of "consciousness" and "the self"' (*MGM*, 84), but also of rhetorical features? Indeed, she admits that 'the element of metaphor is unavoidable in philosophy, especially in moral philosophy; it is simply more or less evident' (*MGM*, 177)—in the same way as in the Magee interview she had discussed 'huge schemes' constructed by philosophers 'involving a lot of complicated imagery' (Murdoch 1997, 7). How is it possible to 'avoid rhetoric' in a discourse in which 'metaphor is unavoidable'? Can there be a metaphor without rhetoric? Peter Conradi, ever alert to nuance, points out that the voice in *MGM* is interesting in itself; and that:

> it often feels like someone talking to us, even thinking out loud. Like her admired Schopenhauer, Murdoch exhibits puzzlement and has the courage to embark on excursions and diversions, to repeat, to stray, to make odd connexions. (Conradi 2001, 356)

Murdoch was clearly trying to sort these problems out herself in her discussion of Wittgenstein and his vexed relations with language. She writes, 'language is full of art forms, full of *values* ... It may be said that if one lets everything in it isn't philosophy. Surely one must have a "system"?' (*MGM*, 281–282). In this same passage, she writes how 'with a free and apt use of metaphor, with swift intuitive imagination, Wittgenstein describes the *experience* of thinking' (*MGM*, 283). Although she stays with the 'old quarrel' and insists that 'philosophy is definitely not poetry', she ends this section with the assertion, or concession, that 'even in philosophy, language is not a cage' (*MGM*, 283). She cannot accept what she sees as Wittgenstein's attempt to set up a system which 'pointedly excludes the individual peculiarity of speaking humans', and she shows how Wittgenstein's own use of language undermines his 'frozen logical example' (*MGM*, 281) by its own individuality and particularity. Stephen Mulhall writes that part of attending to the particularity of individual metaphysicians is attending to their individuality – which means acknowledging what distinguishes them from other metaphysicians as well as acknowledging what connects them with those engaged in the same activity. (Mulhall 1997, 236)

The voice of a philosopher cannot be discounted any more than the voice of a literary writer: any attempt to ignore voice, context, point of view, and other literary qualities of a philosophical text will result in an impoverished and limited reading. The same is, of course, true of literary critics like myself, and I freely admit to deploying rhetorical devices in my own writing.

In a discussion of Plato's *Republic*, Patrick Hayes and Jan Wilm discuss the terms of the 'ancient quarrel' that Murdoch refers to above, that between literature and philosophy. They claim that 'every reader of *The Republic* knows, [that] Socrates' claims are ... ironically undercut by Plato'. They go on to say,

It quickly becomes apparent that even in *The Republic*, Socrates cannot in fact do away with the form of discourse that has been marked out as 'literature'. While his Philosopher Kings must ascend from the cave, to which mere mortals are condemned, to witness the light of truth, they must then descend back from the light into the cave, and communicate the truth through representation. Philosophers, it would appear, are thus always already in some sense poets: they must create the myths and metaphors through which the good and the true can be narrated and understood. Socrates, it turns out, does not therefore reject literature: he merely wishes to domesticate it. (Hayes and Wilm 2017, 9–10)

It is notable that in this passage these authors attribute the myth of the cave to Socrates—a character in Plato's *Republic*—rather than Plato himself. I am not convinced that 'every reader of *The Republic*' is aware that Socrates is not merely a mouthpiece for Plato's views. This quotation comes from an introduction to a book on the philosophical tendencies in the novelist J. M. Coetzee's literary works, and the authors, Hayes and Wilm, are both literary scholars. They are therefore perhaps more attuned than some to the literary features of works of philosophy, and the inevitability of rhetorical devices and figures of speech in discursive prose as well as in narrative. Although there is lively critical debate about the rhetorical status of *The Republic*, there are surely still many who read it as a work transparently expounding the views of Plato, using Socrates as his mouthpiece. This is perhaps confirmed by the warning, in the chapter on the ancient quarrel in the *Cambridge Introduction to Literature and Philosophy*, that:

> one must be alert to inconsistences among the voices, take care not to assume that Socrates is always a reliable spokesperson, and understand that not all the views attributed to him are necessarily those of Plato. There are times when it may be necessary to take what Socrates says ironically. (Cascardi 2014, 26)

Far from 'every reader of the *Republic*' knowing that Socrates's views are ironically undercut, it is assumed that the readers of the *Cambridge Introduction* need to be warned and instructed how to—or how not to—read the *Republic* and Plato's other dialogues. In fact, David Robjant warns that 'it is not obvious that treating Socrates as Plato's satirical voice is any nearer to getting at authorial intention "in the story" than is treating Socrates as Plato's utopian voice' (Robjant 2015, 1).

So although in the 1977 discussion with Magee, Murdoch allows that the *Symposium* is both a work of philosophy and 'work of art', she claims that it is highly unusual in being both, and that philosophy *should be* cool and rational and unsullied by rhetoric, despite often being reliant on imagery. In *MGM*, published 15 years later, she writes that 'metaphor is unavoidable' and that 'language is not a cage'. Further, she proposes that 'the best model for all thought is the creative imagination' (*MGM*, 169). And in her own work of philosophy (*MGM*), as we have seen, she uses metaphors and rhetorical devices, and discusses their use by other philosophers. She told Simon Price in 1984 that she was 'trying to write a book based on [the Gifford Lectures] which will be a very Platonist book'—and criticised those who dismiss Plato's work because it is 'all so poetic that it can't really be saying anything serious' (Price 2003, 152). Her correspondence with Australian philosopher Brian Medlin shows that the 'old quarrel' was a constant preoccupation: in an undated letter early in the 1990s she wrote, 'That you are a poet emerges from your writing. (And it is certainly philosophy.)' (Dooley and Nerlich 2014, 82); and then, in May 1991, she expressed the wish that 'philosophy and poetry (Plato said there was an old feud between them) [may] co-exist peacefully & creatively' (Dooley and Nerlich 2014, 103). As George Steiner writes,

The Platonic challenge will justly confront the creative imagination so long as philosophy and literature co-exist. That co-existence remains charged with the informing tension of the unfinished. Nowhere more so than in the achievement of Iris Murdoch. (Murdoch 1997, xviii)

Miles Leeson sees it as a major challenge in Murdoch's oeuvre 'to make the distinction between two different forms of writing and allow them to enhance each other, or rule out any such influence' (Leeson 2010, 9). I would not wish to deny the distinction, and would certainly never rule out their influence on each other. Steiner's notion of the 'informing tension' is an important insight. In Forsberg's compelling analysis of *The Black Prince*, he asks whether,

perhaps the resonating indecision [is] precisely what we should pay attention to. After all, texts that lack conclusions often do so for a reason. They leave something for the reader to do, and they *mean* to leave something for the reader to do. (Forsberg 2013, 182)

Similarly, I am not sure that Murdoch ever made up her mind one way or another about philosophy and literature, and that this inability, or unwillingness, to decide who to side with in the 'old quarrel' remained a source of creative friction. Maria Antonaccio writes that 'movement between metaphysics and empiricism ... structures *MGM*' and that there is 'a parallel tension in Murdoch's theory of the novel, the tension between form and contingency' (Antonaccio 1996, 112–113). Many other writers have commented on the tensions—usually seen as creative—between form and content, between philosophy and literature, in *MGM* and in Murdoch's work more broadly.[2] It seems likely that her insistence on the clear distinction between literature and philosophy was at least in part a protective strategy to discourage the reading of her novels in a philosophical light, because she preferred not to be thought of as a philosophical novelist. As Bran Nicol writes,

Time and again in interviews she patiently maintained that while her novels did contain philosophical discussions they were certainly not 'philosophical novels', nor did she set out deliberately to dramatize in fiction the philosophical questions that interested her. (Nicol 2001, 580)

This strategy has never been entirely effective and such readings of her novels abound: hardly surprising when she continually introduced philosophical dilemmas and philosophically inclined characters in her fiction. One might argue that whether she deliberately did so is irrelevant to critical practice: once a book is published, the author must let the reader judge. Be that as it may, I am not aware that she ever tried to discourage the contrary tendency—to read her philosophy as literature—perhaps because it has not been such a common practice among her critics and readers.

There is of course a danger in assessing a work on criteria irrelevant to its aims, and I do not intend to read *MGM* in the same way as I would read a novel. However, as I have shown, there are aspects of this book that seem to invite a literary reading—that is, reading for tone, character and rhetoric—reading not so much for *what* is said, as for *how* it is said. Antonaccio observes that in *MGM*, Murdoch 'has produced a kind of metaphysics which, not unlike a novel, incorporates some of the accidental, aimless and humorous character of human life within an essentially loose-textured but coherent form' (Antonaccio 1996, 136). In fiction, we expect a lot of things to be shown to us, rather than told; we expect events as well as ideas; perhaps it could be said that we read metonymically rather than metaphorically. A philosopher will use metaphors and examples to illustrate an argument, while a novelist will tell a story in its particulars, using any number of rhetorical techniques, and usually leaving the 'point' of the story for the reader to fathom. An essential difference, especially in novels of Murdoch's generation and tradition, is the prevalence of free indirect discourse—the fact that contemporary novelists, as she herself says, 'won't ... describe his characters from the outside; he will describe them from consciousness, or if he suddenly describes them from the outside, this will be an obvious literary device' (Murdoch 1978, 535). But fiction is not the only kind of literature, and not all literature needs to have a narrative element. Leaving aside the obvious example of poetry, creative non-fiction prose is a branch of literature, including essays with no narrative element. Where to draw the line between 'creative non-fiction' and philosophy may not be as clear as it at first seems. According to Cascardi, 'to say they are different kinds of writing or different discourses says both too much and too little' (Cascardi 2014, 3). Leeson wonders in passing whether the chapter on Schopenhauer in *MGM* might be better thought of as an 'essay' (Leeson 2010, 124), suggesting an open-ended, relaxed kind of composition rather than a tightly-structured and closely argued philosophical text. And Murdoch herself says, that though they are so different, philosophy and literature are both truth-seeking and truth-revealing activities. They are cognitive activities, explanations. Literature, like other arts, involves exploration, classification, discrimination, organised vision. Of course good literature does not look like 'analysis' because what the imagination produces is sensuous, fused, reified, mysterious, ambiguous, particular. Art is cognition in another mode. (Murdoch 1997, 11)

Towards the end of *MGM* Murdoch writes, 'in thinking about the work of the great metaphysicians one has to seek a balance between "faithfulness to the text" and a tendency to invent one's own metaphysician', and she speaks of her own 'danger of inventing my own Plato' (*MGM*, 510). My impression is that she reads with a novelist's sensitivity—or at least a novel-reader's sensitivity—to the personality of each philosopher whose work she is discussing, and the context in which he or she is writing. This is more pronounced in respect of some philosophers that of others. She might be in danger of inventing her own Plato, but does not seem inspired to do so with others, like Kant and Hegel. Wittgenstein, on the other hand, is described in various imaginative ways: at the time of writing the *Tractatus*, Wittgenstein is 'a brave young man' who 'offers a strong impression of his own moral style' (*MGM*, 54). In the *Investigations*, 'there is a sort of strained anguish ... thought being constantly stretched to its limit' (*MGM*, 274). She had met Wittgenstein personally, and in her May 1991 letter to Medlin she says, mischievously, 'The idea of "reading him as poetry" would annoy him very much' (Dooley and Nerlich 2014, 104).

The philosopher who brings out the novelist in *MGM* even more than Wittgenstein is Schopenhauer. Murdoch compares the two, in telling terms, using the extended string of adjectives so characteristic of her descriptive prose: 'Schopenhauer represents what Wittgenstein shudders from: an insatiable omnivorous muddled cheerful often casual volubility' (*MGM*, 79). One could almost see this same dynamic in the contrast between Jake and Hugo in *Under the Net*, or even more clearly in Arnold Baffin and Bradley Pearson in *The Black Prince*. As George Steiner writes in his Foreword to *Existentialists and Mystics*, 'The game of recognition is tempting' (Murdoch 1997, x). However, I am not intending to pursue that 'game'; merely to point out some affinities between the character-drawing in *MGM* and that in her novels. As Steiner points out, 'the strangeness, the solitude, the psychological and social risks inherent in the "examined life" are central to her imagined world' (Murdoch 1997, xi), and I believe that, having assembled throughout her career a large cast of *Dramatis Personae* many of whom are engaged in that kind of life, she could hardly help seeing some of her philosophical forbears in rather the same way when it came to writing about them at length—and, Antonaccio writes, 'it *matters* in literature, morals, and politics, how we portray the human person' (Antonaccio 1996, 117).

Schopenhauer, as Conradi points out, is one of Murdoch's 'heroes' in *MGM*, along with Kant and Plato. He is barely mentioned in her previous philosophical works, only appearing four times in the writings collected in *Existentialists and Mystics* (apart from her discussion of him with Magee, quoted above, and Steiner's Foreword). Most of these references to him in the earlier philosophy are parenthetical or dismissive. However, for reasons I will leave others to fathom, this changes with *MGM*. Schopenhauer has a chapter to himself and is referred to *passim* throughout the book. Murdoch notices not just his ideas, with which she is often enough at variance, and which she has described elsewhere as 'somewhat confused and incoherent' (Dooley and Nerlich 2014, 203), but his voice—his 'relation to his reader is relaxed, amicable, confiding, that of a kindly teacher or fellow seeker. He tells stories and makes jokes' (*MGM*, 79). Conradi's description of Murdoch's voice in *MGM* quoted above, specifically making the connection between Schopenhauer and Murdoch as writers, is couched in remarkably similar terms. By contrast, Murdoch writes, 'Wittgenstein does not relate to a reader ... Even the imagined interlocutor in the *Investigations*, the "someone" who "might say", is isolated from us inside the text' (*MGM*, 80). This distinction between the two writers is important enough to Murdoch for her to end her Schopenhauer chapter (or essay) with it.

Although I can describe, see, and feel many technical differences between the voice and point of view of *MGM* on the one hand and Murdoch's novels on the other, there is a parallel between my affective responses to the two forms, exemplified by two passages in *MGM* and her puzzling 1989 novel *The Message to the Planet*. In *The Message to the Planet*, I believe, there are unwritten tensions and contradictions embedded in the primary plot, and these are connected with the character of Alfred Ludens. As I argue in my 2014 article, Ludens is 'officially' heterosexual but the narrative is full of hints of homoeroticism in his feelings towards several male characters.[3] Much of the novel is taken up with description of the actions of Ludens, who is singularly unperceptive about his own feelings and motivations, which makes the novel in many ways frustrating to read. I have been unable to decide whether Murdoch intended these contradictions in Ludens' character, or whether there was some more complex reason for this effect. However, there is a secondary plot in this novel, concerning Franca, the wife of Ludens' friend Jack, and in the passage where she is first introduced the novel suddenly opens, like a flower. After the rather perfunctory opening section, combining exposition and conversation, containing much past tense and passive voice, we are taken into the present-tense conscious-ness of Franca: 'Franca had seen the pale white moon in the evening, and now again pale white in the early morning' (Murdoch 1990, 22). Every time I read this transition I am again struck by the contrast, and the difference in registers continues throughout the novel as the two plot lines alternate. The effect of this change is to capture the reader's interest—the reader's *attention*—more completely than the opening section. The importance of attention in Murdoch's moral philosophy can hardly be overstated. Although it is usually discussed as an essential part of a moral agent's capacity to deal justly with the world and with other people, rather than a literary effect, it is surely also important to acknowledge the effect skilful writing has on the nature and intensity of a reader's attention to the text. Murdoch talks about literature as 'a dis-ciplined technique for arousing certain emotions'. The challenge, for the artist, is to harness that technique in the service of 'truth-seeking and truth-revealing': 'Art is close dangerous play with unconscious forces' (Murdoch 1997, 10–11).

Though the reading experience is different in many ways between the two forms, fiction and philosophical prose, I did find on reading *MGM* that the early chapters were intellectually interesting but somehow dutiful, the prose hard-won and therefore slow to read. The transition in this case was not so abrupt: however, I was not far into Chapter 3, the Schopenhauer chapter, when I perceived a change. Murdoch often disagrees with Schopenhauer, and finds fault with his arguments, but she writes about him with a kind of engaged affection, ascribing to him qualities such as 'felicitous daring' (*MGM*, 59) and 'irrepressible empiricist gaiety' (*MGM*, 70); 'he cannot resist rambling, he constantly makes jokes' (*MGM*, 76) and 'finds the ordinary world full of interesting wonders' (*MGM*, 77).

These phrases that she uses to characterise Schopenhauer have none of the poetry, the distillation of feeling in image, that characterises her introduction of Franca, although she perhaps comes close when she writes that he is 'fascinated by the world and its bright diversity' (*MGM*, 62). As a novelist, Murdoch is not usually thought of as particularly poetic in her style, but the extent to which she uses imagery and poetic diction in her novels is foregrounded in Carol Sommer's unique book *Cartography for Girls*, in which Murdoch's sentences are removed from their functional context as part of a narrative structure and reassembled in a kind of random poetic assemblage. However, though technically the two styles of writing are quite different, and of course their aims are quite different, the way Murdoch describes Schopenhauer also engages the reader's attention: she does not often use the 'cold clear' voice she recommends (Murdoch 1997, 5). It is more like literature: 'reified, mysterious, ambiguous, particular' (Murdoch 1997, 11). It does more than present and discuss Schopenhauer's ideas. Although it is not the kind of imaginative assumption of a person's subjectivity which often happens with fictional characters, when we are drawn to empathise with a particular character whose point of view is inhabited by the writer, it is a way of recruiting sympathy for him, and directing the reader's attention to him, on account not of what he says, but of his personality and character—of who he is.

> Antonaccio writes that the actual experience of reading *MGM* confronts us not so much with a systematic metaphysical treatise as with a transcript of a brilliant thinker's stream of consciousness, full of detailed reflection and analysis, but also dense with seemingly random associations, humorous asides, and profound insights. (Antonaccio 1996, 135)

While Antonaccio's use of the term 'stream of consciousness' is perhaps misleading here, bringing to mind a quite specifically modernist aesthetic Murdoch would certainly eschew in her philosophy, if not in her fiction, I think this passage conveys well the richness and density of Murdoch's philosophical writing, with its suggestion of '*seemingly* random associations'. Murdoch wrote, of 'the truth, terrible, delightful, funny, whose strong lively presence we recognise in great writers', affirming that 'it is impossible to banish morality from this picture', and that an 'important part of human learning is an ability to generate and to judge and understand the imagery which helps us to interpret the world' (*MGM*, 215). The vivid imagery she often uses herself is full of colour and vitality, often enlivened by strings of rhetorical questions, some of which she answers, while leaving others unanswered. As she says of Schopenhauer, she 'is prepared to exhibit [her] puzzlement and to ramble' (*MGM*, 251). She apologises, when discussing Wittgenstein's *Philosophical Investigations*, for 'rushing in where angels fear to tread' (*MGM*, 277), but these are the passages where she, like Schopenhauer, abandons caution and ventures to the 'border-line of what is expressible, [which] is very blurred'. Perhaps this is, like art, another kind of 'close dangerous play with unconscious forces' (Murdoch 1997, 10–11), but Murdoch affirms that 'out at this edge', beyond the domain of the angels, 'is often a good place to be' (*MGM*, 295).

Acknowledgements I am grateful to Nora Hämäläinen, Frances White, David Robjant for their helpful comments on earlier drafts of this chapter.

NOTES

1. In May 1986, she told Brian Medlin that she was 'writing some philosophy which may be hopelessly bad. It is an addiction'. And five years later: 'I'm not really a philosopher anyway' (Dooley and Nerlich 2014, 7, 104).
2. See for example Nicol (2001) and Mulhall (1997).
3. See Dooley (2014).

REFERENCES

Antonaccio, M. 1996. Form and contingency in Iris Murdoch's ethics. In *Iris Murdoch and the search for human goodness*, ed. Maria Antonaccio and William Schweiker, 110–137. Chicago: University of Chicago Press.

Baldick, C. 1990. *The concise Oxford dictionary of literary terms*. Oxford: Oxford University Press.

Cascardi, A.J. 2014. *The Cambridge introduction to literature and philosophy*. New York: Cambridge University Press.

Conradi, P. 2001. *The saint and the artist: A study of the fiction of Iris Murdoch*. London: HarperCollins.

Dooley, G. 2014. The pursuit of love in Iris Murdoch's *The message to the planet*. *Journal of Language, Literature and Culture* 61 (3): 167–176.

Dooley, G., and G. Nerlich (eds.). 2014. *Never mind about the bourgeoisie: The correspondence between Iris Murdoch and Brian Medlin 1976–1995*. Newcastle upon Tyne: Cambridge Scholars.

Forsberg, N. 2013. *Language lost and found: On Iris Murdoch and the limits of philosophical discourse*. New York: Bloomsbury.

Hayes, P., and J. Wilm (eds.). 2017. *Beyond the ancient quarrel: Literature, philosophy and J.M. Coetzee.* Oxford: Oxford University Press.

Leeson, M. 2010. *Iris Murdoch: philosophical novelist.* London: Continuum.

Mulhall, S. 1997. Constructing a hall of reflection: Perfectionist edification in Iris Murdoch's *Metaphysics as a guide to morals. Philosophy* 72: 219–239.

Murdoch, I. 1977. *The fire and the sun: Why Plato banished the artists.* New York: Viking.

Murdoch, I. 1978. 'Iris Murdoch on natural novelists and unnatural philosophers.' [Interview with Bryan Magee.] *The Listener* 27 April: 533–535.

Murdoch, I. 1990. *The message to the planet.* London: Penguin.

Murdoch, I. 1992. *Metaphysics as a guide to morals* (Abbreviated *MGM*). London: Chatto & Windus.

Murdoch, I. 1997. *Existentialists and mystics: Writings on philosophy and literature,* ed. Peter Conradi. London: Chatto & Windus.

Nicol, B. 2001. Philosophy's dangerous pupil: Murdoch and Derrida. *Modern Fiction Studies* 47 (2): 580–601.

Price, S. 2003. Iris Murdoch: An interview with Simon Price. In *From a tiny corner in the house of fiction: Conversations with Iris Murdoch,* ed. Gillian Dooley, 148–154. Columbia: University of South Carolina Press.

Robjant, D. 2015. What use is literature to political philosophy? Or the funny thing about Socrates's nose. *Philosophy and Literature* 39 (2): 322–337.

Sommer, C. 2016. *Cartography for girls: An A–Z of orientations identified within the novels of Iris Murdoch.* York: Information as Material.

CHAPTER 8

Disciplines of Attention: Iris Murdoch on Consciousness, Criticism, and Thought (*MGM* Chapters 6–8)

David J. Fine

Scholars in philosophy and religious studies have done much to clarify Iris Murdoch's account of consciousness and moral vision. I aim, with this analysis of *Metaphysics as a Guide to Morals* (henceforth *MGM*), to bring Murdoch's concept of consciousness to literary studies. In particular, I examine the significance of literary criticism in Chapters 6–8. This focus situates Murdoch's concern with language and helps explain the division of 'Consciousness and thought' into two non-consecutive chapters. In the intervening chapter, 'Derrida and structuralism', Murdoch censures a relation to art characterised by detachment and suspicion, and this interruption not only signals criticism's importance to the larger argument but also stresses structuralism's neglect of individual consciousness. Pointedly, Murdoch rejects the theory-driven approaches to literature that emerge from structuralism. She condemns critical theory's elitism and endorses, instead, an attentive encounter with art and others. Murdoch envisions a practice that moves beyond critique, and

D. J. Fine (✉)
University of Dayton, Dayton, OH, USA

© The Author(s) 2019
N. Hämäläinen and G. Dooley (eds.),
Reading Iris Murdoch's Metaphysics as a Guide to Morals,
https://doi.org/10.1007/978-3-030-18967-9_8

she does so in defence of both the individual's inner life and art's moral efficacy.

My reading foregrounds Murdoch's engagement with literary criticism for two reasons. I aim, firstly, to clarify the role criticism plays within the overarching argument of *MGM* and, secondly, to situate Murdoch's position within recent debates in literary studies. These debates centre on critique, a reading practice characterised by the hermeneutics of suspicion, and assess its predominance in the field. To this end, I explore Murdoch's depiction of consciousness, explaining its connection to an individual's moral capacity and showing how structuralism erodes its base. In the second section, I address this tension more fully by way of literary criticism. Art proves central to these three chapters, and from them I isolate both Murdoch's rebuke of structuralism and her picture of the good critic. The latter drives the concluding section's exploration of Murdoch's continued relevance, which emerges, I argue, from her sense of attention. As she suggests at the conclusion of 'Consciousness and thought II', 'we all, not only can but *have to*, experience and deal with a transcendent reality, the resistant otherness of other persons, other things, history, the natural world, the cosmos, and this involves perpetual effort' (*MGM*, 268). This chapter dilates on the shape this effort takes in literary studies in order to clarify the relationship between criticism and consciousness.

Consciousness: Inner Life

The moral claims of *MGM* rest, to a large extent, on Murdoch's depiction of consciousness. As this opening section demonstrates, Murdoch thinks carefully through—and accounts for—the torrent of considerations, desires, rationalisations, fantasies, and judgments that constitutes self-being and frames the challenge of ethics. Modern shifts in both the analytic and continental traditions of philosophy have, however, bracketed—if not sponged away—the subject's inner life. This eclipse of interiority threatens philosophers' ability not only to describe moral activity adequately but also, and most alarmingly, to recognise the individual as such. For Murdoch, one must begin with the perception of real individuals, and her metaphysics hinges on the link between a person and his consciousness. As she makes plain, 'I want there to be a discussable problem of consciousness because I want to talk about consciousness or self-being as the fundamental mode or form of moral being' (*MGM*, 171). It is therefore essential, at the outset, to elucidate the scope of this problem and to define the challenge structuralism poses to self-being.

Philosophers have struggled to register inner life, but Murdoch upholds the centrality of consciousness for two related reasons. Firstly, a concept of consciousness, however hard to pin down, witnesses one's unique selfhood. 'Our present moment, our experiences, our flow of consciousness, our indelible moral sense,' Murdoch asks, 'are not all these essentially linked together and do they not *imply* the individual?' (*MGM*, 153). Secondly, it allows one to discuss the moral refinement that occurs within consciousness. The work of morality begins in this inner space and gives shape to the unique, contingent individual. She recalls how

> the layman lives at peace with 'consciousness', with all its obscure impli-
> cations of 'ownership' and 'presence'. It is what is most his own, he is
> responsible for it, even though it may seem to include so much that is not
> momentary or personal or private or clearly visible. (*MGM*, 173)

Moral philosophy must heed, then, 'our dense familiar inner stuff, private and personal, with a quality and value of its own, something which we can scrutinize and control' (*MGM*, 153). Murdoch retains this everyday sense of consciousness—'its vague ordinary-language meaning as an awareness of self as continuous being' (*MGM*, 148)—and it grounds her ethics.

The conscious mind does not, however, naturally envision the world with clarity and grace. On the contrary, human beings adopt self-protective illusions that block reality. Murdoch shows how effortlessly the egoism that arises from consciousness clouds awareness. Therefore, one must work to see clearly. This labour functions as the keystone of morality, since accurate perception depends on egoism's reduction. One must cultivate habits of attention and look outside the ego-soaked morass. In this sense, 'consciousness is a form of moral activity: what we attend to, how we attend, whether we attend' (*MGM*, 167). Moral philosophy's questions—of what to do and when—make sense, for Murdoch, only in relation to inner life. Ethical action necessitates good consciousness, because morality rests on one's ability to perceive the world beyond self-preoccupation. People do not choose in a vacuum or act in a laboratory; rather, they struggle to see clearly, and only then might they do good things in the world. This world remains drenched in value, and the individual's stream of consciousness—'surely if we are searching for "being" this is it' (*MGM*, 173)—interacts with this outer realm. One is, thankfully, able to speak of this stream's quality in terms of better and worse. Indeed, one must.

This portrayal of consciousness and the articulation of its place in moral life rank among Murdoch's chief contributions to philosophy. She first makes this case in a series of influential papers in the 1950s. With *MGM*, the argument's context shifts, however, from existentialism to deconstruction. These conceptual systems have much in common, according to Murdoch, but deconstruction presents a graver threat with its 'anti-individualistic determinism' (*MGM*, 157). Deconstruction—which she classifies, along with poststructuralism, modernism, and postmodernism, as 'structuralism'[1]—poses an acute risk to ethics, because, on its account, human beings become subject to the texts they only apparently author. Murdoch's objection concerns language, specifically how structuralism depicts subjectivity in relation to speech. On this postmodern scene, people 'are not masters of language, we are ourselves, as utterers, simply parts of language, we do not and cannot really know what we are saying, or possess any intelligible "present" which is "our own"' (*MGM*, 153). The structure subsumes the individual: the system of signs effects the subject who speaks words not quite her own. The self is here an illusion, the product of false consciousness.

The meaning of consciousness thus shifts from an individual's cognitive capacity—over which she has some control—to the historical consciousness of Hegel and Marx. Consciousness, in this latter sense, belongs to the social group or to the historical epoch: it refers, in ordinary speech, to an awareness of systemic injustice. Here, Murdoch does not denigrate recognition of social injustice; instead, she highlights the tendency of this overriding social consciousness to obviate individual particularity and moral agency. This shift is not all that surprising. As she notes, 'Marxists regarded the bourgeois concept of the individual as moribund', and Derrida picks up where Marx left off. 'Language and feeling and value (and thoughts and emotions, etc.) are henceforth,' Murdoch explains, 'not "owned" by "private persons" in the old familiar sense.' Talk of inner life reeks of the retrograde; hence, the '"metaphysics of presence" is to be rejected: the notion that "the present" is what it seems to be as a reality in the consciousness and experience of the individual' (*MGM*, 151). False consciousness now fills the subject's mind as he becomes a container for larger, ideological forces. Structuralists, in turn, employ the jargon of their specialists to diagnose this condition.

Murdoch dismisses this position vis-à-vis language and defends its ordinary users. She rejects structuralism precisely because it pathologises inner life and thus obfuscates the moral effort that takes place continuously within consciousness. For Murdoch, structuralism begins with an inadequate, counterintuitive formulation of the subject, and this starting point distorts the individual's ability to attend to the world. In fact, one finds, among these thinkers,

> that further steps have been taken which purport to deny our ordinary sense of a transcendent (extra-linguistic) real world 'out there'; indeed there is no 'out there' since language, not world, transcends us, we are 'made' by language, and are not the free independent ordinary individuals we imagined we were. (*MGM*, 151)

The world's quiddity, which surpasses the ego, dissolves in the language that people once, naïvely, took to describe it. The individual follows suit, since that 'old concept of the self as a unified active consciousness, living between appearance and reality (the traditional field of the novel), is being dislodged by psychoanalytical psychologists and "literary" deconstruction' (*MGM*, 162). Murdoch makes it clear that literary critics have, after Derrida, had the greatest success extending the structuralist vision (*MGM*, 151).

This theoretical account, still influential in literary studies, appears rather macabre: agency lessens, and reality thins. What makes it so attractive? Murdoch's discussion of consciousness, I believe, provides a clue: structuralism appeals to the academic ego. The individual and her freedom fade, but a new elite emerges. 'People who cannot think, who fail to think, who choose not to think, are pictured,' Murdoch explains, 'as being sunk in a dark muddled consciousness, composed of feelings and associations and fragmentary awareness. Such people live by unreflective conventions, they are afraid of action and change and free creative thinking.' These ordinary folks—unlike the liberated critical theorists—suffer from bad faith and take the world as it comes. Here, structuralism echoes Marxist critique of class relations but with a twist. 'Structuralist thinking contains', according to Murdoch, 'an aestheticized version of this concept, only the ordinary people (the new "proletariat") are now inert (like the old dull bourgeoisie) and the "battlefront" is the linguistic front line, the playground of creative poeticized writers and thinkers' (*MGM*, 156). Unlike their forebears, these revolutionaries take to the classroom and launch their critique.

It is not difficult to see why this picture charms deep thinkers. As Murdoch demonstrates, structuralism responds to the sluggishness of political change and to real limitations of human agency. Its practitioners analyse texts, then, to reveal what casual readers miss: namely, the forces that maintain the status quo. They employ critique, a mode of reading grounded in the hermeneutics of suspicion, and unveil impediments to social change.[2] This purportedly radical stance has, though, real implications for moral and political life. One witnesses, in structuralism,

> fact actually becoming value, as quasi-scientific technical modes of discourse (psychoanalysis, anthropology, semiology, grammatology, etc.) are treated as ultimate truths, and *contrasted* with a conceptually vague 'ordinary language' composed of conventional assumptions and illusions, and which if solemnly uttered by some non-technical thinker is inevitably in bad faith. (*MGM*, 162)

Everyday truth-seeking falls from view as critics expose the counterintuitive. Structuralists thereby exalt the unconventional.

Murdoch includes a passage from *The Golden Bowl* in 'Consciousness and thought I' to shift focus. With a turn to literature, she shows the centrality of consciousness to moral growth by way of Maggie Verver, who comes to see the world outside self. Murdoch enacts a particular form of criticism, one that prioritises attention. While she develops this thinking in the following chapter, her brief analysis of Henry James highlights the place of consciousness in art and morality. Consciousness remains, for Murdoch, tied to the individual, cognitive effort one takes— or fails to take—in order to see situations and people clearly. 'Knowledge informs the moral quality of the world,' and, for this reason, she insists that

> the selfish self-interestedly casual or callous man *sees* a different world from that which the careful scrupulous benevolent just man sees; and the largely explicable ambiguity of the word 'see' here conveys the essence of the concept of the moral. (*MGM*, 177)

As Murdoch's metaphor of vision suggests, literature's moral value resides not only in its nuanced illustration of consciousness but also in the opportunity it gives readers to see a new.

CRITICISM: ART OBJECT

Thus far, I have sketched Murdoch's depiction of consciousness and shown how it informs her assessment of structuralism. In what follows, I deepen this account by way of criticism and art. I aim, in this section, to identify the issue Murdoch takes with structuralist methodology and to juxtapose it with her critical practice, which she grounds in attentive truth-seeking. After all, Murdoch's rejection of structuralism stems, in large part, from how these thinkers interpret literary texts. They arrive at literature with Marx, Nietzsche, and Freud in tow and locate its meaning in the hidden, atypical, and deep. I will suggest that Murdoch posits three main objections to this approach: (1) critical texts displace literature; (2) critics become a scientific elite; and (3) language's truth-seeking function disappears. Murdoch rejects these trends and emphasises, instead, the individual's encounter with art. She demonstrates this aesthetic experience's value for ethics and argues that, in their writing and teaching, critics must respect the individual and support his truth-seeking practice.

Murdoch closes 'Derrida and structuralism' with a poignant reminder:

> the limits of my language which are the limits of my world fade away on every side into areas of fighting for concepts, for understanding, for expression, for control, of which the search for the *mot juste* may serve as an image. Everyone, every moral being, that is every human being, is involved in this fight, it is not reserved for philosophers, artists and scientists. (*MGM*, 216)

Clumsily, all human beings use words to grasp at a reality that eludes them. 'Language', therefore,

> must not be separated from individual consciousness and treated as (for the many) a handy impersonal network and (for the few) an adventure playground. Language, consciousness and world are bound together, the (essential) aspiration of language to truth is an aspect of consciousness as a work of evaluation. (*MGM*, 216)

Structuralism wrongly reserves meaning for a select group. A feeling of liberty rewards its practitioners, who have insiders' access to the system, while determinism clouds uncritical minds. Murdoch condemns this elitism, which isolates language's free players from its damned pawns.

Structuralism's relationship to literary texts drives Murdoch to this conclusion. She characterises deconstruction as 'Linguistic Determinism, since it presents a picture of the individual as submerged in language, rather than as an autonomous user of language' (*MGM*, 185). The individual dissolves into a network of signs, which the critic's reading discloses. Suggestively, structuralists use 'text' to describe both literature and the critical product, and this conflation merits pause. As Murdoch explains, '"text", as a technical term, conveniently allows the critic to bracket himself with the imaginative writer. The novel and the criticism of it are both "texts", the latter being potentially the true one.' From there, criticism easily displaces literature: the former does not suffer from the bad faith that the astute critic shows to reside in the latter. In this sense, 'the work of criticism *is* the real work of art' (*MGM*, 206). Structuralist readings reveal something important about larger systems, but, as a result, they downplay, if not all but obfuscate, the space between art and other. Literature and its readers are both products: writer, book, and reader all hold places in the linguistic system and merge into its whole. The critic, rather than artist, displays this reality.

This prioritisation of structuralist texts forecloses what literature might do to discipline individual vision. Art's moral potential fades. 'In effect,' Murdoch claims,

> structuralism is anti-religious, the idea of 'God' being connected with old 'logocentric' ideas of divinely established pre-linguistic meanings. It is also non-moral, since it erases the idea of truthfulness and the common-sense idea of freedom which goes with it. (*MGM*, 200)

Literature confesses historical wrongs; it plays, and it perpetuates, too. It does not, however, provide a picture of reality, at least not in the way it once did. Critics do the real work of revealing things as they, counterintuitively, are. This disclosure permits, then, 'a certain proud "authenticity"', one which 'is to be achieved by those who are no longer duped by outmoded ideas' (*MGM*, 200). The critic gains prestige and power as a sort of seer, one who knows just how dark the times are. He henceforth demystifies. His pointed critique reveals the unpleasant facts of social existence—no God, no truth, no love—from which ordinary people take flight into religious superstitions and political delusions.

This focus on the counterintuitive encourages scholars to set themselves apart. With pressure to publish widely and assess quantitatively, Murdoch notes how the 'belief that literature is an easy subject may lead academics to defend themselves by becoming specialists who know everything about one period, or indeed one writer, and nothing about anything else'. This pressure does not stop with specialisation. 'It may also,' Murdoch suggests, 'lead them to embrace an obscure and difficult theory which looks like a science, which other people do not understand, and which provides the consoling feeling of having a special private expertise, and so being just as good as a physicist or a biologist' (*MGM*, 207). Professional anxiety easily leads critics to master an arcane insider tongue and to assume a scientific, medicalised stance, where literature becomes something to dissect. To establish legitimacy, humanists flee the murky world of value and transform into clinicians of fact. 'Paradoxically, the motives, or ideals, of structuralism have,' Murdoch insists, 'as their nemesis or accompaniment the wish to establish oneself as a member of an elite' (*MGM*, 207–208). This technocratic exclusivity consoles the chosen few.

As texts displace literature and humanists turn scientist, language's relation to truth alters. Things are not what they appear:

> the ideal deconstructionist is more like a scientist who shows that things are *absolutely not* what they seem (they really are made of atoms). He will tell us that the literary object, as we have hitherto understood it, is pure phenomenon, below which lies something quite different from what its naïve creator believed and intended, or what the naïve reader imagines he perceives. (*MGM*, 190)

Critics disclose the text's non-obvious, highly specialised significance. The theoretical agenda subsumes the artwork, showing its meaning to exist elsewhere. Literature's significance now lies apart from the common reader. Indeed, structuralism reserves art for specialists, who have the training to analyse it properly, because, in unskilled hands, it disseminates false consciousness. 'Our whole concept of what literature *is*', Murdoch writes, 'is here in question. This *quest* for the hidden deep (primal-language) meaning of the *text* (to use the jargon) is now said to be the main and essential part of the critic's task' (*MGM*, 189). Critics study literature to expose covert meanings rather than to respect something at once independent and beautiful.

Murdoch admits that readings driven by critique may, at times, prove valuable (*MGM*, 189). She worries, though, that structuralism's primacy will invalidate other reading methods. As an all-encompassing explanation, structuralism tends to wrangle everything into its corral of seeing: its picture of linguistic subjection might easily dominate all criticism. This ubiquity risks the loss of particularity and individuality, since, 'as in other metaphysical "totalities," system obliterates a necessary recognition of the contingent' (*MGM*, 194). Structuralism fails to see that which resists or troubles its picture. Critics fit the world into their structure: 'they in effect "disappear" what is individual and contingent by equating reality with integration in system, and degrees of reality with degrees of integration, and by implying that "ultimately" or "really" there is only one system' (*MGM*, 196). Suspicious readers overlook the jumbled bits and locate proof for the thesis that they bring to the text. This approach distorts human beings' relation to truth, because it neglects the particular.

Structuralism undercuts truth's value within the humanities. As Murdoch explains, the 'fundamental value which is lost, obscured, made not to be, by structuralist theory, is truth, language as truthful, where "truthful" means faithful to, engaging intelligently and responsibly with, a reality which is beyond us' (*MGM*, 214). Art provides people with the chance to attend to that 'which is beyond' their egos. Aesthetic encounters serve, in Murdoch's philosophy, as an exemplum of what people do all the time: they look, and they interpret. One works—on a continuum of illusion and truth—to clarify one's consciousness: to get things right. Good readers interact with a reality that resists both annihilation by ego and encapsulation by system. Critics should help rather than hinder this process, because criticism is akin to consciousness: it too strives after an accurate interpretation. As such, literary criticism must retain truth-seeking as one of its prime virtues. Language, Murdoch explains, 'performs its *essential* task, through its ability to be truthful; and its truthfulness is a function of the struggle of individuals creatively to adjust language to contingent conditions outside it' (*MGM*, 216). This work weaves human beings into the world, one they share—by virtue of language—with others.

Good art gets one closer to reality than bad art, which, for Murdoch, peddles in consolatory fantasy. Still, art and truth remain in close relation, and criticism should evaluate both truth and falsehood. 'The often difficult explanation of the *truth* of great art is,' Murdoch suggests, 'a proper task of criticism. The concept of language-using must imply that of an individual person as a presence, that is, it must imply responsibility and the possibility of truth, upon which the possibility of falsehood depends' (*MGM*, 211). The good critic brings a love of literature to her vocation, along 'with a sophisticated liberal-minded judgment and a refined sense of value' (*MGM*, 207). She minds the gap between the art object and the eyes that view it. In this manner, she foregrounds the struggle to see the poem—and, *mutatis mutandis*, the world—as it is. This labour of patient attention is, of course, less exciting than critical theory. Murdoch describes how an 'attractive esoteric theory, incomprehensible to laymen, may be felt to be more lively and amusing than the vaguer, less easily stated objectives of traditional critics' (*MGM*, 207), but the ordinary tasks of literary criticism remain. The analysis of metaphor, the scan of verse, the consideration of character: these skills exercise one's moral capacity.

Although many people fail to recognise it, 'the study of literature is something *difficult*.' It requires a generosity of spirit and generality of knowledge too often absent. 'A good teacher of literature (and a good literary critic) not only understands poetry (which not many people do) and other literary forms, but is a historian, a linguist, a connoisseur of other arts, and a sophisticated student of human nature. He is in the best sense', Murdoch adds, 'a jack of all trades' (*MGM*, 207). Good critics specialise but use their understanding to connect with a big, messy planet. They accept 'that statements are made, propositions are uttered, by individual incarnate persons in particular extra-linguistic situations, and it is in the whole of this larger context that our familiar and essential concepts of *truth* and *truthfulness* live and work' (*MGM*, 194). Literary studies must accept art's unassailable relation to reality and acknowledge criticism's moral call. In practice, this work might look more like patiently seeing with others than displaying expertise to peers, but, in any case, the good critic desires truth and teaches others how to admire—justly and lovingly—the world's beautiful recalcitrance.[3]

THOUGHT: JUST VISION

I have withheld discussion of the contemporary scene, because I am arguing that it is only after the interruption of 'Derrida and structuralism' that the full relevance of 'Consciousness and thought' becomes clear. In Chapter 7, Murdoch's interlude with the theorists not only reaffirms the centrality of consciousness to moral vision but also shows how quickly things go awry if one obstructs criticism's relation to truth-seeking. This valuation resonates, in important ways, with the postcritical turn in the humanities. In fact, Murdoch's assessment of structuralism anticipates this conversation. She does not, however, offer a solution; instead, she brings clarity to the problem of a suspicious approach to literature. Put plainly, critique refuses the ordinary. This refusal feeds into perceptions, however misguided, of the humanities' irrelevance. For this reason, I conclude with Murdoch's sense of attention and articulate what it offers to literary studies today. Current debates about critique do merit attention, which, for Murdoch, means waiting—avoiding the temptation to theorise away the difficulty—and really looking in order to get a clear view of the problem.[4]

Murdoch's engagement with literary theory is not without its critics. In his review of *MGM*, Terry Eagleton argues that its account of Derrida functions as 'a kind of composite bugbear or handy straw target for all that Murdoch finds nightmarish about modernity'. He describes Murdoch's approach as, in fact, 'the kind of slipshod conflation of one's bêtes noires which no academic would tolerate in a first-year undergraduate's essay' (Eagleton 2003, 260). Bran Nicol reaches a similar conclusion, confirming that 'what we know as structuralism does not encompass poststructuralism, deconstruction, modernism, and postmodernism as she claims it does.' On his view, Murdoch wrongly characterises Derrida as a structuralist and thus misreads his philosophy. Her reading, ultimately, 'seems to play into the hands of those who regard Murdoch as a theoretical dinosaur, still harping on about "truth" and "greatness" as if literary criticism and philosophy remained rooted in the Oxbridge Commons Rooms of the 1950s' (Nicol 2001, 588–589). Whether demon or caricature, Murdoch's Derrida has alienated many literary critics.

It is not surprising, given the publication of 'Derrida and structuralism' at the height of the critical theory boom, that this chapter has received harsh and sustained critique. Still, Niklas Forsberg rightly cautions against a quick dismissal of Murdoch based on her engagement with other philosophers (Forsberg 2013, 64). She does paint with broad strokes, but, as Stephen Mulhall has argued, Murdoch's style complements her ethics. For Mulhall, *MGM* 'works hard to avoid presenting the texts it discusses in ways which falsify their unity or their multiplicity' (Mulhall 1997, 235). This tactic ensures that the concepts and systems examined remain, in Mulhall's words, 'limited wholes' (Mulhall 1997, 232). Here, one might take Murdoch's structuralism as a case in point. She not only illuminates the similarities among poststructuralism, deconstruction, modernism, and postmodernism but also maintains—indeed emphasises—their differences, thereby impeding closure. The list of terms that she yokes together with 'structuralism' is, I would suggest, meant to be jarring. She then pulls on a thread of similarity—largely disguised by the 'post' prefixes—and unpacks the moral implications of a shared heritage, one anchored in Ferdinand de Saussure (*MGM*, 235).[5]

As they explore critique's limitations, contemporary scholars make a similar move. In her work, Rita Felski has criticised suspicion's 'pervasive presence as mood and method' (Felski 2015, 1), one that cuts across critical schools. For her part, Toril Moi identifies as 'post-Saussurean' 'anyone in literary studies who draws on Saussure's linguistics, particularly after World War II. The term includes both structuralists and poststructuralists' (Moi 2017, 16). Moi's classification links poststructuralism with structuralism, and Felski captures their predominant orientation toward literature. Increasingly, scholars agree that critique's different strands—feminism, deconstruction, New Historicism—share a family resemblance. In his assessment of critique's legacy, John Michael claims that

> despite their differences in vocabulary and purpose, each of these approaches subscribes to a sense of textuality that Derrida himself characterised in the opening sentence of 'Plato's Pharmacy', one of deconstruction's founding texts, 'A Text is not a text unless it hides from the first comer, from the first glance, the law of its composition and the rules of its game.' (Michael 2017, 253)

In this tradition, language has something to hide. As a result, it endlessly rewards suspicion.

One might say that critique is the voguish term for what Murdoch wanted to call structuralism. Her misgivings certainly find their contemporary analogues. In their introduction to *Critique and Postcritique*, Felski and Elizabeth Anker identify characteristics of critique—a diagnostic stance that privileges expertise and detachment, a heroic flight from everyday life, and 'a paranoid vision that translates every possible phenomenon into yet another sign of the ubiquity of ideology or disciplinary power' (Anker and Felski 2017, 15)—that echo Murdoch's

appraisal. Of course, critique evades the problem with Murdoch's structuralism, because, as an umbrella term, critique speaks to a variety of
traditions with less confusion. Still, Murdoch's criticism of structuralism
anticipates these debates by twenty years. In 1992, she firmly rejects a
view of literary studies, 'where the codified many may be thought of as
sunk in a deep ocean while the (aesthetically, intellectually) enlightened
few disport themselves upon the surface, rising up into the sunshine
while still belonging to the sea. (Like dolphins perhaps.)' (*MGM*, 267).
Her metaphor clarifies the problem: structuralism obscures the difficult
yet quotidian labour of attention—necessary to all literary criticism—and
instead legitimates a playful spirit of rising-above.

For good reason, Murdoch opens 'Consciousness and thought II'
with a meditation on attention. Unlike structuralist theorising, attention necessitates looking at the particular and waiting to know. One
must withhold cognition, for a time, in order to see clearly; after all, 'one
must see what is happening, what is there, in order to be able to see what
ought to be done' (*MGM*, 218). One heeds a reality that exceeds ego,
pausing and, notably, not thinking. 'A discipline of meditation wherein
the mind is alert but emptied of self enables this form of awareness,'
Murdoch explains, 'and the disciplined practice of various skills may promote a similar unselfing, or "*décréation*" to use Simone Weil's vocabulary. Attend "without thinking about"'. Good critics look at literature
without devouring its reality. They notice its independence. 'This is
"good for us"', Murdoch insists, 'because it involves respect, because it
is an exercise in cleansing the mind of selfish preoccupation, because it is
an experience of what truth is like' (*MGM*, 245). Disciplined attention
respects literature's separateness. One relates—by seeing and waiting—to
an unassimilable difference. This encounter with beautiful contingency
silences self-absorption and burns away egoistic haze.

Critique's detachment isolates critics, however, from the labour of
attention that might refine their literary attachments. Structuralism's
rejection of the ordinary elevates critics above not only the populace
but also, and more significantly, moral struggle.[6] Murdoch shows how
the traditions arising from the hermeneutics of suspicion break the tie
between consciousness and morality. Firstly, in the switch of false for
individual consciousness, structuralism nullifies the process of moral
clarification that the study of art might effect. Secondly, in its elevation
of professional over ordinary users of language, structuralism absolves

scholars from the need for attention, which means that, in effect, their moral vision persists unchecked. These two shifts have disrupted art's moral capacity and undermined inner life. It follows that the attention demanded by the postcritical turn—attention that would involve both clarification of critics' moral vision and (potential) change to their conceptual systems—requires the very concept of consciousness that critique has diluted.[7]

To reinforce the centrality of consciousness to moral vision, Murdoch returns to literature. She insists that readers, ordinarily, 'have no difficulty in understanding novelists, and it is natural here to speak of awarenesses, perceivings, experiences, consciousness, and of someone's "world"' (*MGM*, 264). Narrative literature illustrates, according to Murdoch, 'the importance and omnipresence of a reflective experimental background to moral decision and action, and with this the omnipresence of value (an opposition between good and bad) in human activity' (*MGM*, 259). Readers come to this sense naturally, and Murdoch's perfectionist morality rests on the purification of this stream of consciousness. 'We understand,' she claims, 'what a bad texture of consciousness is like, equally we understand what a good one is like, and what sort of changes lead from one to the other. Consider what novelists can do, and how variously and successfully they can do it' (*MGM*, 261). Moral philosophy must speak to this inner space and 'focus attention upon the experiential stream as a cognitive background to activity' (*MGM*, 267). As she reconsiders Chapter 6's arguments after Chapter 7's theorising, Murdoch offers, in Chapter 8, what one might call a postcritical view.

When Murdoch revisits *The Golden Bowl* in 'Consciousness and thought II', she witnesses what literature does. Novelists depict individuals' streams of consciousness with subtlety, showing that the 'place, where we are at home, which we *seem* to leave and then return to, which is the fundamental seat of our freedom, has moral colour, moral sensibility'. In an ordinary way, novelists highlight, for common and professional readers alike, inner life's moral significance. 'The concept of consciousness, the stream of consciousness, is *animated* by indicating a moral dimension' (*MGM*, 260), and all human beings share in Maggie Verver's struggle to see. Literary critics are no exception: they, too, must really look at particulars and avoid the temptation to flee complexity through abstraction. They must invite moral and conceptual change, which means they must pay attention to their inner life. This invitation holds true for the postcritical, where one must see, purged of professional and personal egoism, the situation as it is. After critique, literary critics have this work before them: in the distance between self and other, in the space between fiction and truth, in that interruption between consciousness and thought.

NOTES

1. My use of 'structuralism' retains Murdoch's capacious sense of the term. I unpack what I take to be its contemporary significance in the third section.
2. Throughout this chapter, I draw upon Rita Felski's sense of critique, which she outlines in her influential *The Limits of Critique* (2015).
3. This chapter is no exception. I am grateful for the editors' thoughtful feedback on earlier drafts. In addition, I must thank Emily Shreve and Jenna Lay for their tireless eyes.
4. Toril Moi's insightful work on attention, from the perspective of ordinary language philosophy, has influenced this formulation (Moi 2017, 226–231).
5. Nicol acknowledges that 'a general "Saussurian" worldview' unites the various components of Murdoch's structuralism (Nicol 2001, 589).
6. Heather Love has helpfully traced the elitism and class bias of critique (Love 2017, 365). Her examination of critics' ensuing detachment is particularly relevant here (Love 2017, 367).
7. Here, I evoke Forsberg's argument for Murdoch's difficulty, especially the need 'to overcome one's own limitations and distortions' (Forsberg 2013, 217).

REFERENCES

Anker, E.S., and R. Felski. 2017. Introduction. In *Critique and postcritique*, ed. Elizabeth S. Anker and Rita Felski, 1–28. Durham: Duke University Press.

Eagleton, T. 2003. Iris Murdoch. In *Figures of dissent*, 259–262. London: Verso.

Felski, R. 2015. *The limits of critique*. Chicago: University of Chicago Press.

Forsberg, N. 2013. *Language lost and found: On Iris Murdoch and the limits of philosophical discourse*. New York: Bloomsbury.

Love, H. 2017. Critique is ordinary. *PMLA* 132 (2): 364–370.

Michael, J. 2017. Tragedy and translation: A future for critique in a secular age. In *Critique and postcritique*, ed. Elizabeth S. Anker and Rita Felski, 252–278. Durham: Duke University Press.

Moi, T. 2017. *Revolution of the ordinary: Literary studies after Wittgenstein, Austin, and Cavell*. Chicago: University of Chicago Press.

Mulhall, S. 1997. Constructing a hall of reflection: Perfectionist edification in Iris Murdoch's metaphysics as a guide to morals. *Philosophy* 72 (280): 219–239.

Murdoch, I. 1993. *Metaphysics as a guide to morals.* (Abbreviated *MGM.*) New York: Penguin Books.

Nicol, B. 2001. Philosophy's dangerous pupil: Murdoch and Derrida. *Modern Fiction Studies* 47 (3): 580–601.

CHAPTER 9

Iris Murdoch as Educator

Megan Jane Laverty

Good – learnt through *everything*, as Plato thought. A light shining everywhere. But to be *learnt*, through all learning. That's what I think anyway.
(Iris Murdoch to Suguna Ramanathan, in Horner and Rowe 2015, 505)

INTRODUCTION: THE PROGRESSING LIFE OF A PERSON

Rarely is Iris Murdoch considered a philosopher of education.[1] And yet,
there are references to education-as-formation in almost every chapter of
Metaphysics as a Guide to Morals (henceforth *MGM*), and it is a unifying
theme of her entire philosophical and literary *oeuvre*. Murdoch took her
college teaching seriously (at St. Anne's and Royal College of Art). She
thought extensively about what and how children should be taught,[2] and
her novels are replete with schools and school teachers. In Murdoch's
fiction, the school teacher is often a 'figure of good', as in the case of
Jenkin Riderhood in *The Book and the Brotherhood* (1987). Murdoch's

M. J. Laverty (✉)
Teachers College, Columbia University, New York, NY, USA

© The Author(s) 2019   125
N. Hämäläinen and G. Dooley (eds.),
Reading Iris Murdoch's Metaphysics as a Guide to Morals,
https://doi.org/10.1007/978-3-030-18967-9_9

interest in education, and her view that all education is essentially moral education—in this as in much else, her orientation is Platonic—inform her readings of Kant, Kierkegaard, Schopenhauer, and Wittgenstein, as well as her analysis of art and literature.

Some philosophers of education have recognised Murdoch's concept of attention as a moral necessity of teaching and learning.[3] Others have defended the value of her Neo-Platonism for the theory and practice of moral education in schools.[4] However, few have addressed the central and vital role of education in Murdoch's thought. In this chapter, I seek to redress this omission by offering a more adequate account of Murdoch's interest in ordinary activities that involve what she terms 'truth-seeking' or 'purification' (*MGM*, 243), which I shall show are fundamentally educational experiences. Such activities include craftsmanship, scientific work, learning a second language, artistic endeavours, mathematical study, gardening and prayer. I argue that Murdoch's interpretation of these activities sheds light on elementary features of our moral lives and what is involved in becoming morally better. In both contexts, there exists a standard that inspires and purifies desire; the process brings about continuous and holistic change; it results in a greater imaginative grasp of reality; and the world is revealed as an occasion of wonder and joy. In short, these shared elements serve to illuminate moral progress and clarify Murdoch's view that individuals should perform activities at which they can improve.

The touchstone of Murdoch's philosophy is the progressively changing quality of consciousness which consists of 'active "reassessing" and "redefining"' (Murdoch 1997, 320). According to Murdoch, we are all always in a process of change, constantly 'deploying and directing our energy, refining or blunting it, purifying or corrupting it' (*MGM*, 495). Her choice of terms—'refining or blunting', 'purifying or corrupting'—reveals that she thinks this change is characterised by 'a process of deepening or complicating, a process of learning, a progress' (*MGM*, 31). Murdoch illuminates this progress by comparing it to being a traveller 'upon a "road"' (*MGM*, 462). Her recurring image of pilgrimage conjures an image of life as a spiritual journey 'inspired by intimations of reality which lie beyond what can be easily seen' (*MGM*, 399). The pilgrim walks along a well-trodden path, seeking not simply the destination—although the destination is not unimportant—but a transformation made possible by undertaking the journey itself. In the words of poet Anne Carson, the pilgrim undertakes such a journey 'in the belief that a question can travel into an answer' (Carson 1995, 122–123). Impelled by a deepening desire for the good, the pilgrim is drawn into the gap between the 'imperfect hurly-burly' (*MGM*, 399) of ordinary life, and a vision of how life *should* be lived.

Murdoch uses this notion of life as a spiritual pilgrimage to summarise Plato's philosophy:

> Life is a spiritual pilgrimage inspired by the disturbing magnetism of *truth*, involving *ipso facto* a purification of energy and desire in the light of a vision of what is *good*. The good and just life is thus a process of clarification, a movement toward selfless lucidity, guided by ideas of perfection which are objects of *love*. Platonic morality is not coldly intellectual, it involves the whole man and attaches value to the most 'concrete' of everyday preoc-cupations and acts. It concerns the continuous detail of human activity, wherein we discriminate between appearance and reality, good and bad, true and false, and check or strengthen our desires. (*MGM*, 14; see also 11)

This passage, which could easily serve as a summary of Murdoch's philosophy, underscores key aspects of her thought that I highlight in this essay. In the following section, I explain Murdoch's conviction that morality is 'connected with the whole of our being' (*MGM*, 495) as implied by her belief in the progressively changing quality of con-sciousness, which I consider the hallmark of Murdoch's perfectionism. If consciousness is progressive, then it follows that all of life's moments, even the mundane ones, are pedagogical. They propel us to distin-guish between appearance and reality, allowing us to become more or less truthful and good.

The view that life is a form of education in itself informs Murdoch's interest in such pedagogical activities as learning a second language, practising meditation, and studying mathematics. In the essay's third sec-tion, I examine Murdoch's analysis of these activities—which she refers to elsewhere as 'intellectual and craft studies' (*MGM*, 242)—and her argument that they force 'a concept of the good upon us' (*MGM*, 415). Murdoch considers these activities to be among the experiences that offer a kind of proof for the existence of the Good—she considers them analogues (and instances) of 'the progressing life of a person' (Murdoch 1997, 320; see also Diamond 1996). Bearing this in mind, I suggest that Murdoch's analysis of these activities can prove philosophically instruc-tive, particularly against the background difficulty of having to theorise about moral progress. In Murdoch's view, this difficulty accounts for Plato's use of myths and the failure of Freudian psychoanalysis to establish itself as a science (Murdoch 1997, 341–343).[5] It also accounts for her interest in literature.[6] It is literature's focus on characters that make novels ideally suited to reveal the progressive quality of consciousness. It does not follow from this, however, that novels have a monopoly on moral truth—nor does philosophy, for that matter.

Further, according to Murdoch, conventional models of learning are not the only activities that lead to truth and goodness. Although Murdoch understands intellectual and artistic studies as analogues (and instances) of moral progress, she does not think that the ability to learn or a formal education is what makes individuals morally better— hence her esteem of the virtuous peasant (*MGM*, 324). In this chapter I expand upon Murdoch's thought that we are most like spiritual pilgrims when engaged in artistic and intellectual activities, but I wish to emphasise that throughout her work, Murdoch appropriately and perceptively acknowledges the profound disanalogies: these activities are undertaken *in* a life; we set them as tasks for ourselves and life cannot (and should not) be approached as a task; moral perfection is manifestly distinct from artistic or intellectual perfection; and the 'measure' of an individual is incommensurate with that of a philosopher, pianist or scientist.

THE PILGRIM'S PROGRESS

Murdoch never wavered in her conviction that consciousness 'is a form of moral activity' (*MGM*, 167), characterised by 'a deep continuous working of values, a *continuous present and presence* of perceptions, intuitions, images, feelings, desires, aversions, attachments' (*MGM*, 215, italics hers). Cora Diamond endorses this 'extremely central theme' in Murdoch's philosophy (Diamond 1996, 82). In an article engaging with Diamond's scholarship, Danièle Moyal-Sharrock objects to the claim's 'militant or postmodernist flavour' and likens it to the claim that 'all our thoughts and actions are *political*' which she rejects as 'ideological rumbling'. According to Moyal-Sharrock, while such claims are trivially true, in the sense that 'anything can be read into anything if one is intent on it', they are offensive to our common sense. She takes it is as a given that 'we distinguish between the sentences: "The neighbor was brutally murdered" and "I'm making pea soup"' in moral terms (Moyal-Sharrock 2012, 234, italics hers).[7] The sentence 'I'm making pea soup' is intended to reveal that most of our thoughts and activities are far too mundane to be of moral consequence. For Moyal-Sharrock, the moral import of making pea soup derives from a certain context, as in the case of an individual continuing to prepare it directly after being informed of her neighbour's murder.

Murdoch anticipated something like Moyal-Sharrock's criticism as early as 1970 (Murdoch 1997, 328), and in *MGM* she explicitly and repeatedly states that the evaluative character of consciousness 'need not imply that all states of consciousness are evaluating or can be evaluated' (*MGM*, 167). She does not deny that we make scientific or commonsense statements. To this end, she acknowledges that 'the proposition that "the cat is on the mat" is true, indicates a fact, if the cat is on the mat' (*MGM*, 26). Similarly, propositions can express aesthetic evaluations, as, for example, when we admire a person's elegant bearing, take delight in a charming flower, or marvel at an imposing cathedral. Taking up the question of aesthetic consciousness, also in response to Diamond's scholarship, Sabina Lovibond argues that we need not adopt a morality-centred answer to the question of what makes life valuable. She interprets Wittgenstein (of the *Notebooks*, at least) as characterising the good human life by its contemplative, rather than explicitly moral, character. In such a life, we look upon the world with 'a happy eye', experiencing it '*as if*' it were a felicitous composition'. We can thus live a good life 'from simply *being in the world*' (Lovibond 2007, 308, italics hers).

Murdoch acknowledges aesthetic consciousness of the kind Lovibond describes—we only need to think of her kestrel example (Murdoch 1997, 369). Unlike Lovibond, however, she does not countenance that aesthetics may constitute an alternative to morals in regard to what gives life meaning. Neither does she suggest that aesthetic, commonsense and scientific concepts be conflated with moral concepts. Rather, Murdoch argues that progress within any of these concepts involves learning.[8] Learning a concept is not a discrete activity and neither does it result from the sheer effort of will. We do not simply pick and choose our concepts or how we are to go about understanding them. The labour involved in deepening and refining our conceptual understanding is diffuse. This is because a concept is less like 'a ring' and more like an orientation or way of 'grasping' experience (Murdoch 1997, 40). Individuals are always conceiving reality, even in moments when they are not think-ing or deliberating about it. While conceptual labour might be diffuse, we know that learning is possible in light of how it transforms vision and brings reality into view. Inspired by real and increasingly well-discerned standards of perfection—whether commonsensical, scientific or aes-thetic—we make progress in our understanding and appreciation of what is perfect.

Thus, learning confers a moral significance upon progressively chang-ing consciousness, regardless of whether it results in new or modified action. Consciousness becomes more, or less, discerning as a result of its own activity. Moreover, as consciousness becomes more truth-ful, the individual's understanding—indeed, his or her entire orienta-tion to the world—moves further away from appearance toward reality. Egoistic vision and energy (Eros) is purified and made more spiritual. As Murdoch explains, 'what we attend to, how we attend, whether we attend' matters because our experiences—whether situations, things, people or activities—are not available to us under generic descriptions (*MGM*, 167). Rather, their descriptions reflect our unique, contempo-raneous position in the world, as well as our orientation to it, in terms of what we desire and value. To quote Diamond, we do not 'inhabit the same perceptible, describable world' because our understanding of sit-uations, people and things is always 'irreducibly evaluative' (Diamond 1996, 85).

Whether we attend, how we attend and what we attend to matters, because these acts of attention have a formative impact on the changing quality of consciousness. The problem is that we cannot precisely predict what the formative impact of these efforts will be. Our ability to manage and direct the progressive process is so limited that Murdoch compares it to breathing (*MGM*, 458). As with breathing, the progressive process is continuous, and so much a part of the background that it is hard to know what effect, if any, our mental states and behaviours will have on the quality of our consciousness now and in the future. Simone Weil conveys this idea when she writes about what it is like to labour over a geometry problem for an hour and be no closer to a solution:

> We have nevertheless been making progress each minute of that hour in another more mysterious dimension. Without our knowing or feeling it, this apparently barren effort has brought more light into the soul ...

Moreover, it may very likely be felt in some department of the intelligence in no way connected with mathematics. Perhaps he who made the unsuccessful effort will one day be able to grasp the beauty of a line of Racine more vividly on account of it. (Weil 1951, 58)

Everything, including cooking pea soup and working on a geometry problem, informs the changing quality of consciousness, even if we cannot determine that formative influence. For this reason, Murdoch concludes that morality has to do with 'all apprehensions of others, all lonely reveries, all uses of time' (*MGM*, 177). The import of how we occupy ourselves in these moments will only become apparent with time and experience.

Consciousness is characterised not only by qualitative change, but also by a 'searching for coherence ("making sense of things")' (*MGM*, 195). In Murdoch's account of this search for meaning, she is—despite being a novelist—surprisingly silent on the subject of the narrative unity of a life.[9] Instead, she derives her conception of unity from art, which includes listening to a symphony, reading a poem, or admiring a painting. Stories count as artistic wholes but are not privileged. I suggest that Murdoch, like her fellow perfectionist, Stanley Cavell, believes that the endlessness of the task requires us, as a matter of principle, to remain open to new and imaginative ways of unifying consciousness and understanding life (Crary 2014). Moreover, she is attuned to the fact that any apprehension of absolute value is going to unify life qualitatively (as opposed to episodically): life's meaning is less a matter of what we do and more a matter of the values that get expressed in the pattern of our doings.

While Murdoch thinks that we cannot do without such limited wholes, she cautions us against seeking refuge in them. According to Murdoch, some of our unifying pictures or stories 'arrest our progress' because they are too dramatic or consoling—'tragic' 'is another comfort word' (*MGM*, 456, 458). No life is so bleak that it prohibits learning. Despite the moral failings—ignorance, injustice, and evil—Murdoch concludes that life is subject to 'the remarkable continued return to the idea of goodness as unique and absolute' (*MGM*, 427). Inspired by real standards of perfection, we make real progress. In the final analysis, the experience of learning teaches us—we finite, flawed, erotic creatures—the necessity and sovereignty of the Good.

EDUCATION AS THE FINDING, FOUNDING, AND FUNDING OF VALUES

Murdoch understands better than most philosophers that humans find the promise of a progressive understanding or genuine growth deeply alluring. As finite, flawed, erotic creatures, we yearn to voyage and to return home, to seek new frontiers and to find refuge, to innovate and to conserve, to give birth to children and to mourn the dead. These universal, abiding and multi-faceted yearnings disclose values that are authoritative, necessary and transformative. These values are determinations of an inexhaustible reality that calls upon us to respond in appropriate ways. The progressive nature of our understanding and our lives—the fact that both can become deeper, more nuanced, and more refined—undermines the view that such values are merely subjective, arbitrary, hypothetical or contingent. For Murdoch, we cannot imagine life without such values: they cannot be 'thought away' from human existence (*MGM*, 427). This is not because we have been taught to believe in them—as we might have been taught to believe in God—but because without them we would be unable to make sense of our experience—unable to make even the most trivial decisions that beset us daily, let alone the large and life-altering decisions that inevitably confront us.

Put differently, what is found to be most perfect is found to exist necessarily—thus, Murdoch refers to certainty as the alternative face of necessity. We discern our experiences more clearly as we deepen our appreciation of the values that claim us. These values are found to be 'fundamental, essential and necessary' because they uniquely foster 'our sense of reality' (*MGM*, 430, 399). In such contexts, judgments of appreciation and approbation arise, not as 'expressive attitudes', but as 'themselves a grasp of reality' (*MGM*, 418). Values enhance our grasp of reality in two principal ways. First, they allow aspects of our experience to 'show up' in ways that were previously unavailable to us: we see subtle variations in colour, the solitary silhouette of a tree, the wistful expression on a dog's face, or a child's intense consternation. In the words of Murdoch, 'the selfish self-interestedly casual or callous man *sees* a different world from that which the careful scrupulous just man sees' (*MGM*, 177, emphasis hers). Second, and not unrelated, these values illuminate our own failings and faults in a manner that opens the way for the work of overcoming and fixing them. Our growth is a constant source of new knowledge and understanding because we are continually coming to recognise the unimportance of what we once deemed important (*MGM*, 430).

This process of becoming progressively more conscious of what is worth desiring is a fundamental aspect of our intellectual and artistic activities. We discover that, just as there is a more elegant solution to a mathematical problem, there is a better way to cope with a troubled relationship. Eventually we understand that life itself can be lived well or badly and that we can become better or worse individuals (*MGM*, 438). Nor is our yearning to make meaningful progress in our lives separate from our yearning to make music, study history, take photographs, paint pictures, perform plays, sail ships, build houses or write literature. The standards belonging to such activities inspire love and, because love cannot be willed, these standards are experienced as real and binding. For example, philosopher and poet Jan Zwicky evocatively describes the experience of our philosophic spirit encountering an authentic philosophical gesture:

> our hearts leap to our chests, the tears come to our eyes, we are prone to think we are crazy and we would like often enough to set the whole thing down, to turn or tear ourselves away. But we are done for, claimed: we belong to what we have scented – unquenchably, uncompromisingly, and indeed sometimes unhappily – until we die. (Zwicky 2015, 286)

To pursue how Zwicky invests a familiar moment with dramatic significance, we only need to consider our desire to set apart certain books, music or art as truly great because we believe that they, above others, are 'revelatory' (Gaita 2001, 9). Zwicky conveys the spellbinding power of such artistic and intellectual achievements by dramatising the magnetic force that philosophical excellence has on the consciousness of a philosopher. Zwicky's description also reveals how this magnetism might motivate a philosopher to undertake the long and arduous task of learning how to do it better: seeking to eliminate what is bad or faulty to allow for the integration of only the good elements (Zwicky 2015, 287–289).

Artistic and intellectual activities exercise a magnetic pull on our consciousness and desires because they constitute innumerable forms of what is truly good. The magnetism of these activities makes us willing to persevere: we struggle to learn piano or painting, despite the slow progress, and the demanding nature, of the task, because the imagined goodness of this activity has a powerful hold on our consciousness. Motivated by love of the activity and its perceived value, the individual undertakes it, becoming more practised over time. It is by such means that the individual acquires aptitude and understanding and is transformed by the experience. Murdoch refers to this entire process as a 'love of perfection' (*MGM*, 438) and argues that the activities we pursue reward us for our dedication and discipline by affording us new insights, new powers, and significant breakthroughs.

Murdoch illustrates this educative process with her analysis of the slave boy in Plato's dialogue *Meno*. The dialogue opens with the title character, Meno, posing a set of questions: 'Can you tell me, Socrates – is virtue something that can be taught? Or does it come by practice? Or is it neither teaching nor practice that gives it to a man but natural aptitude or something else?' (Plato 1972, 115/70a). Socrates responds with the proposal that they first answer the logically prior question regarding the nature of virtue. At a certain point in the inquiry, Meno begins to show signs of frustration and appears as though he might abandon the conversation. In an effort to entertain and instruct Meno (and perhaps also to shame him), Socrates guides Meno's slave to discover the solution to a geometrical problem by asking him a series of leading questions. Of the slave's learning, Murdoch writes:

> The slave solving the geometrical problem is orienting himself towards, bringing his attention to bear upon, something dark and alien, on which light then falls, and which he 'makes his own'. He 'sees' an object invisible but grasped as 'there', he is able to concentrate and attend. (To attend is also to wait.) These familiar metaphors are important. It is then as if he always knew it and was remembering it. The process of discovery is to be thought of as accompanied or motivated by a passion or a desire which is increased and purified in the process ... This is something which we can all recognise and which can be illustrated in many different kinds of activity. (*MGM*, 400)

The terms of Murdoch's analysis are eminently pedagogical. Solving the geometrical problem involves struggle: the slave must make himself concentrate and attend. This is particularly difficult because the object of his attention is 'something dark and alien'. He needs to concentrate without being apprised of what he needs to concentrate on. The slave must wait for the solution to dawn upon him as the problem comes into view. Ideally, his desire to solve the geometrical problem is increased, intensified and purified as his process of discovery progresses. Finally, echoing Plato, Murdoch claims that once the discovery has been made, it is as if the slave always knew it and only needed it to be recalled.

Such 'certainties' or 'recollections' are not, as Murdoch points out, 'solitary revelations' (*MGM*, 400). They occur against the background of a shared disciplinary practice. This is important, because sustained involvement in geometry, for example, increases the student's confidence in his or her own judgments. The student grows to trust his or her own thinking about geometry precisely because that thinking has been disciplined by the sustained and self-corrective practice of having to undertake the work of solving geometry problems. Admittedly, learning geometry involves 'learning all sorts of strange tricks, but fundamentally it is learning how to make a formal utterance of a perceived truth and render it splendidly worthy of a trained purified attention without falsifying it in the process' (*MGM*, 458–459). Here, Murdoch is speaking of art, not geometry, but Murdoch's assessment is also applicable in this context because the kinds of activities that Murdoch considers educative or truth-seeking need not be overtly artistic, intellectual or removed from everyday life (*MGM*, 195).

Put simply, a truth-seeking activity is any activity that admits of being perfected, and the effort, discipline, and dedication involved in perfecting the activity serve to perfect those individuals engaged in it. To learn an instrument is to learn to play that instrument *well*; to learn philosophy is to learn how to philosophise *well*. Experts and novices alike discern a gap between the way that they undertake an activity and the way in which it *ought* to be undertaken. To discern that gap *is* to want to close it, to strive to perfect the activity. These activities provide a sense of direction and of how we might move in that direction: of what we need to improve. Our engagement in them reveals that 'we are changed by love and pursuit of what we only partly see and understand' (*MGM*, 22).

Learning to become skilful in such an activity is also rewarded by what R.F. Holland describes as 'an indefinite progression of the work, with the possibility of advancement and the growth of comprehension and the natural joy that attends the exercise of a human faculty' (Holland 1980, 56). This long-term feature of truth-seeking activities is illustrated dramatically in the following passage from Simone Weil's essay on reading:

> For the sailor, for the experienced captain, his boat has become in a sense an extension of his own body; it is an instrument by which to read the

tempest, and he reads it very differently than a passenger does. Where the passenger reads chaos and unlimited danger, the captain reads necessities, limited dangers, resources for escaping, and an obligation to be courageous and honorable. (Weil 2015, 26)[10]

The captain in Weil's example trusts his reading of the situation because over time his progressive understanding has proved increasingly trustworthy. Moreover, he appreciates that his reality will continue to yield up its secrets the longer he sails. Truth and progress are the rewards for trained effort (*MGM*, 400).

Drawing upon the scholarship of Talbot Brewer, we might attribute the indefinite nature of progress in truth-seeking activities to their *dialectical* nature (Brewer 2009; see also Cordner 2015 and Laverty 2015). According to Brewer, individuals engage in dialectical activities 'on the strength of an as-yet-indistinct intimation of their intrinsic value'. Such activities have 'a self-unveiling character' in that their constitutive ideals and internal goods are progressively clarified by means of the learner's ongoing engagement in them. Thus, that engagement is characterised by a dialectic of searching and finding. And, if the constitutive ideals and internal goods are 'complex and elusive enough', then 'this dialectical process can be reiterated indefinitely' (Brewer 2009, 37). Nothing about our progressive achievements 'annihilates the task' because the fulfilment of one constitutive ideal in turn reveals another, more demanding one. For Holland, this dialectical progression 'relates to betterment, not in the sophistical sense, but in the absolute sense of getting better and being better' (Holland 1980, 57–58): betterment in the sophistical sense connotes advancement in relation to someone else or to getting ahead in the world, whereas betterment in the absolute sense connotes achievement that is determined internal to the activity or practice and that can be indefinitely reiterated.

Murdoch gives the example of learning Russian, having studied it for much of her adult life. When learning Russian, she is 'confronted by an authoritative structure which commands [her] respect. The task is difficult, and the goal is distant and perhaps never entirely attainable.' The language exists independently and is something that her 'consciousness cannot take over, swallow up, deny or make unreal' (Murdoch 1997, 373). It presents her with an arduous task which, if she is to persevere and make progress, requires piety, honesty, and humility. The reward is a 'knowledge of reality' that finds expression in a vocabulary of secondary normative terms—colourful, elegant, facile, sloppy, delicate, tender, noble, delightful, parsimonious and forceful—that Murdoch can then use to describe and defend her love and progressive understanding of Russian language and literature (see Higgins 2018, 139–145). As her understanding progresses, she becomes a more adept speaker and reader; she is more discriminating in her choice of Russian words and more discerning in her appreciation of their meaning.

Truth-seeking activities imply mastery—a concept that has a long history in education. Murdoch, like Weil, focuses on the role of attentiveness or 'attentive waiting' (*MGM*, 323) to accentuate that while someone (like herself) might yearn to be fluent in Russian, the progress that she makes is not deliberate or willed.[11] Although truth-seeking activities require discipline and practice, improvement is at best 'piecemeal' and does not occur at our behest. Our efforts simply prepare us for the occasion of being taught. Mastery arrives—it is bestowed upon us as an occasion of grace—and is never made final. Because mastery comes to us from 'the outside', it makes us feel that our human endeavours have been given 'supernatural assistance' (Murdoch 1997, 334). Mastery invites humility not because there is more to do and to know, although this is indeed true, but because it establishes the necessary existence of that which is not of the self: the hypothetical (everything about us) is temporarily eclipsed by the categorical (a reality that transcends us). It is a mistake to think that Murdoch values truth-seeking activities because we lose ourselves in practising them; rather, her interest is inspired by the fact that incremental improvements in knowledge, technique and expertise persuade us of, and return us to, a reality that is experienced as absolutely good. Although a masterly artistic performance must come to a close, its spellbinding beauty endures.

Progress in a truth-seeking activity implies attentiveness which Zwicky illustratively defines as 'an egoless availability' (Zwicky 2015, 292). To acquire mastery is not to zero in on a target; rather, it comes from a place of quiet silence or internal stillness. This ready receptivity allows values to 'show up' as stretched between the truth-seeking mind and the world. Reality is made radiant with a beauty that invites us to feel at home in a world uniquely sustained by love.[12] Education does not just wake us up to the world: it bids us to 'be at home in [it] … despite the ill' (Holland 1980, 59). To be at home in the world despite the ill is to find refuge (*MGM*, 8)—a condition of absolute safety. It is to feel held by the world's absolute goodness and is, according to Murdoch, 'a pure untainted source of spiritual power' (*MGM*, 430).

Wittgenstein refers to the feeling of absolute safety as an ethical stance which he contrasts with a 'relative stance' (Wittgenstein 1965, 5). According to him, whereas the relative stance can be justified empirically—examples include 'This man is a good runner' and 'This is the right way to Granchester' (Wittgenstein 1965, 6), the ethical stance is not a matter of empirical fact. Other instances of the ethical stance include 'I *wonder* at the existence of the world' (Wittgenstein 1965, 8; Murdoch 1997, 269) and 'I have found in you my soulmate'. Empirically speaking, no one is absolutely safe nor can they imagine the world not existing. Nonetheless we find the ethical stance intelligible. It encapsulates our desire both to go beyond anything we might say or do in our lives with concepts, and to reflect upon the whole of life's meaning with the very same concepts. In Wittgenstein's terms, Murdoch argues that truth-seeking activities invite the ethical stance.

For the eighteenth-century French philosopher Jean-Jacques Rousseau and the twentieth-century neuroscientist Oliver Sacks, the pursuit of science—botany in the case of Rousseau and chemistry in the case of Sacks—contributed to a deep sense of the world as absolutely good, allowing each of them to feel at home in it, despite the persecution, war, strife, corruption and isolation that they saw around them. Their passion for science filled them with wonder, excitement, joy, fulfilment, and gratitude. Within the context of their scientific pursuits, they were able to experience the constancy of the new: for Rousseau, there were new places to visit and new plants to identify; for Sacks, there were new chemicals to experiment with in new ways. Another appeal of these scientific persuits was the sense that beyond the familiarity and variety of nature, they were making contact with 'a dark, hidden world of mysterious laws and phenomena' (Sacks 1999, 58). By studying plants and elements, Rousseau and Sacks would occasionally discover 'the reason and purpose of their varied structures' (Rousseau 1992, 115). This gave them many happy moments, and filled them with gratitude—what Rousseau called the 'admiration of the hand that allows me to enjoy all this' (Rousseau 1992, 115).

Activities like these intimate a sense of the sacredness of life but need not be accompanied by any metaphysical commitments. The cellist, composer, and conductor Pablo Casals, echoes and exemplifies the idea.

> For the past eight years I have started each day in the same manner. It is not a mechanical routine but something essential to my daily life. I go to

the piano, and I play two preludes and fugues by Bach. I cannot think
of doing otherwise. It is a sort of benediction on the house. But that is
not its only meaning for me. It is a re-discovery of the world of which
I have the joy of being a part. It fills me with awareness of the wonder
of life, with a feeling of the incredible marvel of being a human being.
The music is never the same for me, never. Each day it is something new,
fantastic and unbelievable. That is Bach, like nature, a miracle! (Casals
1970, 17)[13]

Casals describes Bach's music as miraculous because despite having
played the preludes and fugues for eight years, his experience of the
music is always new. There is no accounting for the newness of the music
and rediscovery of the world that accompanies it. We expect the routine,
no matter how pleasant, to produce ennui. It simply should not be the
case that the same music played each day by Casals for eight years turns
out to be 'never the same'. Yet, the more Casals plays these preludes and
fugues, the more remarkable and life-giving they become. The more
time and energy dedicated to mastering such an art, the more the activity opens the world up, not only to our understanding but also to our
appreciation of what is absolutely valuable and we experience this appreciation as wonder and joy.

It must not be overlooked that Casals was a professional cellist who
started each day by playing the piano; Murdoch was a contemporary
author and a philosopher who dedicated part of her adult life to learning Russian; Sacks was a neuroscientist with a love of chemistry; and
Rousseau discovered botany in his twilight years. It is impossible to
know in advance the truth-seeking activities that will inspire us and how
they will live on in our futures. It is also true that our truth-seeking
activities can idle (Murdoch 1997, 334). In such moments, we pursue
these activities (speaking, writing, cooking, sailing, or playing the piano)
practically, failing to attune ourselves to their truth-seeking or perfectionist dimensions. In these moments, we must be reminded that no matter
how accustomed to, or expert in, an activity we have become, new possibilities for growth reside in the gap between what is and what *could*
be the case. Once back on the path of truth- or perfection-seeking, the
activity resumes as a journey toward understanding of self and the world.
The activity then once again informs our broader conception and love of
what it means to do anything well, including, and perhaps most importantly, what it means to live well.

Conclusion

In this chapter, I have addressed the central and vital role of education in Iris Murdoch's philosophy. Against the backdrop of her (Platonic) idea of life as a spiritual pilgrimage, I have considered two essential aspects of her thinking. First, I interpreted her belief in the omnipresence of morality as an implication of her perfectionism. Second, I considered activities that Murdoch thinks provide a kind of proof for the necessity and sovereignty of the Good. My analysis suggested that a fuller understanding of these activities can prove philosophically instructive. With an infinite set of activities that might be classified as truth-seeking, individuals are capable of pursuing many of them at once: their learnings can take place on plural paths. In fact, our lives are made up of many, various and complex combinations of these very activities. There is thus an isomorphism between the singular life each of us leads and the individual activities that comprise it. Such activities deepen the meaning of our lives and move us toward a sense of the absolute.

Acknowledgements Thanks to René Arcilla, Diana Barnes, Gillian Dooley, Maughn Rollins Gregory, Nora Hämäläinen, David T. Hansen, Rachel Longa, and Laurance J. Splitter for discussion and helpful comments on earlier drafts.

Notes

1. One exception is Evans (2009).
2. See Murdoch (1993, 1998) and Dooley (2003).
3. See Buchmann (1989), McDonough (2000) and Olsson (2018).
4. See Jonas (2016) and Nakazawa (2018).
5. Freudian psychoanalysis figures more prominently in *Metaphysics as Guide to Morals* than in *The Sovereignty of Good* which indicates that Murdoch grew to appreciate Freud's affinity with Plato. In *MGM*, she refers to Freud more than once as a 'self-styled modern disciple of Plato' (*MGM*, 20).
6. For discussion of Murdoch on philosophy and literature, see Forsberg (2013, 2015) and Hämäläinen (2015, 133–184).
7. See also Cordner and Gleeson (2016).
8. See Laverty (2007, 2009) and Forsberg (2013, 2017).
9. See Gaita (1991, 134–136), MacIntyre (2007) and Brewer (2009).
10. See also Yoda (2017).
11. For discussion of Murdoch on attention, see Cordner (2009, 2016) and Forsberg (2017).

12. See Gaita (2001, 199–200), Holland (1980) and Zwicky (2015).
13. For discussion of this passage, see Holland (1980, 59–60), Gaita (1991, 214–215).

REFERENCES

Brewer, T. 2009. *The retrieval of ethics*. Oxford: Oxford University Press.
Buchmann, M. 1989. The careful vision: How practical is contemplation in teaching? *American Journal of Education* 98 (1): 35–61.
Carson, A. 1995. *Plainwater: Essays and poetry*. New York: Random House.
Casals, P. 1970. *Joys and sorrows: His own story as told by Albert Kahn*. New York: Simon and Schuster.
Cordner, C. 2009. Waiting, patience, and love. In *Waiting*, ed. Ghassan Hage, 169–183. Carlton, VIC: Melbourne University Press.
Cordner, C. 2015. Dialectical activity, ritual and value: A critique of Talbot Brewer. *Philosophical Investigations* 39 (2): 1–14.
Cordner, C. 2016. Lessons of Murdochian attention. *Sophia: International Journal for Philosophy of Religion, Metaphysical Theology and Ethics* 55 (2): 197–213.
Cordner, C., and A. Gleeson. 2016. Cora Diamond and the moral imagination. *Nordic Wittgenstein Review* 5 (1): 55–77.
Crary, A. 2014. A radical perfectionist: Revisiting Cavell in light of Kant. *Journal of Aesthetic Education* 48 (3): 87–98.
Diamond, C. 1996. 'We are perpetually moralists': Iris Murdoch, fact, and value. In *Iris Murdoch and the search for human goodness*, ed. Maria Antonaccio and William Schweiker, 79–109. Chicago: Chicago University Press.
Dooley, G. 2003. *From a tiny corner in the house of fiction: Conversations with Iris Murdoch*. Columbia: University of South Carolina Press.
Evans, W. 2009. Iris Murdoch, liberal education and human flourishing. *Journal of Philosophy of Education* 43 (1): 75–84.
Forsberg, N. 2013. *Language lost and found: On Iris Murdoch and the limits of philosophical discourse*. London: Bloomsbury Publishing.
Forsberg, N. 2015. The categorical and the everyday: On Coetzee, Murdoch, and Cavell on the presence of philosophy in novels. *Philosophy and Literature* 39: 66–82.
Forsberg, N. 2017. M and D and me: Iris Murdoch and Stanley Cavell on perfectionism and self-transformation. *Iride: Journal of Philosophy and Public Debate* 30 (81): 261–372.
Gaita, R. 1991. *Good and evil: An absolute conception*. London: Palgrave Macmillan.
Gaita, R. 2001. The pedagogical power of love. *Journal of the Victorian Association for the Teaching of English* 37 (2–3): 8–20.

Hämäläinen, N. 2015. *Literature and moral theory*. London: Bloomsbury Publishing.

Higgins, C. 2018. Education in a minor key. *Educational Theory* 68 (2): 139–145.

Holland, R.G. 1980. *Against empiricism: On education, epistemology and value*. Totowa, NJ: Barnes and Noble.

Horner, A., and A. Rowe (eds.). 2015. *Living on paper: Letters from Iris Murdoch, 1934–1995*. Princeton and Oxford: Princeton University Press.

Jonas, M. 2016. Three misunderstandings of Plato's theory of moral education. *Educational Theory* 66 (3): 301–322.

Laverty, M.J. 2007. *Iris Murdoch's ethics: A consideration of her romantic vision*. London: Continuum.

Laverty, M.J. 2009. Learning our concepts. *Journal of Philosophy of Education* 43 (1): 27–40.

Laverty, M.J. 2015. 'There is no substitute for a sense of reality': Humanizing the humanities. *Educational Theory* 6 (6): 635–654.

Lovibond, S. 2007. 'In spite of the misery of the world': Ethics, contemplation, and the source of value. In *Wittgenstein and the moral life: Essays in honor of Cora Diamond*, ed. Alice Crary, 305–326. Cambridge, MA: Massachusetts Institute of Technology.

MacIntyre, A. 2007. *After virtue—A study in moral theory*. Notre Dame, IN: Notre Dame University Press.

McDonough, S. 2000. Iris Murdoch's notion of attention: Seeing the moral life in teaching. *Philosophy of Education Society* 2000: 217–225.

Moyal-Sharrock, D. 2012. Cora Diamond and the ethical imagination. *British Journal of Aesthetics* 52 (3): 223–240.

Murdoch, I. 1993. *Metaphysics as a guide to morals*. London: Penguin Books.

Murdoch, I. 1997. *Existentialists and mystics: Writings on philosophy and literature*, ed. Peter Conradi. London: Penguin Books.

Murdoch, I. 1998. *Occasional essays by Iris Murdoch*, ed. Yozo Muroya and Paul Hullah. Okayama: University Education Press.

Nakazawa, Y.M. 2018. Iris Murdoch's critique of three dualisms in moral education. *Journal of Philosophy of Education: Early Access* 52 (3): 397–411.

Olsson, A.-L. 2018. A moment of letting go: Iris Murdoch and the morally transformative process of unselfing. *Journal of Philosophy of Education* 52 (1): 163–177.

Plato. 1972. *Protagoras and Meno*, trans. W.K.C. Guthrie. London: Penguin Books.

Rousseau, J.-J. 1992. *The reveries of the solitary walker*, trans. Charles E. Butterworth. Indianapolis: Hackett Publishing Company.

Sacks, O. 1999. Brilliant light: A chemical boyhood. *New Yorker*, 20 December.

Weil, S. 1951. Reflections on the right use of school studies with a view to the love of God. In *Waiting for God*, trans. Emma Crauford, 57–66. New York: G. P. Putnam's Sons.

Weil, S. 2015. *Simone Weil: Later philosophical writings*, trans. Eric O. Springsted and Lawrence E. Schmidt. Notre Dame, IN: Notre Dame University Press.

Wittgenstein, Ludwig. 1965. A lecture on ethics. *The Philosophical Review* 74 (1): 3–12.

Yoda, K. 2017. An approach to Simone Weil's philosophy of education through the notion of reading. *Studies in Philosophy and Education* 36 (6): 663–682.

Zwicky, Jan. 2015. Alcibiades' love. In *Philosophy as a Way of Life: Ancients and Moderns—Essays in Honour of Pierre Hadot*, ed. M. Chase, S.R.L. Clarke, and M. McGhee, 283–298. Wiley Blackwell.

CHAPTER 10

'I Think I Disagree': Murdoch on Wittgenstein and Inner Life (*MGM* Chapter 9)

Anne-Marie Søndergaard Christensen

INTRODUCTION

After receiving a copy of *Metaphysics as a Guide to Morals* (henceforth *MGM*) from Iris Murdoch, her friend Brian Medlin writes back: 'your beautiful big book arrived a few days ago and I have been dipping into [it?] with pleasure. So far I think I disagree with what you say in "Wittgenstein and the Inner Life," but I'll have to make sure that I've understood you aright (so there!) before I launch into a complaint' (Dooley and Nerlich 2014, 174). Reading Murdoch's chapter, many may tend to be of the same opinion as Medlin without being able to pinpoint precisely what Murdoch gets wrong in her treatment of Wittgenstein's later philosophy—it is telling that Medlin never returns to the question in his later letters. The aim of this chapter is to untangle Murdoch's reading of Wittgenstein's investigations of the inner, and I will argue that one important problem with this reading is that

A.-M. S. Christensen (✉)
Syddansk Universitet, Odense, Denmark

© The Author(s) 2019
N. Hämäläinen and G. Dooley (eds.),
Reading Iris Murdoch's Metaphysics as a Guide to Morals,
https://doi.org/10.1007/978-3-030-18967-9_10

it is ambivalent. On the one hand, Murdoch explicitly notes how Wittgenstein is concerned with 'what philosophers, and laymen, wrongly picture or imagine' (*MGM*, 288), and that he aims to dissolve preconceived, but illusory ideas of the inner. On the other hand, she treats several of Wittgenstein's investigations as if they are in fact constructive pieces of philosophy aimed *to change* our conception of the inner, especially in her remarks on Wittgenstein's example of sensation S and his notion of lifeform, which leads her to the conclusion that 'Wittgenstein has been *forcing upon us* a certain picture of experience as a kind of illusion, thereby discrediting the density and the real existence of inner thinking ("inner life")' (*MGM*, 279).

In the following, I will trace Murdoch's involvement with Wittgenstein's philosophy and reconstruct her reasons for this conclusion, which, among other things, include her acceptance of Saul Kripke's sceptical reading of the rule-following considerations, and I will show that she is wrong to read Wittgenstein's therapeutic involvement with certain philosophical mistakes as substantial, philosophical theses. In closing, I will argue that if Murdoch had not misread the *Investigation* in certain ways, she may have found Wittgenstein to be, if not a companion, then an ally in her own endeavour to restore and re-direct philosophical interest in how the inner can play a transformative role in relation to language and moral life.

PREPARATIONS AND ANTICIPATIONS

In order to identify what worries Brian Medlin and many other readers of Murdoch's treatment of Wittgenstein's later philosophy in *MGM*, I will begin by considering some of the remarks on Wittgenstein's philosophy that precede the discussion in Chapter 9. In several places, Murdoch discusses Wittgenstein's first work, *Tractatus logico-philosophicus*, especially his remarks on ethics and the idea 'that ethics cannot be put into words' (Wittgenstein 1961, 6.421), and she expresses some sympathy for what she sees as Wittgenstein's attempt to 'segregate value in order to keep it pure and untainted' (*MGM*, 25), that is, to indicate the area of value by being silent about it, even if Murdoch ultimately sees this attempt as misguided, resting on a mistaken acceptance of a philosophical separation of fact and value.[1] More important for an understanding of Chapter 9 is what Murdoch writes about Wittgenstein's later philosophy, and I think it may prove instructive to consider three distinctive and representative remarks on the *Philosophical investigations*:

One of the emotions likely to be aroused by reading the *Investigations* is a sense of loss. ... What we 'lose' in the *Investigations* is some sort of inner thing. As we pursue Wittgenstein's arguments, and do his 'exercises', about 'following a rule' and how meaning is not a 'mental process', we may (rightly) become convinced (for instance) that we do not need mental samples to recognise chairs, or memory images to have memories. But we may also end up feeling that we cannot now justify the reality or identity of our most important thoughts and most precious awarenesses. We are losing the *detail*. (*MGM*, 49)

These forms of arguments in removing old Cartesian errors, may indeed seem to render problematic the common-sense conception of the individual self as a moral centre or substance. [We] feel that we have lost something: our dense familiar inner stuff, private and personal, with a quality and a value of its own, something which we can scrutinise and control. (*MGM*, 153).

'Do not try to analyse your own inner experience' (*Investigations* II, xi, 204) may be seen also as a suggestion that one should not attach too much significance to (probably egoistic and senseless) inner chat. Silence becomes the inner as well as the outer person ... It is one thing to present sound anti-Cartesian critical arguments about sense data, momentary inner certainties, or the role of memory images in remembering; it is quite another to sweep aside as irrelevant a whole area of our private reflections, which we may regard as the very substance of our soul and our being, as somehow unreal, otiose, without relevant *quality* or *value*. (*MGM*, 157)

There is a lot to take note of in these quotes, but I will try to focus on the two most obvious points. One such point is that Murdoch here uses a (for a philosopher at least) highly emotional language; the remarks are pervaded with a sense of loss, of alarm and worry, and a fear of overlooking or even eliminating a tremendously important element in human life, and through her remarks flows a current of frustration with or even resentment towards Wittgenstein for not seeing the dangers that his way of doing philosophy pose to our inner lives. Something important is at stake for Murdoch, and this leads us to the second point, namely her ambivalent or conflicted attitude towards Wittgenstein's later writings. Wittgenstein's work is presented as constructive and necessary, but also as disappointing and even dangerous, as if Wittgenstein, in working to alleviate Cartesian influences on our thinking about the inner, also does something else which endangers invaluable features of our inner lives. Even if Murdoch does not initially see Wittgenstein as opposed to the inner, she does see him as negligent, irresponsible and blind to the workings of his writings in a way that is both philosophically and morally reproachable.

We may find it surprising that Murdoch does not take a more straight-forward, critical stance in relation to Wittgenstein's later philosophy because what she thinks it endangers is, according to the above quotes, really no small matter; it is nothing less than 'the reality or identity of our most important thoughts and most precious awarenesses', 'the *detail*', 'the individual self as a moral centre or substance', 'our private reflections', in sum, 'the very substance of our soul and our being'. These are serious allegations, but are they really appropriate? This question is difficult to answer, especially because Murdoch does very little to situate her critique, she does for example not engage in any close readings of the *Investigations*. It is therefore not entirely obvious *how* she thinks Wittgenstein's reflections of the inner can lead us astray.

One way to trace the source of Murdoch's worries is to look at the one sentence that she does quote from the *Investigations*: 'Do not try to analyse your own inner experience.' Murdoch presents this quote to support the idea that Wittgenstein rejects representations of the inner that lead us into mistakes in philosophy, but she then adds that it may also be seen as warning against placing too much significance on 'inner chat'. Furthermore, when she re-quotes the sentence again in Chapter 9, she offers an even stronger interpretation: 'This sounds more like moral or religious advice: do not spend time scrutinising your conscience' (*MGM*, 270), adding, later in the chapter, 'Perhaps Wittgenstein was pointing to the necessity, at least the desirability, of an inner silence' (*MGM*, 282). We may speculate that Murdoch transfers the Tractarian emphasis on silence to her reading of the *Investigations*, but the question is whether this transferral is justified with regard to this particular sentence.

The quoted sentence is taken from what was originally published as the second half of the *Investigations*, in the latest edition renamed the *Philosophy of Psychology—A Fragment*, and it occurs in a section where Wittgenstein discusses an example of a person who describes her particular impression of a picture. Wittgenstein writes, 'So a perfectly specific description was given.—Was it *seeing*, or was it a thought?', to which he notes, 'Don't try to analyse *the experience* within yourself' (Wittgenstein 2009, PPF §187–188, 215; italics mine). The central question is *what use* the sentence quoted by Murdoch has in this context. It certainly appears as if it is an integrated part of this specific investigation of experiences of pictures, warning us that the answer to the preceding question is not to be found within a particular mental experience. This interpretation of the sentence is supported by the new and improved translation of the *Investigations* (which, of course, was not available to Murdoch), where the German 'das Erlebnis' is translated as 'the experience', showing that the phrase straightforwardly refers to the specific experience of the person of the example and does not imply anything general, either positive or negative, about Wittgenstein's view of the significance of attending to inner experience, in contrast to Elizabeth Anscombe's original translation, where 'das Erlebnis' became 'your own inner experience'. At least in this instance, Brian Medlin's reservations towards Murdoch's readings of Wittgenstein seem to be justified. However, we still have not discovered the reasons for Murdoch's general mistrust of Wittgenstein's treatment of the inner, and the aim of the investigation of Chapter 9 will therefore be to identify these reasons.

WITTGENSTEIN AND THE INNER LIFE

At the start of Chapter 9, Murdoch provides a framework for her reading of Wittgenstein's work: 'Modern philosophy, in parting company with Descartes, has also rightly disposed of various metaphysical entities postulated by previous philosophers' she writes, adding, 'Yet for instance, when reading Wittgenstein, we may worry about "inner life". Can there not be too fierce a removal of entities deemed to be unnecessary and unknowable?' (*MGM*, 269–270). In the attempt to identify how the *Investigations* may involve a 'too fierce removal' of inner life, I will focus on two topics, Murdoch's discussion of the example of sensation S and her understanding of Wittgenstein's notion of lifeform, largely influenced by Saul Kripke.

In §258 of the *Investigations*, Wittgenstein imagines an example where he (and not Wittgenstein's S man', as Murdoch writes) writes the sign 'S' every time he has a particular sensation. What makes this example special is that Wittgenstein's writing of the sign is guided *only* by his inward attention to the isolated experience of sensation S; as the example is made out, he therefore cannot refer to a definition or any other form of criteria in order to determine whether he uses the sign 'S' correctly. Sensation S is, in this way, essentially private, and, according to Wittgenstein, this means that in the example, 'I have no criterion of correctness. One would like to say: whatever is going to seem correct to me is correct. And that only means that here we can't talk about "correct"'

(Wittgenstein 2009, §258). Wittgenstein thus challenges philosophical ideas of essentially private inner entities and ostensive definitions, and the possibility of establishing a meaningful sign that does not have any connections to our actions, practices, or other uses of language.

Murdoch reacts quite strongly to this example, remarking that 'Wittgenstein's S man is a prisoner of Wittgenstein's relentless thinking, part of a general attack upon the (his) concepts of "private language" and "inner process"' (*MGM*, 273). In arguing for this conclusion, Murdoch describes the example as 'a tailormade situation designed to show the emptiness of the inner when not evidently connected with the outer', and she objects that:

> in real life, the owner of S would be an individual living in time. Wittgenstein's example suggests but a perfunctory interrogation. The truth or falsehood of the claim is not allowed into the picture, which would include an immense number of details about character and situation. (*MGM*, 273)

Leaving aside the fact that the owner of S, Wittgenstein, was at some point a living individual, it seems safe to say that Wittgenstein would completely agree with Murdoch's description. This is the *point* of his example, this is what it is meant to capture: the futility involved in philosophical attempts to refer to sensations without relying on the 'immense number of details' that would allow for meaningful talk of such sensations. Wittgenstein's is not attacking sensation S, he is trying to show that sensation S is a philosophical fiction that has nothing to do with our experiences of sensations, because these experiences presuppose and connect to numerous details in our ordinary lives which also breathe life into the way we talk about sensations in ordinary language. Wittgenstein is making the grammatical point that we cannot make sense of philosophical pictures of sensations as absolutely private, isolated inner entities; he is not, as Murdoch seems to think, making the substantial or positive point that we never have any personal or individual sensations. Murdoch's remark is in fact not an objection to Wittgenstein's treatment of the example of sensation S, but rather support for the very point of his example: that S is not really anything, precisely because it does not connect to anything in our ordinary lives.

Murdoch actually allows that Wittgenstein's investigations are *not* intended as an attack directed against the inner as such. She asks, 'Surely

Wittgenstein's attack on the inner-outer-thing dualism concerns a philosophical mistake and is not intended by him to suggest there is no such thing as private reflection, or to support a behaviourist ethics?' (*MGM*, 270), and she notes that 'indeed Wittgenstein at moments declares he is not analysing it [the intense lively privacy of the individual "inner life"] away. Only pointing out "grammatical mistakes"' (*MGM*, 278). Nonetheless, Murdoch still holds that *the way* Wittgenstein pursues and develops his philosophical aim subjects the inner to an unjustified form of regimentation, and she substantiates this worry by an objection to Wittgenstein's point in presenting the example of sensation S: 'Wittgenstein's image of "outer criteria" seems, in his use of it, unbearably narrow; and, one feels, *motivated* by a desire to restrict and curtail the jumbled field of our inner musings' (*MGM*, 275). Murdoch expands on this critique one page later, writing:

> The vast concept of 'experience' subsists as something inward (perhaps images or toothache) but dependent upon, situated by, a public outer, which has consequences ... Truth is not exhibited by an account of an inner process (all right) but by criteria of truthfulness. How is truthfulness tested? How is memory tested? By consequences! (*MGM*, 276)

There is a lot to be untangled here. Murdoch is right that Wittgenstein uses the example of sensation S, as well as numerous others, to make the point that references to sensations stand in need of outer criteria or 'outward criteria' as Wittgenstein's original German 'äusserer Kriterien' is best translated. But how are we to understand this point? In Murdoch's interpretation, it means that all criteria of truthfulness that can be applied to the inner ultimately refer to 'consequences!'

To a certain extent, this is in line with the way that Wittgenstein describes uses of criteria, for example in this short discussion of confessions, where he notes that

> the importance of the true confession does not reside in its being a correct and certain report of some process. It resides, rather, in the special consequences which can be drawn from a confession whose truth is guaranteed by the special criteria of truthfulness. (Wittgenstein 2009, PPF §319, 234)

Whether we live up to criteria, of meaning, of truth or of truthfulness for example, is, according to Wittgenstein, judged by consequences.

However, the consequence requirement does not mean that we can only take something to be meaningful or truthful if it has *observable, outer* consequences. We can imagine a case, where I confess to a friend that I have harboured hidden feelings of envy and resentment towards her through all our years of friendship, for example because of her unmistakeable talent or her privileged background, and that I now promise to work to change these feelings. What would confirm the truthfulness of this confession? It may of course be confirmed by observable consequences, that I for example come to express more support in relation to her successes in life. However, it is also possible that the confession will not have any 'outer' consequences, that it will not make any observable difference. Maybe I am a skilled hypocrite, or maybe I have flawless manners that have previously made it possible for me to behave beautifully towards my friend, and because of this, my way of behaving towards her will not change. Still, if the confession is truthful, it will have what we may call inner consequences: I will stop indulging in my feelings of resentment, I will practise feeling happy about my friend's achievements etc. The point is that, within a Wittgensteinian framework, such inner doings also count as consequences that show the truthfulness of my confession because they are *in principle* assessible for others. I can relate them to my friend for example if she later asks whether my feelings towards her have changed.

What Wittgenstein is objecting to in his discussion of sensation S is that *the very possibility* of using outward criteria and of looking for the consequences of the use of the sign 'S' is ruled out beforehand. It is in this sense that questions of meaning and truth depend on a relation to a public outer. Wittgenstein is *not* saying that we can only ascribe meaning and truth to something that does in fact have overt, observable, outer consequences, and the Wittgensteinian example of the confession is in fact quite close to one of Murdoch's most discussed examples. This is the case of M and D, where a woman, M, who initially dislikes and disdains her daughter-in-law, D, comes to see that the fault lies not with D, but with her own perception of and her feelings towards D and therefore decides to change these. M 'observes D or at least reflects deliberately about D, until gradually her vision of D alters' (Murdoch 2001, 17), but without this change having any influence on her behaviour towards D which has been impeccable from the beginning. Nothing that Wittgenstein writes excludes the possibility of such an example, because even if the change in M's vision of D is inner and personal, it is not private *in principle* (as sensation S). It is related to many other aspects of M's life, and if she wants, M may later talk to others about this change.

THE 'GREAT CLARITY' OF KRIPKE

So, we return to the question: Why does Murdoch think that the richness and the reality of the inner is threatened by Wittgenstein's writings? I think that part of the reason is Murdoch's acceptance of the interpretation of the rule-following investigations presented in Saul Kripke's influential book, *Wittgenstein on Rules and Private Language*, which she found had 'discussed with greater clarity the matter with which I have been engaged' (*MGM*, 283). The focal point of Kripke's interpretation of the *Investigation* is §201, where Wittgenstein writes:

> This was our paradox: no course of action could be determined by a rule, because every course of action can be brought into accord with the rule. The answer was: if every course of action can be brought into accord with the rule, then it can also be brought into conflict with it. And so there would be neither accord nor conflict here.

Kripke reads §201 as presenting a genuine sceptical paradox arising from the insight that neither subjective, inner 'facts' about particular humans nor objective, outer 'facts' such as forms of platonic rules can serve as criteria of correct rule-following and ultimately of correct language use. Importantly, Murdoch also understands Wittgenstein as engaged in a fight against a fundamental form of scepticism and remarks on the *Investigations*: 'The question is, as Kripke points out, very like that posed by Hume. How can we be sure that the future will resemble the past?' (*MGM*, 284).

On Kripke's reading, Wittgenstein is worried that the (apparent) sceptical conclusion of §201 endangers the very possibility of meaning and language, and he therefore offers a 'solution' to the paradox. On Kripke's reconstruction, the solution is to adopt a model according to which the question of meaningful use will have to be dealt with on two different levels, one that concerns the individual and one that concerns the linguistic community. According to Kripke, the sceptical paradox means that, at the level of the individual, it is impossible to distinguish between what *seems* right and what *is* right. In this way, the problem identified by Wittgenstein in relation to the use of the sign

'S' for sensation S is in fact completely general, and Kripke thus sees Wittgenstein's remarks on private language as really a sub-part of the rule-following investigations. If we look at language use from the perspective of the individual, we have no criteria of correct use; the individual is in fact simply doing what she is 'inclined to' (Kripke 1982, 88). We should therefore give up the idea that we can ever talk about meaning in relation to isolated individuals.

According to Kripke, we should instead change our perspective to that of the linguistic community. From a third-person perspective, we can establish or rather reconstruct a criterion of correct rule-following, namely that the individual acts in a way that accords with the actions of other competent users of her language, that is, we regard an individual as a competent language user if her observable behaviours and uses of language are consistent with the behaviours and uses of other members of her language community under suitable circumstances. However, if an individual uses a concept in a way that is statistically deviant and 'no longer conforms to what the community would do in these circumstances, the community can no longer attribute the concept to him' (Kripke 1982, 95). On this view, the notion of correct language use simply rests on the possibility of the shared reactions of a group of people, and the criteria for meaningful language use are fundamentally reduced to just one, namely that of consistency with the actions of the majority of members of one's linguistic community. Moreover, as this criterion does not involve references to a shared reality or our inner lives, no criterion of correctness can be applied in relation to the collective behaviour of the linguistic community. In Crispin Wright's succinct phrasing, 'the community does not go right or wrong, rather it just goes' (qtd in McDowell 1998, 268).[2]

What is important in the present context is that Murdoch seems to accept Kripke's 'community view of language' as the right way to understand Wittgenstein's notion of criteria of meaningful language use, and she also uses Kripke's understanding of language community as a guide to understand Wittgenstein's notion of lifeform. Before the section on Kripke, she notes that 'Wittgenstein's *Lebensformen* are introduced as fundamental (logical?) judges of the possibility of meaning' (*MGM*, 276), and she asks, 'Is the substratum, what is ultimate, a reliance upon "general agreement" in a community as an arbiter of sense?' (*MGM*, 280–281). Later, she picks up on this idea and notes that Wittgenstein 'returns to the idea of *Lebensformen* as something absolutely fundamental

... A "community" here suggest an enclosure, a dominant group of judges, or a thoroughly reliable general will' (*MGM*, 285). This interpretation of lifeform as the 'arbiter of sense' and 'dominant group of judges' provokes Murdoch, morally and philosophically. What if the community is despotic, she asks, what if the statistical dissenters, the nonconformists, are the truly free, artistic renewers of language? Does this view of lifeform allow for the role and the value of the individual? By reading Kripke, Murdoch comes to believe that Wittgenstein is engaged in a fight against scepticism that makes him jeopardise the importance of the individual and of truth. As she writes, 'how does all this leave us, the individuals, where does it leave our thought-stream, our private reflections, where does it leave *truth*, if our foundations are so shaky and our judgements so shadowy?' (*MGM*, 272).

My point is that Murdoch is reacting, not to the writings of the *Investigations*, but to the 'great clarity' of the writings of Kripke. Many interpreters have objected against the idea that Kripke's community view represents an adequate reading or even an adequate reconstruction of the central parts of the *Investigations*, and that there is something wrong with this reading is indicated by the fact that the presentation of the apparent sceptical conclusion of §201 is immediately followed by a sentence beginning, 'That there is a misunderstanding here ...'[3] Wittgenstein is *not* addressing a real sceptical challenge, rather, he is showing how scepticism may arise from certain philosophically mistaken ways to approach rule-following and language. In §201, he is diagnosing a specific type of philosophical mistake, namely that of seeing basic rule-following as dependent on interpretations, and what he goes on to do, is to offer an alternative picture according to which rule-following and criteria for meaningful language use is considered dependent on, but *not reducible to* 'agreement ... in judgments', 'the common behaviour of mankind' (Wittgenstein 2009, §242, §206).

For the later Wittgenstein, any adequate understanding of language must take into account an understanding of the common human lifeform consisting of basic human ways of acting, what he sometimes calls 'the natural history' of human beings, the fact that 'Commanding, questioning, storytelling, chatting are as much a part of our natural history as walking, eating, drinking, playing' (Wittgenstein 2009, §25). Wittgenstein certainly does not reduce criteria for correct language use to the verdict of 'a dominant group of judges' within a community; he rather holds that the criteria for correct language use will have to be settled in each particular instance of use. In fact, the notion of lifeform *is not meant to do any positive work* in explaining correct language use; as an object of comparison (cf. Wittgenstein 2009, §130), this notion is meant to do work in relation to particular philosophical problems, reminding us of certain basic facts about humans (for example that they act and react alike in many ways) that can help us dissolve certain tempting confusions such as the sceptical confusion that we need 'a something', for example a community of judges, to secure the meaningfulness of language. The role of Wittgenstein's notion of lifeform is in fact very different from the role of the linguistic community in Kripke's interpretations of rule-following, and it is also very different from the understanding of '*Lebensformen*' criticised by Murdoch, for example in her ongoing critique that Wittgenstein's notions of lifeform and language game are not sufficiently well-defined and explained to serve as a foundation of language. What Murdoch is missing is that Wittgenstein does not in any way intend these notions to serve as a foundation of language or meaning, and this shows that the target of Murdoch's worries about the dominance of the community and the elimination of the importance of the individual is fuelled by Kripke's writings rather than by Wittgenstein's.

'THE WILDEST STRANGEST MOST INDIVIDUALISTIC REGIONS OF HUMAN EXISTENCE'

What I have argued above is that Murdoch probably would have been in a much better position to understand Wittgenstein's treatment of the inner, if she had not turned to Kripke as a guide to the *Investigations*. In this last section, I do, however, also argue that there is another reason why Murdoch comes to see herself in opposition to Wittgenstein's work, a reason that is internal to her own thought and connected to the difference between her philosophical interests and the interests of Wittgenstein. One of the aspects of language that Wittgenstein wants to bring to the fore in the *Investigations* is the shared background of action, activity and practice that makes up the human lifeform. In contrast, Murdoch's primary interest in *MGM* is to bring out how a person's inner life is shaped by a unique web of values, attitudes and emotional responses that influences and shapes not just that person's actions and judgements, but also her experience of reality. Murdoch is interested in the aspects of experience which are individual and personal, but which at the same time also have a potential to develop our moral attention.

In the middle of Chapter 9, Murdoch states this aim by saying that experience 'directs us towards the messiness of ordinary life and its mysteries', and she continues, 'At the borderline of thought and language we ... have to *wait* and attempt to formulate for ourselves and convey to others our *experience* of what is initially beyond and hidden. We look out into the abyss, into the mystery, intuiting what is not ourselves' (*MGM*, 283). Wittgenstein's interest in language's embeddedness in a background of shared human interests and ways of acting makes him attentive to some of our simplest and most common language-games, while Murdoch's interest in what appears at the border of individual experience makes her explore the possibilities of truly individuated experience and expression, the places where 'the "goings-on" of language recede from "clear cases" into the wildest strangest most individualistic regions of human existence' (*MGM*, 285–286).

The individualistic aspects of experience and language are important to Murdoch because of her two-sided, but also fundamentally individualistic, view of moral vision and development. From Simone Weil, Murdoch gets the idea that the possibility of moral change is intimately connected to the quality of our attention towards the reality of what surrounds us (cf. *MGM*, 52). This form of attention depends on an effort to truly to attend to 'what is there' and to hold on to a fundamental (but in philosophy all too often neglected) truth about moral life, namely that 'in order to be able to see what ought to be done, one should see the faces of strangers as well as friends' (*MGM*, 218). Still, Murdoch is not saying that attention grants us something like a direct access to our moral reality, because, according to her, there is no form of seeing that is not shaped by imagination; when we see a situation, we have already 'imagined it in a certain way' (*MGM*, 314). For Murdoch, there is a 'moral sense of "see" which implies that clear vision is a result of moral imagination and moral effort' (Murdoch 1992, 36), and in this way she thinks that 'Perception itself is a mode of evaluation' (*MGM*, 315). What we see will on the one hand often be influenced by our egoism and self-serving fantasy, which means that we must work to minimise the distorting influence of the self, to cast away our egoistic drives and fantasies and engage in what Murdoch calls 'unselfing'. However, if we succeed in this process of unselfing, attention on the other hand also depends on our experiences, concepts and abilities to imaginatively and creatively explore and expand our understanding of the world in an effort to come closer to an adequate understanding of what is really there (cf. *MGM*, 320–323). In this way, the act of attending is a creative task that carries a great potential of moral transformation.

A consequence of Murdoch's view of attention is that experience and the inner are never neutral, they are always to some extent morally coloured. 'Our ordinary consciousness is a deep continuous working of values, a *continuous present and presence* of perceptions, intuitions, images, feeling, desires, aversions, attachments. It is a matter of what we "see things as", what we let, or make, ourselves think about' (*MGM*, 215). On this view of experience as the result of a creative and moral attention to the world, experience is essentially individuated and personal, but it is also, at least if we manage to do the work of unselfing, a source of insight into the good.

Murdoch thus works to unfold a view of individual experience that for her connects to Plato's idea about the reality of goodness, the idea that, despite all our failings and frailties, 'We know about good and evil' (*MGM*, 15). Experience may move or unsettle us, for example through the feelings of happiness in face of goodness or of acute unease in the face of wrongdoing. However, one consequence of this view is that we can never be completely sure that others see the reality in the same way as we do, that they have the same experience of moral importance. As Cora Diamond remarks, Murdoch's view is here in opposition to a (standard) philosophical view of reasons as public because Murdoch thinks that there can be 'great difficulty in one person's communicating reasons to someone else; reasons for her are not essentially public' (Diamond 2010, 67). From the idea that personally shaped and morally coloured experience of the world may be a possible source of insight into the good follows the possibility that such insight may not be readily expressible in public terms.

Again and again, Murdoch returns to the problems of finding the right expression for new moral insights, and she talks about these as mysteries, as 'muddled and complex', as something we see but 'cannot say' (*MGM*, 280, 283). The question is how we best describe these problems? Do they arise because moral insights are *essentially* inner and private, in principle inaccessible for others? Or do they arise because we have not yet fully developed the concepts that can give such insights a fully determinate form, because the attainment of moral insight and the development of concepts are two sides of the same coin?

Actually, Murdoch seems to take both views. Firstly, in her dealings with Wittgenstein, she seems to be occupied with securing a private inner sphere, as when she writes that 'Our *whole* moral-aesthetic intellectual creativity abounds in private insoluble difficulties, mysterious half-understood mental configurations' (*MGM*, 280; italics mine). It is hard to know what to make of this idea, how to ascribe such essentially private and half-understood insights a role in our lives. Maybe this is what Murdoch ought to have taken with her from her engagement the example of sensation S, that to picture something as *essentially* private is not to secure it from the corrupting influences of the community, but to picture it in a way where it cannot play a role in our lives, where it really is not anything at all. Murdoch seems to be caught in a picture of the inner and outer as two isolated realms, because of a worry that if we give up this picture the inner will be overflown and obliviated by the outer, and she is here in conflict with Wittgenstein's point that this picture is unsustainable as a general understanding of the inner and the other.

Murdoch does, however, not always use the picture of two realms in order to show the importance of the inner, because she also describes the role of personal experience as that of de-stabilising our moral concepts and forcing us to engage in the development of new ones. In fact, much of Murdoch's work centres around the problem of developing concepts which can adequately express our moral difficulties, and which may help us reconcile our personal values with what is real and establish a moral world in which we actually want to live. Here, language 'performs its *essential* task, through its ability to be truthful; and its truthfulness is a function of the struggle of individuals creatively to adjust language to contingent conditions outside it' (*MGM*, 216). For Murdoch, in Diamond's words, 'moral concepts in a sense "set up" a world: they show what sorts of thing there are, what it means to recognize them, what it is to live in a world with such things' (Diamond 2010, 62). On this view, the problems with expressing our personally shaped moral insights arise because we have to work with concepts that are too narrow, poor or misdirected to allow us to fully see and express our moral experiences, or because we are in a process of developing concepts that will allow us to do so. That is, the reason why the individual or personal aspects of inner life are often difficult to express is because they concern moral insights that are still in the making, still finding their form in language.[4]

Murdoch's understanding of language as a site of moral change does not invite the temptation of seeing the inner as isolated from the outer. Instead, it suggests a model where inner and outer are two different aspects of moral life, where our moral lives are considered as a unity of a personal inner *entangled with* a public outer, and where language is the place for our continuous development of or setting up of our moral world. This model is not in any way in conflict with the writings of the *Investigations*; in fact, if Murdoch had seen the full potential of Wittgenstein's later work, she could have come to consider him an ally in the attempt to show how we in language can work to develop adequate moral concepts in a dynamic interplay between our personal moral insights and the reality of 'what is there'.

NOTES

1. See e.g. *MGM*, 30–43. For a different understanding of ethics in the *Tractatus*, see Christensen (2011).
2. In the article, McDowell shows how Wright reads Wittgenstein in a way that parallels Kripke's reading.
3. For influential criticisms of Kripke's community view as a reading of Wittgenstein, besides that of McDowell, see Baker and Hacker (1984) and Goldfarb (2014).
4. See also Murdoch (1956).

REFERENCES

Baker, G.P., and P.M.S. Hacker. 1984. Critical study: On misunderstanding Wittgenstein: Kripke's private language argument. *Synthese* 58 (3): 407–450.

Christensen, A.-M.S. 2011. Wittgenstein and ethics. In *Oxford handbook of Wittgenstein*, ed. Oskari Kuusela and Marie McGinn, 776–817. Oxford: Oxford University Press.

Diamond, C. 2010. Murdoch the explorer. *Philosophical Topics* 38 (1): 51–85.

Dooley, G., and G. Nerlich (eds.). 2014. *Never mind about the bourgeoisie: The correspondence between Iris Murdoch and Brian Medlin 1976–1995*. Cambridge: Cambridge Scholars Publishing.

Goldfarb, W. 2014. Kripke on Wittgenstein on rules. In *Rule-following and meaning*, ed. Alexander Miller and Crispin Wright, 92–107. London: Routledge.

Kripke, S. 1982. *Wittgenstein on rules and private language*. Oxford: Basil Blackwell.

McDowell, J. 1998. Wittgenstein on following a rule. In *Mind, value, and reality*, 221–262, Cambridge, MA: Harvard University Press.

Murdoch, I. 1956. Vision and choice in morality. *Proceedings of the Aristotelian Society* 30: 32–58.

Murdoch, I. 1992. *Metaphysics as a guide to morals*. (Abbreviated *MGM*.) London: Chatto and Windus.

Murdoch, I. 2001. *The sovereignty of good*. London: Routledge.

Wittgenstein, Ludwig. 1961. *Tractatus logico-philosophicus*, trans. D.F. Pears and B.F. McGuinness. London: Routledge.

Wittgenstein, Ludwig. 2009. *Philosophical investigations/Philosophische Untersuchungen*, 4th ed., ed. P.M.S. Hacker and Joachim Schulte. Chichester: Wiley-Blackwell.

'We Are Fantasising Imaginative Animals' (*MGM* Chapter 11)

Hannah Marije Altorf

READING *METAPHYSICS AS A GUIDE TO MORALS*

I first read *Metaphysics as a Guide to Morals* (henceforth *MGM*) twenty years ago. I had just finished my *doctoraal* (more or less the equivalent of an MA or an MPhil) at the University of Nijmegen and had been given the title *doctorandus*, 'he who has to become a doctor'. I was looking for a way to do exactly that and *MGM* fascinated me, even though, or perhaps because, I understood very little of what I was reading.

MGM starts *in medias res*, in the midst of things. The work is in this respect not all that different from Murdoch's novels, which often start in the middle of conversations or death bed confessions.[1] In her philosophical work, this approach has brought discerning thoughts, as well as puzzlement. Take for instance the beginning of 'On "God" and "Good"', one of the three essays in *The Sovereignty of Good* (1970): 'To do philosophy is to explore one's own temperament, and yet at the same time to attempt to discover the truth' (Murdoch 1997, 337). This is an inspiring, but not a common understanding of philosophy. Yet, Murdoch never makes clear why this is so or why it needs stating

H. M. Altorf (✉)
St. Mary's University, London, UK

© The Author(s) 2019
N. Hämäläinen and G. Dooley (eds.),
Reading Iris Murdoch's Metaphysics as a Guide to Morals,
https://doi.org/10.1007/978-3-030-18967-9_11

at the beginning of the essay, though she returns to the importance of temperament briefly.[2] To start a work in such a way suggests both intimacy and urgency. It is as if we as readers enter an ongoing conversation, not unlike Plato's *Symposium*, just at the moment when Murdoch starts speaking. Yet, unlike in *The Symposium*, there is a sense of urgency to the conversation. There is no time to lose.

MGM lacks many of the framing elements found in other works of philosophy. There is no acknowledgement that this text is based on Murdoch's 1982 Gifford Lectures. There is no preface with thanks to friends and colleagues for their contributions or to a spouse for putting up with long periods of withdrawal to one's study. No introduction places the book in the context of recent discussions and scholarship. Instead, the contents page, the dedication to Elizabeth Anscombe and an epigraph in French by Paul Valéry (about which more later) are immediately followed by Chapter 1: 'Concepts of Unity. Art', of which the first sentence reads: 'The idea of a self-contained unity or limited whole is a fundamental instinctive concept' (*MGM*, 1).

'The idea of a self-contained unity or limited whole is a fundamental instinctive concept.' I have read this sentence many times and it still baffles me. Why start thus? Why start with unity, or more precisely with 'the idea of a self-contained unity or limited whole' (and, by the way, are these the same)? What is 'a fundamental instinctive concept' and can an idea be a concept? The consequent sentences provide some insight. Murdoch writes: 'We see parts of things, we intuit whole things. We seem to know a great deal on the basis of very little' (*MGM*, 1). This makes more sense. I only see the front of the faces of the people opposite me in the British Library, but I assume there is a back to them and even a complete human being, sitting on a chair. When I look down at my laptop and look up again, I assume that the faces I saw before are the same as those I see now and that they have not been exchanged for seemingly identical, but in reality different faces. I see parts of things, I intuit whole things. I seem to know a great deal on the basis of very little. However, it is still not clear to me why Murdoch starts with this idea and whether it is indeed a fundamental instinctive concept or, even, what a fundamental instinctive concept is.

I don't remember why I kept reading twenty years ago. Perhaps I was then much better at knowing a great deal on the basis of very little. I may have been inspired, or warned, by the epigraph, the quote from Valéry: '*Une difficulté est une lumière. Une difficulté insurmontable est un soleil.*' The quote returns halfway through the book, where Murdoch writes, though without mentioning Valéry: '(An insuperable difficulty may or may not be the sun, but it gives some light.)' (*MGM*, 251).[3] I suspect that twenty years ago, I intuited what I perceive more clearly now: *MGM* is the work of an exceptionally erudite and original philosopher. As readers we witness her thinking. We are aware of a close engagement with thinkers and arguments, even when we are also likely to miss several references, because they are without acknowledgement and not part of our knowledge or vocabulary. Murdoch assumes intimate knowledge of texts and ideas and she does not always make explicit what is quotation, what her own thought and what the thought of someone else.

All the same, there have been times when I lost heart, reading the same sentences over and over again and not being able to make much sense of them. I once discussed with my students what an editor could have done. (Nothing meaningful, we suspected, without changing the text beyond recognition.) Readers have experienced the book as 'a bewilderingly dense and impenetrable confluence of several seemingly distinct ways of addressing its central concerns', as Stephen Mulhall writes. 'To put it more bluntly: the trouble with *Metaphysics as a Guide to Morals* is that in general its sentences, its individual chapters and its overall structure appear to be extremely disorganized' (Mulhall 1997, 219–220).

These comments are not without justification. Yet, I do not hold, as Mulhall does, that 'these formal aspects ... are ... a carefully calculated achievement' (Mulhall 1997, 220). Instead, I understand *MGM* as a radical attempt to retain and rethink ideas and concepts about what it is to be human. As in attempts of a similar radical nature, structure and clarity have occasionally yielded to sheer audacity and novelty of thinking. *MGM* is not the first book in the history of philosophy that has baffled its contemporaries.[4] What is more, Murdoch has always been keenly aware of ideas that challenge or counter her line of argument. She knows them intimately and is almost too eager to acknowledge these, at times without spelling them out. *MGM* thus reads like a dialogue, in which speakers eagerly interrupt each other.[5] Lastly, Murdoch does not write for purely academic purposes, as is for instance evident at the end of 'On "God" and "Good"', where she writes: 'For both the collective and the individual salvation of the human race, art is doubtless more important than philosophy, and literature most important of all' (Murdoch 1997, 362). If this sounds over the top, that is because it is deliberately so.

Murdoch wants to save our souls—even those souls who feel queasy about being called 'souls' and, I suspect, Murdoch would be one of them. Yet, ultimately, salvation trumps queasiness.

Reading *MGM* can be a struggle at times. Though I am not convinced this is on purpose, I don't think Murdoch would have wanted it otherwise. Struggle is an essential part of her moral philosophy and more than once she confesses to struggling herself.[6] Any introduction to *MGM* should perhaps not promise any more than this, in language that is no more religious than that used in the work: one will struggle and may be saved. Such struggling also characterises imagination. As will become clear, it can be a struggle to use one's imagination well. What is more, Murdoch struggles with the notion throughout the chapter. She fears it is empty, even when she judges it essential (*MGM*, 322).

This does not mean, of course, that readers are without resources (as Murdoch would probably affirm, see *MGM*, 329, 335). It helps to acknowledge that one is witnessing a thinker struggling to address urgent problems. It helps also to read Murdoch's earlier work, especially *The Sovereignty of Good*, as a *prolegomena* to *MGM*. It helps not to expect framing. Having reread most of *MGM* over the last year or so, I find myself returning to one of the earliest introductions to the work. In *Iris Murdoch and the Search for Human Goodness* Maria Antonaccio and William Schweiker distinguish two guiding images: that of moral pilgrimage and the hall of reflection. Murdoch understands life as a journey or moral pilgrimage, in some ways similar to Plato's allegory of the Cave. Her writing can be a guide on this journey, but not in any straightforward sense. The other image, that of the hall of reflection, is taken from the work itself. *MGM* can indeed be compared to 'a huge hall of reflection full of light and space and fresh air, in which ideas and intuitions can be unsystematically nurtured' (Antonaccio and Schweiker 1996, xv).[7]

To read *MGM* is then to take part in a conversation, 'in which ideas and intuitions can be unsystematically nurtured'. We are unlikely to surmount all difficulties. Perhaps we should not even try to, as we experience that some light may come from insurmountable difficulties. With these thoughts in mind I now turn to the chapter. What follows is intended as a guide to reading and it will be helpful to have the book at hand. I start with a general commentary on the text and then discuss the chapter in three sections: one on Kant, one on Plato and the last on 'soul-talk'.

'IMAGINING IS *DOING*, IT IS A SORT OF PERSONAL EXPLORING'[8]

Murdoch starts the chapter on imagination again *in medias res*. She writes: 'Kant ... establishes imagination as a mediator between sense perception and concepts, something between sense and thought.' Reflections on Kant's notion of imagination take up the first nine pages of the chapter (*MGM*, 308–316). The significance of Kant for Murdoch's understanding of imagination is confirmed by his reappearance throughout the remainder of the chapter, as he appears throughout *MGM*.[9]

The chapter falls roughly into two parts, which are separated by an asterisk on page 325. The first part consists of two larger sections discussing Kant and Plato. The second part consists of several sections, which are less easily characterised, because a range of different topics is discussed. My focus will be on the first half of the chapter and I shall repeat some of the findings from an earlier discussion of this chapter.[10]

The significance of the earlier part is twofold. It confirms the importance of imagination for Murdoch's thinking and it does so by showing how her notion of imagination, as well as the distinction between imagination and fantasy, are firmly grounded in her reading of philosophy, especially Kant and Plato. The distinction between imagination and fantasy is not new, but in her earlier writing it appears without much philosophical context. There, it is explained by referring to art and literature rather than philosophy.[11] The sections on Kant and Plato in Chapter 11 of *MGM* show Murdoch, in contrast, as a close and creative reader of philosophical classics. The distinction between imagination and fantasy is experienced when contemplating art and has been developed through close reading of major thinkers from the history of philosophy.

In addition to the rough structural device that Murdoch introduces by separating sections, I would like to suggest two more. The first is perhaps best characterised as 'refrain'. Throughout *MGM* Murdoch keeps returning to phrases and images. In Chapter 11 one finds, for instance, what is at least the third appearance of the enlightened man in Zen Buddhism who 'begins by thinking that rivers are merely rivers and mountains are merely mountains, proceeds to the view that rivers are not rivers and mountains are not mountains, and later achieves the deep understandings that rivers are really rivers and mountains are really mountains' (*MGM*, 244; see also 325, 189). Another prominent refrain, specifically in Chapter 11, is 'Perception itself is a mode of evaluation' (*MGM*, 315, 328, 329, 334; see also 25–26.) The repetition of the latter in particular signifies its importance in understanding Murdoch's notion of imagination. I shall return to this later.

The other structural device is to read the different parts of this chapter as it were 'backwards'. Murdoch's reflections at the end of the different sections help understand what precedes. In Chapter 11 I perceived four such instances: near the end of the first part of the chapter (*MGM*, 323), at the end of the discussion of Plato (*MGM*, 321), at the end of the discussion of Kant (*MGM*, 316) and at the end of the chapter (*MGM*, 346). The latter two are more clearly defined than the first two.

'KANT WAS MARVELLOUSLY NEAR THE MARK'[12]

I start the discussion of Kant at the end of the first part, where Murdoch confirms the importance of imagination and fantasy, writing: 'We are fantasising imaginative animals' (*MGM*, 323). While this statement is likely to jump out more to someone who is familiar with Murdoch's earlier work and with the scholarship, it also draws attention to itself by the way it is formulated.[13] It is, after all, a direct play on the classical understanding of human beings as 'rational animals'. Moreover, it immediately follows a set of challenging questions: 'What do you do with your mind when you are in prison? Or bereaved or suffering irremediable injustice, or crippled by awful guilt? What you are able to do with it then will depend very much on what you were doing with it before' (*MGM*, 323).

These questions reinforce that for Murdoch the notions of imagination and fantasy are not so much isolated objects of study as they are as part of her moral philosophy and its emphasis on the inner life. To see how Murdoch came to write 'we are fantasising imaginative animals', I turn two pages back. Here, Murdoch introduces the notions of imagination and fantasy:

> To mark the distances involved we need for purposes of discussion, two words for two concepts: a distinction between egoistic *fantasy* and liberated truth-seeking creative *imagination*. Can there not be high evil fantasising forms of creative imaginative activity? A search for candidates will, I think, tend to reinforce at least the usefulness of a distinction between 'fantasy' as mechanical, egoistic, untruthful, and 'imagination' as truthful and free. (*MGM*, 321, italics hers)

This quotation clearly displays Murdoch's dialogical writing style. She immediately questions the distinction she introduces. ('Can there not be high evil fantasising forms of creative imaginative activity?') She also makes clear that the distinction between imagination and fantasy is made 'for purposes of discussion'. It is 'useful'.[14] It is less likely to be found in reality as such or even in art. Thus, even Shakespeare, who for Murdoch is the standard of great art, merges imagination and fantasy.[15] The distinction between imagination and fantasy is, moreover, moral. Imagination is truthful, free. Fantasy is untruthful, egoistic. 'Imagination suggests the searching, joining, light-seeking, semi-figurative nature of the mind's work, which prepares and forms the consciousness for action' (*MGM*, 323).

As I argued before, the distinction between imagination and fantasy is not new. What is new is that it appears in conversations with Kant and Plato.[16] *MGM* shows the importance of these two thinkers for Murdoch's understanding of imagination. Kant allows Murdoch to argue that imagination permeates all our activities, whereas Plato offers a distinction between better and worse imagination, or between imagination and fantasy. Murdoch's argument is best reconstructed by now turning to the end of the section on Kant. Here Murdoch writes:

> How flexible can a deep concept be? is a founding question of philosophy. Kant, in his precision, is careful not to demand too much of the concept of imagination. He distinguishes the empirical imagination, which spontaneously yet 'mechanically' prepares a sensuous manifold for subjection to the synthetic *a priori* and empirical concepts of the understanding, but which is not independently creative or aesthetically sensible, from the aesthetic imagination which is spontaneous and free and able to create a 'second nature'. But are 'fine art' and 'genius' as described by Kant really such a small corner of human faculty and experience? The concept of genius itself emerges from an appreciation of the deep and omnipresent operation of imagination in human life. (*MGM*, 316)

The quotation displays Murdoch's approach in reading Kant. What she writes is not an exposition of his thought, but critical and creative engagement. She notices Kant's careful balancing of the flexibility of a concept against precision, but also makes clear that it is not hers.[17] The quotation also introduces three important stages in Murdoch's discussion of Kant: the empirical imagination, the aesthetic imagination and the notion of genius. I shall briefly discuss each here.[18]

In the discussion of the empirical imagination, it becomes obvious that this form of imagination already appeared at the beginning of *MGM*, though it was not named there as such. It is the empirical imagination, which allows us to 'know a great deal on the basis of very little' (*MGM*, 1). We imagine a whole human being when we only perceive a face and we imagine them to exist over time, even when we don't perceive them continuously.

In Chapter 11 the empirical imagination is described as 'a mediator between sense perception and concepts, something between sense and thought.' It 'spontaneously yet "mechanically" prepares a sensuous manifold for subjection to ... concepts of the understanding' (*MGM*, 308, 316). The sensuous manifold, i.e. what is supplied by the senses, is brought into an image, to which then concepts can be applied. Thus, the empirical imagination is essential in the process that allows me to perceive the chair on which I am sitting as such and as distinguished from the desk. Without imagination we cannot perceive. This aspect of the empirical imagination Murdoch adopts eagerly. She is less interested in other aspects of the Kantian notion, though my reading of the first lines of *MGM* above suggests that she is aware of these. Her distance from Kant is perhaps most obvious when when she writes: 'One might almost say that "imagination" is the *name* of the transcendental problem, or is used as a convenient blanket to cover it up. Kant *had* to invent the idea' (*MGM*, 310).[19]

In the discussion that follows the differences between Kant and Murdoch become more pronounced, as Murdoch will try to read the aesthetic imagination and the notion of genius back into the empirical imagination.[20] Their differences were already suggested by the quotation marks around 'mechanical', even when Murdoch agrees with Kant that imagination is central to perception. Her reading is also revealed by her use of the image of 'barrier', which she intends to lower to a 'threshold' or transform into 'lungs' (*MGM*, 309, 315). My reading focuses on the notion of genius, as the quotation at the end of the section indicates that that is where Murdoch's interest lies.[21] 'Genius *invents* its own "rules" or modes ... Kant's "genius" is a spontaneous faculty which its owner cannot explain, and whose products offer no general rules for imitators ... The imagination produces something unique' (*MGM*, 313). Is it possible to read this kind of creative imagination back into the empirical imagination? Are we in perception creating and recreating as if without rules? Should we be? Murdoch seems to suggest as much when she writes,

'This idea can go very far, farther perhaps than its author intended' (*MGM*, 314). At this point, the refrain 'Perception itself is a mode of evaluation' appears for the first time in this chapter (*MGM*, 315). Reading this 'superior' form of imagination into the empirical imagination, which Kant so carefully tried to keep separate, Murdoch suggests that we are or should be geniuses even when only looking at the world. Moreover, for her this is nothing unusual: 'We have to "talk" and our talk will be largely "imaginative" (we are all artists)' (*MGM*, 315).

Murdoch then returns to the image of a barrier:

> The point is, to put it picturesquely, that the 'transcendental barrier' is a huge wide various band (it resembles a transformer such as the lungs in being rather like a sponge) largely penetrable by the creative activity of individuals (though of course we are culturally marked 'children of our time' etc.), and this creativity is the place where the concept of imagination must be placed and defined. (*MGM*, 315)[22]

The barrier has now become a 'huge wide various band', resembling 'a transformer such as the lungs in being rather like a sponge'. May not the empirical imagination be also 'independently creative or aesthetically sensible'? We are all artists, even when we 'tell our day', 'rearrange [our] possessions' or are 'looking out of the window' (*MGM*, 37, 334, 329). With this thought Murdoch turns to Plato.

'PLATO IS A GREAT ARTIST ATTACKING WHAT HE SEES AS BAD AND DANGEROUS IN ART'[23]

Whereas Murdoch's reading of Kant allows her to argue that creative imagination pervades all perception, Plato lets her distinguish between lower and higher forms of imagination. Murdoch compares their notion of imagination as follows:

> So it appears that Plato, like Kant, offers two views of the imagination. For Plato the lower level, which for Kant is necessary automatic synthesis, is seen in human terms as the production of base illusions, or perhaps simply of the ordinary unimaginative egoistic screen of our conceptualising. Plato, teaching by images and myths, also acknowledges high imagination as creative stirring spirit, attempting to express and embody what is perfectly good, but extremely remote... (*MGM*, 320)

Plato introduces hierarchy. There are lower and higher forms of imagination.[24] The lowest form Murdoch compares to Kant's 'necessary automatic synthesis', which is 'seen in human terms', which the text suggests to mean a moral light. It is 'base' and 'egoistic'. It is best compared to 'the lowest condition in the Cave ... [Plato] connects egoistic fantasy and lack of moral sense with inability to reflect. Mere uninspired reproductive art ... would then be at the bottom of the scale ... One might take the *Republic* (597) passage about the painter as indicating art which was bad because thoughtless' (*MGM*, 317). Fantasy is characterised by lack: '*lack* of moral sense ... *in*ability ... *un*inspired ... thoughtless'.[25] The highest form of imagination, in contrast, is active: 'High imagination is passionately creative' (*MGM*, 319). This creative imagination is directed towards the reality of others and ultimately to the Good.

These different understandings of imagination tumble somewhat through one another in this section. It is not as easy to discern a line of argument here as it was in the section on Kant. Murdoch starts with a discussion of the Romantics. As I have argued elsewhere, this is a later addition to the text and it does not seem to have changed what follows (*MGM*, 316–317; Altorf 2008, 81–82). Murdoch next explores the distinction between fantasy and imagination. What complicates the writing is Murdoch's ultimate dissatisfaction with imagery and imagination— even with good or high imagination. Her ideal of moral pilgrimage is a constant destruction of imagery until there is none left:

> Moral improvement, as we learn from the *Republic*, involves a progressive destruction of false images. Image-making or image-apprehending is always an imperfect activity ... Images should not be resting-places, but pointers toward higher truth ... the highest activities of the mind ... are imageless. (*MGM*, 317–318)[26]

It seems at times as if Murdoch is more interested in this latter, imageless stage than in any form of imagination. This preference detracts from both the distinction between imagination and fantasy and the understanding of us as 'fantasising imaginative animals' (*MGM*, 323). Have we discussed the useful distinction between imagination and fantasy, its grounding in Murdoch's reading of Kant and Plato, only to have it taken away from us as a 'ladder to be thrown away'? (*MGM*, 323). It is at this stage that I turn to the second part of Chapter 11.

'SOUL-TALK'

I start again at the end of the section. Murdoch writes:

> The inner needs the outer and the outer needs the inner. In these pictures I have tried to 'exhibit' the inner; and resist tendencies which give value and effective function only to the outer (thought of as 'moral acts' or linguistic activity), or regard the 'inner life' as fantasy and dream, lacking identity and definition, even as a fake illusionary concept. (*MGM*, 348)

Murdoch sums up the chapter as an attempt to emphasise the inner against those forms of moral philosophy which merely regard the outer. That this preference is not without difficulty becomes clear in the use of quotation marks around 'inner life'. As in much of her earlier writing Murdoch is here taking issue with dominant forms of moral philosophy ('behaviourist ... existentialist ... structuralist ... utilitarian' (*MGM*, 348)), which are not interested in the inner and even deny its existence. As she writes of utilitarianism: 'Such nullification of the inner may also have a home in utilitarian moral thinking, where it receives understandable lay support from those who hold that 'soul-talk' is a luxury in a world where action to relieve suffering is our main duty' (*MGM*, 348).[27]

The term 'soul-talk' directs us to a central concern in Murdoch's reflections on imagination. What is more, Murdoch's response to this dismissal of the inner can be understood as itself an exhibition of 'soul-talk'. Consider how she starts this section: 'So we may talk and think, constantly examining and altering our sense of the order and interdependence of our values' (*MGM*, 326; see also 325). The second half of Chapter 11 is conversationalist and as a genuine conversation it is constantly altering direction. We are reminded of the 'huge hall of reflection' and indeed this image returns near the end:

> What is needful is inner space, in which other things can lodge and move and be considered; we withdraw ourselves and let other things be. Any artist or thinker will appreciate this picture of inner space ... a private and personal space-time. We might think here of spatio-temporal rhythm; a good person might be recognised by this rhythm. An obsessed egoist, almost everyone sometimes, destroys the space and air about him and is uncomfortable to be with. We have a sense of the 'space' of others. An unselfish person enlarges the space and the world. (*MGM*, 347)

The second part of Chapter 11 can thus be understood as a space-enlarging exercise, in which we contemplate 'whether, on the whole, Mary or Martha led a better life' or whether we 'should also feel socially responsible about what in our society people always or never see ... Urban poverty can impose relentlessly ugly surroundings' (*MGM*, 332, 329). We are urged to contemplate 'Christ upon the cross' or at 'birth, complete with shepherds, kings, angels, the ox and the ass', as well as the eucharist and St Paul (*MGM*, 328, 335, 342, 346). We are admonished to 'teach meditation in schools' and we are told the Tibetan story of the mother who asks her son to bring back a religious relic from the city. The son brings back a dog's tooth from the road, which, when venerated, 'begins miraculously to glow with light' (*MGM*, 337–338).

The word 'soul-talk' reinforces the importance of religion in this second part of Chapter 11. Indeed, many of the images Murdoch offers are religious, in particular Christian and sometimes Buddhist.[28] Murdoch 'assumes that religion is not only a particular dogma or mode of faith and worship, but can exist, and indeed exists, undogmatically as for instance in Buddhism, and potentially everywhere, forming a deep part of morality' (*MGM*, 336). Twice she refers to a quotation from the letter to the Philippians: 'When St Paul tells us to think about whatsoever things are honest, just, pure, lovely and of good report, he believes rightly that we know how to perform this feat of imagination' (*MGM*, 328).[29] She continues: 'How do we know how to do it? Oddly enough we do. (We can distinguish too between doing it in a vague feeble way and attempting to do it better.)' (*MGM*, 328–329). In her continued reflections there is another appearance of one of the refrains: 'With St Paul's admonition in mind, I think that what we literally see is important. Perception is both evaluation and inspiration, even at the level of "just seeing"' (*MGM*, 329).

In comparison to her often 'rather depressing' view of human beings,[30] Murdoch is here surprisingly confident about our ability to use our imagination 'to think about whatsoever things are honest, just, pure, lovely and of good report'. Moreover, she is convinced that we all have 'a collection of such things' (*MGM*, 335). At the same time, she is concerned about the possibility that we may lose this ability and the images. For her, this possibility is closely linked to the disappearance of religion, of religious experience and of our ability to recognise religious experiences as such. She expresses this concern almost as an introduction to this chapter (*MGM*, 307; see also 341). Thus, where the first part of this chapter argues that we are fantasising imaginative animals, the discussion of images in the second part aims to create or retain images which can both 'dislodge … rat-like fantasies or old stale thoughts', and to serve as 'moral illuminations or pictures which remain vividly in the memory, playing a protective or guiding role … refuges, lights, visions, deep sources, pure sources, protections, stronghold, footholds, icons, starting-points, sacraments, pearls of great price' (*MGM*, 332–333, 335).

This chapter thus ends on a hopeful note. We have the ability to distinguish between good and bad imagination and we have the images to protect and guide us. Yet, Murdoch chooses her images mostly from classical art or Christianity and it is debatable whether we still worry about Martha and Mary or even know who they are. As Murdoch acknowledges, 'of course we are culturally marked "children of our time"' (*MGM*, 315). Even if we do not share the intimacy that Murdoch has with the thinkers and artists she quotes and mentions, the urgency of her appeal remains. We are imaginative fantasising animals. As imagination and fantasy pervade our thoughts and our conversations, we need to create and retain good images. Perhaps this is the unsurmountable difficulty that she reminds us of by quoting Valéry.

NOTES

1. Murdoch's twentieth novel, *Nuns and Soldiers* (1980), starts with the exclamation 'Wittgenstein –', which turns out to be a deathbed confession of sorts.
2. 'It is frequently difficult in philosophy to tell whether one is saying something reasonably public and objective, or whether one is merely erecting a barrier, special to one's own temperament, against one's own personal fears' (Murdoch 1997, 359).
3. See also *MGM*, 419: 'Valéry speaks of the sunlight which rewards him who steadily contemplates the insuperable difficulty.'
4. A comparison with Kant's *Critique of Pure Reason* suggests itself.
5. See Altorf (2008, 26, 62, 91–92, 116).
6. See here a comment in brackets in 'The Idea of Perfection': '(There is curiously little place in the other picture for the idea of *struggle*.)' (Murdoch 1997, 317; see also Murdoch 1997, 359 quoted in n.3.)
7. Compare *MGM*, 422 and 296 and *The Fire and the Sun* (Murdoch 1997, 461). Murdoch uses this image more than once, but in the earlier quote in *MGM* the image is used for 'western philosophy since the Greeks' and in *The Fire and the Sun* it is used for literature.

8. Murdoch (1997, 199; emphasis hers).
9. Kant and Plato are the only entries in the index to have *passim* behind their names. Murdoch's reading of Kant especially has received considerable attention in recent years. See for instance Merritt (2017) and Hopwood (2018).
10. See Altorf (2008, Chapter 4).
11. See for instance Murdoch (1997, 11, 215–216, 374).
12. Murdoch (1997, 216).
13. See here especially Midgley's review of *MGM*: '[Murdoch's] counter-theme, if written on a plumstone, would be the importance of the inner, imaginative life—of reflexion, of contemplation, seen as a capacity for watching, discovering, reflecting on and attending properly to what is real in our own lives and in the lives of others—and the need to talk about these things' (Midgley 1993, 334, quoting *MGM* 294, 177).
14. See also the interview with Magee (Murdoch 1997, 11).
15. See for instance the tongue-in-cheek remarks in 'The Sublime and the Good': 'let us start by saying that Shakespeare is the greatest of all artists' and 'Now Shakespeare is great art, and Shakespeare is not play, so Kant must be wrong' (Murdoch 1997, 205, 211).
16. In the first part of Chapter 11 Hume and Coleridge are mentioned as well, but as I have argued elsewhere the comments on their work are later additions to *MGM* and do not affect the argument (Altorf 2008, 75, 81–82, 129n.13 and 14; cp. Murdoch 1986).
17. In this respect Murdoch is exceptional. See Michèle Le Doeuff on the prominence of women in the history of philosophy, where they are better represented than in other fields of philosophy: 'Who better than a woman to show fidelity, respect and remembrance? ... Everyone knows that the more of a philosopher one is, the more distorted one's reading of other philosophers' (Le Doeuff 2002, 125).
18. For a longer discussion and a fuller explanation of Kantian terminology (including synthetic a priori and transcendental) see Altorf (2008) and Warnock (1976).
19. Murdoch is especially critical of the circumscribed role Kant attributes to the empirical imagination. She is not the first or the only one. See Friedrich Nietzsche's more venomous criticism in *Beyond Good and Evil* (see Altorf 2008, 76; Nietzsche 1988, 11).
20. 'Is it misleading simply to read the conscious activity back into the unconscious (transcendental) activity?' (*MGM*, 308–309).
21. For a discussion of Murdoch's understanding of the beautiful and the sublime see Altorf (2008).
22. See also Altorf (2008, 80).
23. *MGM*, 13.

24. See also: 'We can make sense of a scale or series with egoistic fantasies at one end and creative imagination, culminating in genius at the other' (*MGM*, 320).
25. See also *MGM*, 158, 341, 364; Altorf (2008, 83).
26. See also, 'The spiritual life is a long disciplined destruction of false images and false goods until (in some sense which we cannot understand) the imagining mind achieves an end of images and shadows' (*MGM*, 320).
27. See also Murdoch (1997, 307): 'That is, (a) it's no use, (b) it isn't there.'
28. Judaism and Islam are mentioned only to note their avoidance of imagery (*MGM*, 329).
29. See also *MGM*, 335; Murdoch (1997, 345).
30. 'Human beings are naturally selfish ... The psyche is a historically determined individual relentlessly looking after itself ... One of its main pastimes is day-dreaming ... It constantly seeks consolation ... Even its loving is more often than not an assertion of self' (Murdoch 1997, 364).

References

Antonaccio, M., and W. Schweiker (eds.). 1996. *Iris Murdoch and the search for human goodness*. Chicago and London: University of Chicago Press.

Altorf, M. 2008. *Iris Murdoch and the art of imagining*. London: Continuum.

Hopwood, M. 2018. 'The extremely difficult realization that something other than oneself is real': Iris Murdoch on love and moral agency. *European Journal of Philosophy* 26 (1): 477–501.

Le Doeuff, M. 2002. *The philosophical imaginary*. London: Continuum.

Merritt, M.M. 2017. Love, respect, and individuals: Murdoch as a guide to Kantian ethics. *European Journal of Philosophy* 25 (4): 1844–1863.

Midgley, M. 1993. Review of *metaphysics as a guide to morals*. *Philosophical Investigations* 16 (4): 333–341.

Mulhall, S. 1997. Constructing a hall of reflection: Perfectionist edification in Iris Murdoch's *metaphysics as a guide to morals*. *Philosophy* 72 (280): 219–239.

Murdoch, I. 1986. Ethics and imagination. *Irish Theological Quarterly* 52 (1–2): 81–95.

Murdoch, I. 1993. *Metaphysics as a guide to morals* (Abbreviated *MGM*). Harmondsworth: Penguin Books.

Murdoch, I. 1997. *Existentialists and mystics: Writings on philosophy and literature*. London: Chatto & Windus.

Nietzsche, F. 1988. *Jenseits von Gut und Böse. Kritische Studienausgabe 5*. Herausgegeben von G. Colli und M. Montinari. Berlin, New York: Walter de Gruyter.

Warnock, M. 1976. *Imagination*. London: Faber and Faber.

The Metaphysics of Morals and Politics (*MGM* Chapter 12)

Gary Browning

INTRODUCTION

Murdoch's metaphysics is dialectical and historical. It is dialectical in that it establishes a series of internal relations between forms of experience. The personal and the public, the disordered and the ordered and unity and plurality are mutually related constituents of her relational perspective. Past and present function in a similar way. The object of metaphysical understanding is present experience, which at the same time presumes a past from which it has emerged. The historicity of the present entails the time-bound operations of metaphysics. Whereas classical metaphysics as practised by, say, Plato or Spinoza, may be taken as purporting to provide a rational first-order guide to the nature of reality, Murdoch's metaphysics operates by making sense of the relations obtaining between known items within or intimated by our experience. The questions of metaphysics, for Murdoch, arise out of reflection upon contemporary experience and its form develops historically as metaphysicians engage critically with contemporary questions and the work of past

G. Browning (✉)
Oxford Brookes University, Oxford, UK

© The Author(s) 2019
N. Hämäläinen and G. Dooley (eds.),
Reading Iris Murdoch's Metaphysics as a Guide to Morals,
https://doi.org/10.1007/978-3-030-18967-9_12

metaphysicians. Murdoch takes metaphysics to be holistic in its review of how partial forms of experience are only fully intelligible in terms of their location within the whole. Metaphysics identifies the contributions of religion, art, morality to its own integrative understanding of experience. They register the order and unities within experience that metaphysics explains holistically. Like all aspects of experience, religion, art and morals change over time. In modern times, supranatural claims are renounced in favour of what can be known within experience.

Modernity is a time of demythologisation and it forms the context for present philosophical exploration of meaning. Hence the supernatural elements of religion are not to be sustained in the light of the prevailing rationalist temper and a critical philosophical perspective sets limits to a religious perspective as well as identifying its significance. Likewise art is understood critically by philosophy so that its sentimental and consolatory forms are dismissed, but its awareness of underlying unities is respected. Murdoch's metaphysics is not a world-denying Neo-Platonism, in which the ideal is divorced from the apparently real. Her reading of Plato allows for a modern sensibility that links speculation on the absolutely good to the nature of experience as a whole and takes the ideal to be a projection from and reflection back upon the actual. Theory and practice, imperfection and perfection and past and present are mutually implicated in an integrative metaphysics.[1]

Murdoch was aware of the delicacy of her metaphysical thinking. She takes on board a thoroughly modern perspective, in which the limits of knowledge are recognised and empirical understanding is valued. Simultaneously she draws upon Platonic metaphysics to resume an ambitious conception of philosophy's role in framing a broad metaphysical picture of a multidimensional but unitary reality. Murdoch's last published philosophical text, *Metaphysics as a Guide to Morals* (1992) (hereafter *MGM*) focuses upon morality and metaphysics, showing how they are mutually related. Metaphysics descries unity and order, which allows for a moral perspective that goes beyond the individual ego. Morality attests to a vision of goodness that unites the self with others. Morality and metaphysics are here informed by a modern sensibility in that Murdoch highlights the processes of demythologisation that frame the ways in which we understand ourselves in modern times. Science, technology and a stripped-down notion of philosophy set the tone for a modern rational instrumentalism, whereby orienting schemes of metaphysics tend to be excluded. In responding to this context Murdoch enlists a form of

Platonism, which is framed so as to meet and to supersede the philosophical temper of the moment. Murdoch's Platonism is stripped of any associations with otherworldliness. Plato is invoked to provide a sense of the unity and truth which are the goals of philosophical understanding and which can anchor the pursuit of moral perfection. Truth and unity are perceived through art, religious practice and moral engagement, though the working towards truth and goodness is never to be completed.

Murdoch's metaphysics invokes preceding philosophers in establishing a way of seeing the world in which metaphysics is not abandoned but is undertaken so as to work with a demythologised present in recognising aspects of experience that perceive unity and goodness. Metaphysical exploration, for Murdoch, is not a matter of supramundane insight but a historically situated activity that reveals the dialectical interplay between forms of experience and how they constitute a whole that is meaningful. Murdoch's reading of public and private morality, of the political and the personal, exhibits how she operates in providing metaphysical insight by perceiving the relatedness of aspects of experience. Personal morality depends upon public morality just as the point of the public world is to allow individual exploration of the personal. Public forms of morality are also shaped in part by personal exploration of experience just as the goodness of public life demands respect on the part of individual citizens. The moral perfectionism of personal morality underlines a commitment to the order and goodness of experience just as awareness of the calamities that have befallen the public world admits evidence of manifest political imperfection. Order and disorder, goodness and evil, and the public and private are intertwined within experience and the point of Murdoch's metaphysics is to show how they can be seen as working together. Murdoch had registered the distinctness of and connections between the political and moral worlds in her 'A postscript to 'On "God" and "Good"'' (2011) in which she declares, 'The idea of excellence has then a different operation in morals from its operation in politics, since a final acceptance of imperfection and incompleteness is built into politics in a way in which it is not built into morals' (Murdoch 2011, 8).

Metaphysics as a Guide to Morals

Murdoch analyses relations between the personal and the political spheres in Chapter 12 of *MGM*, 'Morals and politics'. It highlights the limits of the public sphere and the perfectionism of personal morality.

The meaning of the one sphere depends upon its relation to the other. In her early novels and philosophical essays Murdoch had entertained diffuse hopes for a socialist renewal. Jake Donoghue in *Under the Net* (1954) is confused about politics but remains a socialist. *The Bell* (1958) rehearses the aspirations and demise of a spiritual community that sets up a co-operative form of life. In her essay 'A house of theory' (1958) she recognises how demythologisation in contemporary culture erodes belief in metaphysics, religion, visionary morals and radical political ideology. Hence, after the Second World War socialism faces challenges, notably due to a quiescent working class, apparent material affluence and a gathering sense that radical ideological theories are untenable in the modern world (Murdoch 1997, 182). In her 'A postscript to 'On "God" and "Good"'' (2011) she recognises how politics is distinct from morals due to the imperfections of the public sphere (Murdoch 2011, 8). By the time she writes *MGM*, Murdoch herself is thoroughly disillusioned with political utopianism. She is alert to the historical evidence that points to the horrors of misguided utopianism. The repressiveness of current and recent socialist regimes, such as Communist China, underpins her distaste for radical socialism and her concern to protect the rights of the individual against the state (*MGM*, 354–357). Her suspicion of totalitarianism is reflected in her novels, where survivors of repressive regimes, such as vulnerable Willy Kost in *The Nice and the Good* (2000) serve as haunting reminders of its dangers. Likewise her letters and journals attest to her recognition of the wreckage of human life that she had witnessed in the aftermath of European dictatorships and the Second World War.[2]

In 'Morals and politics' Murdoch turns decisively away from radicalism and utopian projects. She looks to the wisdom of past political philosophers such as the British empiricists who focus upon the limited but significant task of the state in providing security for individuals. This imperative to protect the individual is acknowledged to involve a distinction between the private and the public. She recognises this distinction to be central to classic liberal thought. She observes, 'Liberal political thought posits a certain fundamental distinction between the person as citizen and the person as moral-spiritual individual' (*MGM*, 357). While accepting the imprecision of the terms of the distinction, she is willing to invoke it so as to limit the power of the state. She remarks, 'Society and so the state *cannot* be perfected, although perfection is a proper ideal or magnet for the individual as a moral agent' (*MGM*, 356). The distinction between the private and the public and the prioritisation of individual freedom are held by Murdoch to be distinctively modern. She recognises how Plato did not recognise the value of individual freedom and notes that Plato's ideal commonwealth of the *Republic* sets the common good above that of individual satisfaction (see Browning 1991).

Murdoch's observation that the distinction between the private and the public is both relatively new and less than clear cut is accurate and is rehearsed by many political theorists.[3] In *On Liberty* J. S. Mill identifies the rationale for governmental activity and its limit to be that of preventing harm to other individuals (Mill 1989, 10). Mill values individual liberty and he rules out governmental regulation of an individual's conduct when other individuals are not affected. Hence Mill distinguishes between self-regarding and other-regarding actions as determining the sphere of liberty to which individuals are entitled (Mill 1989, 34). This distinction is very difficult to specify precisely. All actions in some sense affect others, just as their inspiration is not merely private. Murdoch recognises the indeterminacy involved in separating a private sphere from a public one but maintains a difference between the two in order to protect an individual from violence, coercion and the dangers of an overly powerful state. She sees security to be vital for individual well-being and urges that politics must be regulated by fundamental moral norms. This proposed mode of regulation is distinct from personal morality even if regulatory norms are affected by the latter. She accepts a distinction that is useful even if it is hard to specify in precise terms. She distinguishes between a public political world that is to be governed by highly general axioms prescribing rights and rules, and a personal sphere of moral aspiration to which an individual is to be committed. Personal moral life is perfectionist. An individual is to aspire to do the right thing. Personal morality is a spiritual journey, where the self develops via its moral encounters with others and aims for perfection. Public regulation attends to the imperfect political world where individuals are liable to suffer. It is not perfectionist but rather guards against manifest imperfections by protecting the basic requirements for a decent life. Murdoch observes, 'Society, and so the state, *cannot* be perfected, although perfection is a proper ideal or magnet for the individual or moral agent' (*MGM*, 356).

Murdoch's distinction between private and public morality does not amount to an absolute separation between two spheres and is not sanctioned by unassailable philosophical argument. It is a pragmatic way of drawing a line that works to protect individuals and to guard against the excesses of state intrusion into individual lives. It is a product of reflection upon modern political history. She is critical, however, of the Hegelian project of identifying an overall pattern to the development of history, and of Hegel's Marxist successors who posit an end to history and justify political actions in terms of this endgame (*MGM*, 370). Murdoch is against any totalising political judgements that abstract from a messy contingent world in which rights are to supersede any projected end state. Her political priority is to protect individual rights. She argues, 'The idea of Utopia is a danger in politics, it hints at a rectification of a primal fault, a perfect unity, it is impatient of contingency. The assertion of contingency, the rights of the object, the rights of the individual, these are connected' (*MGM*, 378).

In establishing the limits that have to be respected in considering politics and in her critique of Hegel and Marx, Murdoch invokes Adorno's neo-Hegelian critique of Hegel. Adorno reacts against the Hegelian tradition by critiquing totalising forms of thought. In contrast to Hegel's reading of the inter-relations between subject and object in his *Phenomenology of Spirit*, Adorno admits the independence of the object. He rejects a finalising dialectic that is to yield a final solution to the exigencies of experience. Adorno allows for a negative and continuing open dialectical interplay between subject and object. Murdoch comments approvingly,

> This dialectical give-and-take mutually necessary relation between subject and object is not to be understood in a Hegelian manner as taking place within any sovereign determining totality, whether Hegel's absolute, or a Marxist idea of history as a story with a happy ending. (*MGM*, 370)

Adorno's approach recognises contingent events that cannot be encapsulated in a tight theoretical scheme. Yet he also allows for inter-relations between the elements that are to be theorised. Murdoch sympathy for Adorno sheds light on her thought. She avoids totalising political thought by recognising a distinction between the personal and the public. They allow for differing objectives. In taking her cue from Adorno, however, Murdoch allows for interaction between the public and the private. Public laws are to protect and serve the individual. Perfectionist personal morality depends upon protection of the self from public imperfections. Again, personal moral thinking can contribute to the public agenda by framing ideas on how the welfare of individuals can be best secured by public provision. Murdoch envisages a mutual dependence or a kind of dialectic between the public and the private, though their separation is to be highlighted so as to prioritise the protection of the individual. Murdoch observes, 'The idea of a separation (between the public and the private) is better here than that of dialectic or tension within a totality: it both emphasises a very (general) liberal) political value, and also helps to make sense of political scenes' (*MGM*, 367).

While personal morality is perfectionist, the public sphere is not set on achieving an ideal that might not be realisable. It is flexible and accommodates to the needs of the moment and deals with imperfections and deficiencies that require practical remedies. The dangers to individual welfare that follow from lax or ill-conceived regulation prioritise the maintenance of fundamental axioms that set up clear and firm rules to mediate the transactions of individuals. The rules of the game require to be set so as to protect fundamental needs. Murdoch urges that the public sphere is to be regulated by axioms securing basic requirements for a decent life, for example the human rights of life and liberty should be protected. These rights need to be secured from interference by governments as well by individuals. The rights are to be derived from experience and history, reflecting what has proven to be fundamental to the ordinary pursuit of individual purposes. They demand public respect that is unconditional and unmediated, so these axioms are not to be systematised for that would detract from their immediacy. Public awareness of their absolute significance is dissipated if they are made to fit within an overarching theoretical formula. Murdoch observes, 'They are barriers of principle which are not reducible to a system' (*MGM*, 565). Rights also issue from considered reflection upon a historical changing world. They specify what is thought to be necessary in the public realm from time to time. Hence they are contestable, and they will vary across time and space, even if many of them, such as the right to life, will persist. Their historical piecemeal articulation means that they are not to be seen as the positive enactments of a supervening and universal natural law. Rather they evolve as political experience evolves and throws up issues that demand attention in the light of changing cultural moods and circumstances. There is no precise specification of the ways in which they will evolve. According to Michael Oakeshott, a friend of Murdoch's, there are no absolutes in considering political action (Oakeshott 1962). No ideology can provide for the subtlety of circumstances and we must look to traditions and what they imitate rather than ideological systems. Murdoch recounts a variety of ways in which the agenda for politics develops, noting the activities of feminist movements, and of single issue groups canvassing the rights of animals and the planet (*MGM*, 369). Deeply felt personal moral beliefs, for instance ecological concern for the planet and animal rights, might at one time seem individual eccentricities but, at another point in time might well be absorbed into the norms of the public culture. Murdoch is light on detail in specifying how issues are to be handled by political institutions and more specifically on how sub-stantive aspects of socio-economic policy will be negotiated. Her highly generic account of how axioms are put on to the political agenda by groups is elliptical, but it intimates that she envisages a plural and demo-cratic process by which norms and issues are debated and canvassed.

Murdoch provides no clear-cut recipe for putting axioms on the polit-ical agenda and she recognises the contestable nature of public axioms. Their contestability, however, does not imply that obedience to them is optional. Public order and security depends upon their command of widespread support. Their efficacy depends upon their capacity to elicit obedience, and obedience derives from their moral approval on the part of citizens. Public morality is not entirely separate from personal moral-ity in that individuals agree to public norms in the light of their moral beliefs. The public and the personal are linked dialectically by the for-mation and effective operation of axioms. Personal moral commitments inspire the adoption of axioms and reinforce community solidarity and the maintenance of laws and rights. There are, however, tensions between the public and the personal. While the axioms underpinning the operation of the public sphere demand support and obedience from citizens, on occasions the personal moral commitments of individuals will clash with public rules. Murdoch imagines moral commitments to be more than merely subjective preferences that can be put aside easily; they form part of an individual's spiritual life. A clash between personal principle and public law raises the prospect of civil disobedience on the part of an individual to register their disagreement with the law and to canvas its overthrow. For Murdoch, civil disobedience is acceptable, even necessary, but should be practised sparingly, because there is value in the maintenance of a law insofar as it provides order. Murdoch allows civil disobedience but she takes it to be exceptional and problematic. In undertaking civil disobedience in a democratic society where laws and policies reflect public opinion, an individual must be prepared to argue the case in public debate. If the debate does not lead to a change in the law then disobedience may be legitimate but the individual who refuses to obey the law must accept punishment for an offence. Disobedience is not to be generalised because it may weaken the force of public order, which allows for the very development of personal wide-ranging moral commitments that lie behind the civil disobedience.

Murdoch's account of basic axioms in the public sphere is relatively thin on the detail of how particular axioms are to be decided upon. But it should not be thought that Murdoch is conservative in her emphasis upon order and basic rights. She allows for the possibility of international rights superseding a merely national perspective. Moreover, in *MGM* and in her unpublished 'Manuscript on Heidegger' Murdoch specifically points to the provision of women's rights (*MGM*, 361; Murdoch 1993, 58). Lovibond, though, has argued that Murdoch's novels insinuate a resistance on her part to the full moral and intellectual autonomy of women that is also reflected in her moral philosophy (Lovibond 2011, 7). In a review of Lovibond's *Iris Murdoch, Gender and Philosophy*, Hämäläinen has countered by observing, 'one may suggest that her novels describe what is, rather than what should be' (Hämäläinen 2011).

Murdoch's philosophical views cannot be simply read off from her novels. They reflect the social world so that it is no surprise that in her novels there is a differential treatment of men and women and that men have higher social status and dominate women routinely in the course of Murdoch's narratives. This privileging of the social position of men, however, does not entail that Murdoch's attitude to women is clear cut. Dooley has observed how Murdoch's later novels show a more critical attitude to male adultery (Dooley 2009). Moreover, Murdoch's first-person male narrators do not determine how the novels are to be read. These men tend to be unreliable narrators and the bourgeois family structure, in which men dominate, is critiqued within the narratives.

In assessing the role of women in Murdoch's novels Johnson observes,

> Iris Murdoch's novels pose in new and tantalising ways the question of what it means to write as a woman, to read as a woman. They disconcert and fascinate both female and male readers by continually questioning gender identity and transgressing gender boundaries. (Johnson 1987, 1)

The attitudes towards women of Charles Arrowby in *The Sea, the Sea* (1978) and Hilary Burde in *A Word Child* (1975) are patronising and patriarchal, but as Johnson signals, these attitudes are expressed ironically within self-subverting first person narratives. Murdoch's deconstruction of male domination is of a piece with her critique of bourgeois family structures that are shown to exert sustained damage to children. *A Fairly Honourable Defeat* (1970) represents a devastating critique of the smug, self-satisfied bourgeois family and offers depictions of male attitudes, maintained by Julius King and Rupert Foster that incarnate the demonic and the vain. Simon and Axel, a homosexual couple, manage to achieve a workable relationship but it is outside of traditional male sexual mores and Tallis appears to be good but his saintliness is outside the norm of male attitudes. Murdoch in 'Morals and politics' recognises that axioms establishing sexual equalities are disturbing forms of male power and are likely to be further developed in the future, while her novels pose questions for the prevalent inequalities between men and women. She does not, however, spell out a clear commitment to feminism.

Murdoch's Novels, Morals and Politics

Murdoch's reading of the relations between morals and politics in *MGM* allows for inter-relations between the two. A number of her novels also trace relations between morals and politics. Murdoch's novels do not simply rehearse philosophical doctrines but deal with issues and circumstances phenomenologically that she reflects upon in her philosophical work. Hence novels such as *The Nice and the Good* (1968) and *An Accidental Man* (1971) show characters grappling with tensions between the spheres of morals and politics that are focused upon in her late study of the two spheres in *MGM*. What they show is that characters can feel and appreciate the distinct duties of the moral and political spheres. An individual cannot simply deny an obligation to support his state at a time of war and yet equally he or she has to consider the moral obligations of how others are to be treated. Likewise the state demands that public officials are to be held to account and yet a particular recognition of one's duties to another might be seen as requiring us to relax our concern to hold a public official to account.

The distinction between personal and public forms of morality underlies Murdoch's most expressly political novel, *The Nice and the Good*. Its principal protagonist, John Ducane has to choose between his political and moral obligations. At the request of his head of department, Octavian Gray and the Prime Minister, Ducane, a legal advisor to a government department, leads an inquiry into the death of one of its members, Radeechy. At the same time, Ducane is developing a Platonic relationship with Kate Gray, Octavian's wife, who lives on their Trescombe estate in Dorset. Ducane enjoys the 'niceness' of his relations with Kate, which counterpoint the edginess of his relations with his girlfriend, Jessica, whose insecurity inhibits him from acting on his resolution to end their affair. Kate is warm and expansive in entertaining her friends, Mary Clothier and Paula Biranne, and their children, while enjoying her relaxed relationship with Ducane. She avoids demanding emotions and close observation of herself and others. Her reflecting on her relationship to Ducane is exemplary. 'How lovely it is, thought Kate, to be able to fall in love with one's old friends. It's one of the pleasures of being middle-aged. Not that I'm really in love, but it's just like being in love with all the pain taken away' (Murdoch [1968] 2000, 124).

Kate's self-absorption counterpoints Ducane's close attention to others. He is prepared to offer and receive love, and is affected by the depraved forces contaminating the political world that his investigative work into the affairs of the department has revealed. His own moral sensitivity is heightened in risking his life to save Pierce, Mary's son. In so doing he realises his love for Mary, which contrasts with the ersatz painless 'nice' love that is imagined by Kate. He takes his love for Mary to indicate fundamental goodness in the world, to which he should devote himself. His state of mind is captured in the following observation: 'Her mode of being gave him a moral, even a metaphysical, confidence in the world, in the reality of goodness' (Murdoch [1968] 2000, 332). Ducane's insight into goodness inspires him to set up the reunion of Paula and her husband, Richard Biranne, who is implicated in the death of Radeechy. Due to his moral commitment to help Paula, he refrains from including any damaging reference to Biranne in his official report on the death. Ducane's selfless assistance to Paula reflects his sense of goodness and his personal perfectionist moral commitment. A commitment to the good demands that an individual acts according to a standard of goodness that is distinct from self-interest in its recognition of relational commitments to others. At the same time, Ducane's moral perfectionism that requires his commitment to help Paula and her husband represents a dereliction of his political duty to his department and to the Prime Minister. His political duty is to provide an inclusive report, which might re-establish public confidence in the political establishment and the norms of society. Politics is above all about security and demands that citizens trust in government and its personnel. Ducane's neglect of his political duty is justified by the personal virtue of his action, but the tension between his moral and political duties leads him to resign from his post.

Ducane's resignation over his failure to produce the full facts in his report contrasts with the relaxed attitude of his head of department, Octavian Gray. At the close of the novel the latter accepts the thinness of Ducane's report, because the Radeechy affair is of receding significance. Politics operates by doing what is pragmatically necessary. Trust in public officials is required but if there is no threat to trust then standards can be relaxed. Octavian, like Kate, is nice and bourgeois rather than committed to perfectionist moral ideals. He is temperamentally suited to being a political actor. He is concerned with what works rather than with the good. He is not overly troubled by the demands of personal morality and, as is characteristic of top civil servants, he can be economical with the truth. With a similar worldliness he also conceals his affair with a secretary, just as Kate can renew her social life in the absence of Ducane. Ducane's uneasiness at his failure to discharge his political obligation points to Murdoch's recognition of the delicate balance between political and personal moral obligations. Politics, in *MGM*, is not a utopian project (*MGM*, 356). It is about establishing and maintaining the rules of the game, which provide security in the public world. *The Nice and the Good* shows a related recognition of the differing spheres of morality and politics. Ducane, in his personal life, can be virtuous in pursuing the good but he is also aware of the need to provide security in the public sphere. The value of the world is to be respected but it does not transcend the perfectionist obligation of cultivating goodness.

The tension between the political and the personal, which underpins Murdoch's reading of moral and political life, surfaces in another Murdoch novel, *An Accidental Man* which explores a case of civil disobedience. In the novel Ludwig Leferrier, a young American historian, opts to remain in England rather than to return to the United States to serve his state in the Vietnam war. If he returns home Ludwig faces arrest for avoiding the draft, while if he remains in England he can take up a lecturing post and marry Gracie Tisbourne. Ludwig's parents disapprove of their son's projected marriage and regard avoidance of the draft a being politically dishonourable. They urge him to return home and not to betray political principles. Ludwig is opposed to the Vietnam War on moral grounds and hence considers his decision to remain in England to be morally justified. By the end of the novel, however, and in response to his changing attitude to the marriage and to his moral and political dilemma he decides to return to the United States and to face the consequences. Clearly there are opposing arguments about what Ludwig should do. The Vietnam War excited opposition on many grounds. Indeed Murdoch in her postscript to 'On "God" and "Good"' maintains the rightness of opposition to the war (Murdoch 2011, 8). Ludwig's dilemma is complex and shaped by a number of contingent experiential considerations. His life in the UK appears attractive, he is in love and doubts the cause for which the United States is fighting.

A super power fighting for indeterminate reasons and in controversial and largely ineffective ways appears to be unworthy of support. And yet a state requires a commitment from its citizens to maintain its basic rules which may be said to include its right to wage war. In the novel Murdoch does not take sides on the issue, and records the tension within Ludwig as he battles with his love for Gracie and his strained relations with his parents and also the more general tension between the personal and the political on a leading issue of the politics of the day. Ultimately the novel shows a character facing up to the consequences of civil disobedience, and being prepared to face punishment and popular disapproval, just as in *MGM* she allows civil disobedience just as long as individuals accept civil punishment for their transgressions against the law.

Conclusion

Throughout her career Murdoch tracked political events and was deeply interested in morality. A number of her novels show characters wrestling with political dilemmas. Jake Donoghue in *Under the Net* mixes with political radicals, feels the emotional pull of socialism but cannot articulate a reasoned commitment to its creed. Gerard Hernshaw in *The Book and the Brotherhood* (1987) eschews radical utopianism for the security of a moderate political regime that supports parliamentary democracy. Both Ludwig Leferrier in *An Accidental Man* and John Ducane in *The Nice and the Good* have insight into the importance of the political sphere and respect what it offers. Yet they also recognise the force of personal morality. Leferrier's conscience is stirred by what he takes to be an unjust war and he continues throughout the novel to maintain a principled opposition to the Vietnam War, but by its close he returns to the United States to accept punishment for his civil disobedience. His action respects a political duty to his state, just as John Ducane's resignation from his public post recognises that he owes a loyalty to the public sphere notwithstanding the strength of his moral conviction in aiding a friend in a way that runs counter to official duty.

Murdoch's analysis of morals and politics in *MGM* distinguishes personal morality from public morality and she imagines that the political priority is to protect the individual citizen from harm while the object of personal morality is to pursue an ideal perfection. The dangers of the political arena are rehearsed in a number of her novels, and are intimated in the radical utopianism of Crimond in *The Book and the Brotherhood* that ignores the needs of ordinary individuals (see Browning 2018a). Yet Murdoch also sees connections between the public and the personal in that personal morality depends upon an ordered public world if it is to be undertaken successfully. Hence Ducane recognises the force of public authority while he operates so as to limit what he says in an official report. Likewise political rules and ideas can be questioned and developed via individual morality. A willingness to question American involvement in Vietnam and to practise civil disobedience on the issue is a theme of *An Accidental Man*, and while the novel does not prescribe any lessons to the reader, the practice of civil disobedience is presented as a plausible response to a political situation if respect is also shown to prevailing political authority.

Murdoch's metaphysics operates in order to make sense of experience by showing how forms of life and aspects of experience relate to one another. In her analysis of politics and morality in *MGM* she shows how perfectionist moral aspirations are both supported by the security that is provided by political order but are also necessarily distinct from the imperfect and pragmatic world of politics. Political perfectionism is to be guarded against, given the tendency for political radicalism to generate injustice and violence, and yet the political world is also to be valued and respected as a means of securing order and justice. She recognises that metaphysics cannot provide an absolute set of principles for the political world just as moral life is to be determined by individuals situated in specific situations and making particular judgements. While Murdoch's sense that the axioms of the political world are not absolute represents a reasonable reading of the changeable historical world in which politics take place, her account is elliptical in that it does not provide a rich description of how changes of axioms might take place. She entertains the idea of international rights and governance without specifying how it might operate and she does not expand upon her recognition of women's rights to provide an indication of what further women's rights might be required. Murdoch's account of the metaphysics of morals and politics is elliptical, but it does locate politics and morals on the map of experience so as to guide judgements on what is appropriate in both arenas.

Notes

1. For a discussion of Murdoch's reading of Plato, see Browning (2018b, 178–190).
2. Murdoch's journals are held in Kingston University Library, and a collection of her letters was published in Horner and Rowe (2015).
3. For analysis of the complicated relations between the individual and society, see Browning (1999, 2005, 2016) and Berlin (1969).

References

Berlin, I. 1969. *Four essays on liberty*. Oxford: Oxford University Press.

Browning, G. 1991. *Hegel and Plato: Two modes of philosophising about politics*. New York: Garland Press.

Browning, G. 1999. *Hegel and the history of political philosophy*. Basingstoke and New York: Palgrave Macmillan.

Browning, G. 2005. A globalist ideology of post-Marxism? Hardt and Negri's *Empire*. *Critical Review of International Social and Political Philosophy* 8 (2): 193–208.

Browning, G. 2016. *A history of modern political thought—The question of interpretation*. Oxford: Oxford University Press.

Browning, G. (ed.). 2018a. *Murdoch on truth and love*. London: Palgrave Macmillan.

Browning, G. 2018b. *Why Iris Murdoch matters*. London: Bloomsbury.

Dooley, G. 2009. Iris Murdoch's novels of male adultery: *The sandcastle, An unofficial rose, The sacred and profane love machine* and *The message to the planet*. *English Studies* 90 (4): 421–434.

Hämäläinen, N. 2011. Review of Sabina Lovibond, *Iris Murdoch, gender and philosophy*. *Notre Dame Philosophical Reviews* 12 (10): n.p.

Horner, A., and A. Rowe (eds.). 2015. *Living on paper: Letters from Iris Murdoch 1934–1995*. London: Chatto & Windus.

Johnson, D. 1987. *Iris Murdoch*. Brighton: Harvester Press.

Lovibond, S. 2011. *Iris Murdoch, gender and philosophy*. Abingdon: Routledge.

Mill, J.S. 1989. *On liberty and other writings*. Cambridge: Cambridge University Press.

Murdoch, I. [1968] 2000. *The nice and the good*. London Vintage.

Murdoch, I. 1992. *Metaphysics as a guide to morals.* (Abbreviated *MGM.*) London: Chatto & Windus.

Murdoch, I. 1993. Heidegger manuscript. KUAS6/5/1/4. Kingston University Archives and Special Collections, London.

Murdoch, I. 1997. A house of theory. In *Existentialists and mystics: Writings on philosophy and literature,* 171–186. London: Chatto & Windus.

Murdoch, I. 2011. A postscript to 'on "God" and "good"'. *Iris Murdoch Review* 1 (3): 6–8.

Murdoch, I. Unpublished. Journals, poetry notebooks and other items. KUAS202. Kingston University Archives and Special Collections, London.

Oakeshott, M. 1962. *Rationalism in politics and other essays.* London and New York: Methuen.

Iris Murdoch's Ontological Argument (*MGM* Chapter 13)

Andrew Gleeson

[The] Ontological Proof is mysterious because it does not address itself to the intelligence, but to love.

Simone Weil, quoted in *MGM* three times (401, 425, 504–505)

Iris Murdoch has long sought to replace God with Good. *Metaphysics as a Guide to Morals* (henceforth *MGM*) contains a reiteration and amplification of this theme. Modern science and enlightenment, she argues, displacing religion, have forced a wedge between fact and value that has left us with a picture of ourselves as lonely Cartesian souls and existentialist wills, adrift in an alienating mechanical world. Value survives in deracinated remnants, as a function of practical reason, or as a calculus of pleasures, or as the product of ungrounded choice. Murdoch believes this self-conception is untrue to an indispensable reality of human life, a transcendent and perfect Platonic Good which remains our unacknowledged life-blood. Her ambition is to recover this as a serious philosophical idea, and perhaps beyond that to put it at the centre of a 'de-mythologised' form of Christianity.[1]

A. Gleeson (✉)
Flinders University, Adelaide, SA, Australia

© The Author(s) 2019
N. Hämäläinen and G. Dooley (eds.),
Reading Iris Murdoch's Metaphysics as a Guide to Morals,
https://doi.org/10.1007/978-3-030-18967-9_13

In *MGM* she develops a moral form of the ontological argument (OA) to show how the Good is an essential reality of our lives and thought: a proper conception of the ordinary moral value we experience is a conception of something we can be assured is real, and that reality in some way indicates an ideal, perfect form of itself, the transcendent Good. The argument, normally considered an entertaining conundrum or 'charming joke' (Murdoch quoting Schopenhauer, *MGM*, 392) worth little serious philosophical attention, is thus at the very heart of Murdoch's moral philosophy. Consequently it provides a vantage point from which I try to identify a possible lop-sided tendency in Murdoch's thought, one that places more emphasis on inspiring ideals than on implacable demands.[2] I argue that her version of the argument is handicapped by concentrating on a vision of moral experience which emphasises a slow, calm, contemplative progress towards the attracting ideal of the Good. I contend this does not fully capture the strong sense of the *inescapability* of morality that the moral OA requires. I suggest a modified form of the argument that focuses on our sense of human life as something sacred or inviolable, a sense constituted by the non-negotiable demands other human being make on us not to violate them (in actions like murder, rape, betrayal, etc.). By contrast to the Good as a distant ideal beckoning us forward in a pilgrimage towards ever more wisdom and virtue, the preciousness of human life and its moral demands are the commonplace, proximate substance of our daily lives, albeit so familiar we barely think of them until confronted by their violation.

In the first section I outline Murdoch's moral OA. In the second I introduce three objections and offer replies to them. Two replies are in a spirit I think Murdoch would approve of. The third represents a departure from the main direction of her thinking. Here I develop the moral OA in a form concentring on the preciousness of human life. In the last section I sketch a sense of perfection suitable for my version of the moral OA, and consider the argument's dialectical value.

I

Murdoch's main discussion of the OA is in Chapter 13 of *MGM*. She distinguishes, conventionally, between two versions.

The first (*MGM*, 393) argues that a perfect being must exist since a being perfect in every respect *other than existing* would be less great, less perfect, than a being with the same qualities but which *does* exist. This is the version of the argument vulnerable to Kant's famous objection that existence is not a property. My thought of a perfect island is not made a thought of a better island if I think of it as existing as opposed to not existing.

The second version (*MGM*, 394–395) argues that the concept of God is the concept of a perfect being which *necessarily* exists, and so long as that concept is coherent we cannot but think of God as existing: to think of him as not existing, or indeed as existing only contingently, is not to think of him at all. So either he cannot exist (because the concept of God is incoherent) or he exists necessarily.

Murdoch does not endorse the argument as proving the existence of God. Instead she construes the second version of the OA as a *moral* argument. We should read it as proving the reality of 'some uniquely necessary status for moral value as something (uniquely) impossible to be thought away from human experience, and ... if conceived of, known as real' (*MGM*, 396).

But how do we move from conception to reality? Murdoch's answer is an appeal to Plato, whose philosophy she insists is the context we need to understand the OA. We acquire adequate moral concepts by the kind of learning from moral experience which Plato described and which Murdoch recapitulates (*MGM*, 404–406, 408–412). One of the things we learn, an essential element of the moral conceptions we form, is their *necessity*, their *inescapability* in human life. So this is an argument from experience which gives substance to the concept of something which is necessary to human existence. Summarising the argument with reference to God (but we can substitute 'moral value', as she wants us to) she says, 'God either exists necessarily or is impossible. All our experience shows that he exists' (*MGM*, 405). This nicely encapsulates the conceptual and the experiential elements of the argument.

But this only gets us so far. What the argument to this point establishes is the inescapable reality of the quotidian moral phenomena of ordinary, daily life. Another stage is necessary to take us from these very *imperfect* phenomena—or bundling them together in the singular, from moral value—to the ideal, *perfect* Good. These two stages are not completely distinct, a fact partly reflected in the (perhaps unavoidable) un-clarity (in both Plato and Murdoch) over just how the perfect is discerned in the imperfect. In a sea of images, sometimes it seems like inference, sometimes new concept formation, sometimes intuition (*MGM*, 400), sometimes remembrance (the *Meno*, *MGM*, 400), sometimes aspect-perception, sometimes the faith and hope that loving attention, patiently abided with, will not be disappointed, a faith in something 'apprehended as *there* which is not yet *known*' and which 'comes to us out of the dark of non-being, as a reward for loving attention' (*MGM*, 505, original emphasis)—a kind of creation *ex nihilo*. I cannot pursue these fascinating and profound images here. But at the minimum it is clear that in our moral experience we discover 'degrees of goodness' (*MGM*, 396) which (at least) intimate to us the ideal, perfect Good. Moral understanding, for her, does not consist in the grasp (theoretical or practical) of a moral theory, or even moral principles, applied to a world of value-free fact. We confront a world *already* charged with value. We perceive that value if we can—to use a term Murdoch inherited from Simone Weil—*attend* to (look at) that world purified of the egocentric fantasy which typically holds us in thrall. That purification is a progressive shedding of comforting illusions as our understanding and acquisition of goodness and wisdom is gradually enhanced, achieving both greater depth and greater 'unity'. This is not the unity of a completed theory such as we might get in science, but that most visibly expressed in great art. A lot of life-experience may be necessary to conceive of moral value properly. If my conception is shallow, banal and philistine, then *that* conception will not entail the reality of moral value. The conception may not need to be perfect, but it will need some significant maturity before the claim that what I am conceiving of is something I know to be so will become plausible.

II

But no matter how cultivated my conception, could it not all be illusion? It may be true that moral value cannot be thought away from human experience. It may be true that this conditions our concept of what it is to be human. But (the objection can go) none of that shows that moral experience is experience of something *real*. Perhaps some kind of giant illusion is built into our essential nature (as many philosophers have supposed, not just about morality). It may be true that 'if you can conceive of this entity you are *ipso facto* certain that what you are thinking of is real' (*MGM*, 395, emphasis hers)—but what you are *certain* of is one thing and what is *actually so* can be another.

Murdoch has written: 'Moral concepts do not move about *within* a hard world set up by science and logic. They set up, for different purposes, a different world' (Murdoch 1996, 28, emphasis hers). This suggests her possible sympathy for an answer to this worry that I can only sketch in desperate and dogmatic brevity. The gist is that once a moral judgement has satisfied all the criteria internal to morality itself (and any factual assumptions are correct) then no room remains for coherent doubt about its truth. There are no criteria external to morality by which our most basic moral criteria (which, ultimately, means our most basic moral reactions and attitudes—like, for example, our horror and disgust at torturing children for fun) can be appraised as correct or incorrect. Thus, once we have made our moral judgements, there are no further 'ontological' questions about the reality of properties attributed by those judgements; if the judgement is to be challenged it must be on moral grounds. The same goes for physical (scientific) judgements, aesthetic judgements, mental judgements, and so on. Each domain has its own 'internal' criteria for correctness, but there are no domain-transcendent criteria. If this is right there is no reason to doubt that judgements correct by morality's own criteria are judgements about something real.

This metaphysically 'quietist' line of thought gets powerful resistance from the objection that if we admit the reality of moral properties then we admit the reality of things offensive to science (unless they can be shown to reduce to, or supervene on, scientifically kosher properties). Quietism can, I think, disarm this objection too. There are many things in the world not accountable for in scientific terms. But this does not mean that there are 'weird' non-natural things offensive to science, or indeed to a scientific naturalism. There are moral things, aesthetic things, mental things and so on. It is only the assumption that there is just *one* kind of reality, and so that physical and moral claims must be answerable to *the same* criteria, which creates a conflict and a sense of a threat to science. Moral ideals and moral properties are non-natural in the sense that they are not physical, but not in the sense that they threaten the closedness of the physical universe or the completeness of science. Such notions make sense only *within* the scientific perspective and *its* criteria for correctness. There is no such thing as the world being open or closed, or an account of it being complete or incomplete, *simpliciter*, without specifying a context (physical, mental, moral, etc.)—for without a context there are no criteria to give the assertions sense. The idea of the universe 'in itself', independently of any perspective or gestalt and its internal criteria, is incoherent. A physical or a moral description of the world is *already* a description of the world 'in itself'. (Indeed, what would a

description of the world be that was *not* a description of it 'in itself'?)
Beware moving from the truism that every description is relative to some
set of criteria to the conclusion that they are only descriptions of 'appearances' and not reality, not the world 'in itself'. To demand descriptions
of the world that are from no perspective is to demand descriptions *for
which there are no criteria as to their correctness or incorrectness,* and they
are not descriptions at all. Notice too that quietism is not idealism—
properties (physical or moral) are 'there' whether we see them or not.
In both cases, we cannot make things true just by wanting, wishing or
willing them to be so. Given a set of criteria, the world determines what
is true, not us.

It might be thought that even if this quietist line of thought suc-
ceeds for actual, instantiated moral properties, there remains a distinct
problem for Murdoch's ideal Good. Put pithily, the problem says that
if something is merely ideal, if it transcends what is instantiated in the
actual world, then it is not real. The objection equivocates over the
word 'ideal'. The word is sometimes contrasted (usually by philosophers) with 'real' or 'actual'. But in street speech to talk of an 'ideal'
is typically to talk of a goal or aim, of something someway distant but
highly desirable, optimal or supreme. This need not imply any doubt
of its reality. Modern thought tends to conflate the actual and the real.
They are treated as close to synonyms. But an ancient tradition, to which
Murdoch subscribes (*MGM*, 406–407) sees the ideal as, if anything, *more*
real than the actual, i.e. the instantiated. An actual poem is only as real,
qua poem, as it approaches exhibiting those qualities which constitute
excellence in poetry, the qualities which make an attempt at poetry *most
fully poetic.* Similarly, goodness (in a person, in an action) is more real
the better it is, and only the perfect Good is fully real (is, if you like, *fully
what it essentially is*). The less and more real are both available to us, the
one in the typically confused and obscure flux of immediate experience,
the other as a distant object of contemplation: '[Good] is real as an idea,
and is also incarnate in knowledge and work and love' (*MGM*, 508).
There is no confusion in this so long as we do not think that the ideal
is real in the sense of something we can lay our hands on as I can on my
tennis racquet. And again, if it is feared this introduces weird non-natural
properties into the world, then quietism comes to the rescue.

If something along these overall rough lines in the last two paragraphs
is defensible then the philosophical sceptic's objection to Murdoch's
moral OA can be met: absent any other obstacles, she can make the

move from a moral value being (properly) conceived of, to its *being* real (and not merely *thought of* as real).

There is however a third line of objection to Murdoch's moral OA that is harder to deal with. The problem concerns the characteristic emphasis in her description of the moral life. That emphasis is on the attraction of the distant ideal. Hers is a morality of gradual growth in virtue and wisdom by attention to this ideal as we partially perceive it in good actions, good people and, especially (not just good but) great art. Obviously this is a very important part of morality. I am sure it is indispensable. But *for the purpose of the indispensability claim made by her moral OA* is this the right theme to stress? Many of us are barely responsive to the higher ideals of the moral life. We get by in a rather thoughtless and mediocre way, rationalising our timid and conventional lives. Too many of us never confront our demons or push beyond our 'comfort zone', and perhaps rarely even think of such things. We remain lazily the captive, in Murdoch's striking phrase, of our 'consoling fantasies'. Yet we need not be moral monsters, much less be unrecognisable as human. For pedestrian purposes that suffice for most life contexts we count as 'decent' (or at least not indecent) people. We do not and would not murder, rape, pillage, betray, lie, steal, break promises and so on. To reiterate, I do think that attention to the ideal, and ultimately to something like Murdoch's perfect Good, is fundamental and indispensable. But I do suggest that it is not what in moral life is most urgent, non-negotiable, absolute and resistant to compromise and temporising, and so not what is most suitable as the main meaning of *indispensable* 'moral value' in the moral OA.

So what *is* most indispensable? Here is a remarkable fact of great relevance to morality that goes strangely overlooked: in the last 24 hours none of us has committed a murder, rape or any of the grave evils listed above (so I do my readers the compliment of assuming). That we have not done so is no accident, no mere good fortune. It is not that we may not have been angry enough at someone to punch them in the face, frustrated enough by stress at work or home not to have treated someone unjustly, or worn down enough by the disappointment and sorrow of life to have contemplated self-harm—open the time period wide enough and nearly all of us will have had such violent or nasty impulses sometimes. Yet very few of us ever act on them (and most of those who do are in jail). This is not due to mere habit, which is only too easily perturbed by the course of events. It is not because we are saints, or unusually thoughtful people. But nor is it just a matter of self-interest, the fear of getting caught. We do not do these things because we *cannot* do them. That 'cannot' is of course moral, not physical. No physical constraint stays our hand against our brother and sister. It is a constraint partly of sympathy and partly of conscience. It is our inchoate, practical recognition that to do such things is a terrible violation of something sacred: other human beings.[3] In submitting to this necessity we recognise one kind of absolute moral requirement: that there are certain ways we must not treat other people. So what is *most* indispensable is our robust sense that the evils listed above—murder, rape, etc.—are things we morally cannot do, that there is a certain minimal *piety* owed to other human beings *as* human beings that entails that these things cannot be done, that these things are outrageous violations of something sacred, precious, *inviolable*: human beings.

Most of the time we are blithely unaware of this moral necessity, which we automatically (usually with no sense of forbearance) abide by every moment of a civilised life. When it does come to consciousness, the reflective person may form the conception of this usually unconscious and inarticulate moral necessity, which can serve as the premise of the moral OA, a conception of something definitively indispensable from human life. There is nothing genuinely akin to this in the case of the attraction to the perfect Good. Murdoch often speaks of the ubiquity of value in her sense. Ubiquitous it may be (so is moral necessity) but indispensable it is not. As I have already said, many lives that we can take no great exception to are lived with barely a thought of ideals, let alone of the perfect ideal. The pursuit of them—also often unconscious—readily wanes and expires in a way that our unthinking adhesion to the moral necessities does not (or if it does, produces highly disturbing emotions). Other human beings and the largely unconscious moral force they exert upon us are a far more palpable presence in our lives that the Good.

We become aware of moral necessity on those occasions when it comes to the surface in temptation (and our conscience looms up to warn us) or, more dramatically, in violation—in those transgressions we commit against others (our lies, betrayals, evasions or worse, when shame, guilt and remorse consume us) or that we witness performed by others (occasioning our shock and indignation). And when it does come to the surface, at least in very serious cases like murder, the mark it leaves on nearly every life—or would leave if it happened—is profound and often unconsolable. I may know nothing of the importunate vagabond who, when I angrily shove him out of my way, falls in the river and drowns—but in my desolate remorse I know that his life was of absolute significance, and that the wrong I have done him is forgivable only by him and pardonable only by God. (That remorse is not the product of any attention to the vagabond. If anything it is the product of my *inattention* to him, and if I attend to him now, *it* is a product of the remorse. Or better, perhaps remorse is a *form* of attention—but what I attend to is the only too close *him*, not the remote Good.) Sometimes the Good breaks in dramatically upon a human life—in cases of encounter with great saintliness or beauty, as I have said—but for most of us the effect passes quickly, dissolved back into the busyness of life. Only for relatively rare people do (or would) such experiences make a lasting and deep difference: the priest or doctor called to a vocation of service, the artist to one of creating beauty. Admittedly Murdoch does talk of obedience and submission—but it is obedience to something at least akin to a calling, and failure to obey is not like failure to refrain from violation of others. Jesus said 'Be ye therefore perfect, even as your Father which is in heaven is perfect', but Christians do not treat failure at this, or even failure seriously to pursue it, the way they treat murder, rape, etc.

Moral necessities do not arise from cultivated attention to ideals, but from very basic inter-personal reactive attitudes (sympathy, remorse, indignation: partly innate, partly socialised) that are certainly definitive of human life in distinction from animal life. These attitudes are objects of reflection, but they do not begin from reflection, contemplation or attention. They rule our lives from a position usually beneath the surface. At moments of, and in lives inured in, inattention, they may burst to the surface, sudden, unbidden, unwelcome. They take us by the neck, and force us to attend—but what we attend to is not a good example or a distant ideal, but just the reality of the human being in front of us. Perhaps then we may turn our attention to ideals.[4]

I think we can see Murdoch's accent on the more peaceful aspect of moral life, and perhaps even a shying away from the more dramatic, in her criticism of Norman Malcolm. Malcolm was one of the first philosophers in the twentieth century to develop the second form of Anselm's original argument (Malcolm 1960). Murdoch criticises his reliance on Wittgenstein's notion of a language game, but I shall not address that here. She also takes him to task for suggesting the concept of God is critically conditioned by the experience of overwhelming guilt, and that from that 'storm in the soul' there arises 'the conception of a forgiving mercy that is limitless, beyond all measure' (qtd. in *MGM*, 416–417). Murdoch is right to push back against any suggestion that 'people who lead quiet orderly lives are less spiritual than those who are errant and tormented'. And equally right to suspect that sometimes a harping on sin betrays the histrionic thought that 'extreme sin *deserves* extreme grace' (*MGM*, 417, emphasis hers). I assume she would say similar things to the idea that Malcolm's guilt (if not his forgiveness) applies to morality as well as God. But she goes too far, I think, when she writes:

> if there is any sort of proof from experience via meaning, should not the relevant phenomena be, not esoteric, but of great generality? ... If the meaning of 'God'can be learnt from experience might we not expect the lesson to be everywhere visible? (417)

It may be true (as she says at *MGM*, 430) that many of our best lives are fairly ordinary, unspectacular examples, people whose lives lack dramatic highs and lows. But it remains essential to our moral nature that, as Wittgenstein remarked, we are capable (all of us) of damning ourselves. That possibility, the possibility of such highs and such lows, is a standing condition of our moral lives. How those of us with quiet, orderly lives *would* react *if* we murdered someone is an essential index of our moral humanity—it marks us off from the psychopath: unlike him, we *cannot* murder people. This is hardly esoteric. In truth, the most pedestrian of lives has something dark within it that the moral necessities protect it from.

It is true that the Christian teaching of original sin relates to a condition of 'fallen-ness' that encompasses all of our frailty, including our neglect of ideals, not only those occasions where we commit egregious violations of other people. But that does not mean that such violations do not hold a central place in the sense of sin—that sense (I take it to be the guilt to which Malcolm refers) would not be what it is, would not have the gravity it does, without the standing possibility, for all of us, of such violations, and of our responses to them of remorse, indignation, etc.: 'Cain rose up against Abel his brother, and slew him.' The sense of sin is intertwined with the sense of human life as sacred. Divine love and divine judgement are a package deal. Modern non-Christians do not speak of God or original sin, but we have not (or not yet) lost the responses of remorse and indignation that (together with love, grief and compassion) constitute our sense of human life as something uniquely precious (and that still ultimately animate the language of 'human rights').

III

The OA has always been associated with the notion of perfection, and that notion is of course at the centre of Murdoch's thought: the Good is a *perfect* Good. In that respect, her focus fits the OA. By contrast perfection seems to be lacking from the notion of absolute demand that I have argued should be front and centre in a moral OA. In this last section I want to sketch a sense of perfection suitable for my conception of absolute demand, and then relate it to Murdoch's perfect Good.

Murdoch's perfection of the Good is expressly a form of moral perfection, always remembering that this comprehends moral perception and wisdom, and not merely overt conduct. The notion of perfection I want here is very different. John Legend sings:

> Cause all of me
> Loves all of you
> Love your curves and all your edges
> All your perfect imperfections. (Legend and Gadd 2013)

All your *perfect imperfections*. Love can make the imperfect perfect. Not as a moral agent, or as a physical specimen, but as something infinitely precious, something the lover will give his very life for. Thus does the mother see her child, the lover their sweetheart. Here we are perfected by a love that is blind to the imperfections of body and character that usually dazzle us in our worldly preoccupations, where these things are what matter most. Of course those things are sometimes important (a threatening illness) but they cannot be the things that, in Christian language, 'save' us, i.e. save us from the risk of falling out of the human family, the family of those who are inviolable because they can (unlike an animal or an inanimate object) *be* violated.

In like way, when we recognise the inviolability of human beings in remorse or indignation or compassion we see them as perfect in the same sense. We see them as having a momentous importance (one making absolute moral demands on us) that owes nothing at all to the imperfections (or for that matter the perfections) of body, character, personality, etc. The disabled, the insane, the wicked, the wretched of the earth— we, brothers and sisters, are all sacred. Murdoch's version of the moral OA invites us to conceive of a perfect Good. If we form that conception properly, we can rest assured that we are conceiving of something real.

My version invites us to conceive of human beings as perfect in the sense of sacred. And when that conception is properly formed it too is a conception of something real.

Finally, there is of course a question about the dialectical utility of the OA. Murdoch's discussion of it notes Anselm's prayer in which he confesses to God that 'I do not seek to understand that I may believe, but I believe in order to understand', and she comments on the 'limitation upon the claims of the Proof' these words indicate (*MGM*, 392). The proof 'may be seen as a clarified or academic summary of what is already known, rather than as an argument to be put to an outsider. It may be seen too as a proof which a man can only give to himself' (*MGM*, 392). The argument moves from the proper concept of moral value to moral value being real, from thought to reality. But as we have seen, the success of that move depends upon the moral experience which forms our concepts. Someone with little or twisted experience will not have the proper concept and the argument will fail (they are not thinking of the right thing). So the persuasiveness of the argument depends crucially on the maturity of a person's moral conceptions. The argument is impotent to move a psychopath. It is only a person already in some degree sensitive to moral value—to the extent they have formed mature concepts—to whom the argument will appeal. To appreciate the force of the argument is to feel the demands of morality and the attraction of the Good. But to form mature concepts seems to require (normally at least) some belief in them—a real (non-philosophical) sceptic will just give up too early. And that seems to mean that a person with mature concepts already accepts the conclusion of the argument, at least for some part of morals.

Should we say then that the argument is futile for those who do not already accept the conclusion, and superfluous for those who do? That is too stark. In-between are people tempted by a kind of moral amnesia; tempted to forget or betray what in their heart they know; tempted to lose faith in the argument's thesis, and the promise of moral experience, that 'the "object" of our best thoughts, must be something real ... something fundamental, essential and necessary' (*MGM*, 430). I like to think this is the fool (all of us, sometimes) whom Anselm had in mind when he originated his famous argument. The argument may not ratiocinatively convince—box us into a corner with logic—but it may recall us to our senses, remind us of what we know (Murdoch's allusions to the *Meno*) and of the importance of not loosening our grasp of it, not even when we are offered all the powers of this world. Murdoch may adapt

Anselm's use of the Fourteenth Psalm: 'The fool hath said in his heart, There is no Good' (Anselm 1968, 3).

What stirs inside us at that rebuke? What awakens in our heart? Murdoch says it is the Platonic Eros, not the Good but 'a spirit which moves toward good' (*MGM*, 428), a 'spiritual energy, desire, intellect, love' (*MGM*, 496). Could this be the love that Weil speaks of when she says that the OA is addressed to love? The argument recalls us to direct our loving attention to what is good. And that includes what is sacred, inviolable, what is, in my sense, perfect. 'We *know* of perfection as we look upon what is imperfect' (*MGM*, 427, emphasis hers). But perhaps sometimes, when we look into a human face, we look directly upon what is perfect.

Acknowledgements I am grateful for earlier comments on this paper by Nora Hämäläinen, and to discussions with David Cockburn and Christopher Cordner.

NOTES

1. For a perceptive discussion of this ambition see Mulhall (2007).
2. Maria Antonaccio identifies one of Murdoch's great contributions to moral philosophy in the twentieth century as 'the expansion of the domain of ethics beyond the confines of obligatory action' (Antonaccio 2007, 15). Antonaccio is right and it was a mighty contribution. Nevertheless this paper suggests she tilted things too far in her own distinctive direction. It is important to remember though that the notion of interhuman moral demands that I put at the centre of my argument is very different in a number of ways from the standard philosophical understanding of obligation. For instance, it does not rest on familiar naturalistic assumptions. The rejection of naturalism is one among many things I have learned from Murdoch (and others).
3. The impossibility is not, I think, a literal one (if I do A, then it was not true that I morally could not do A). I take it to mean something roughly like this: if I were to do that, I would suffer a life-blighting remorse (so that if I do it, then it can still be true that it was morally impossible for me): 'Oh, my God! What have I done?' For a classic discussion of moral necessity (sometimes called moral incapacity or impossibility) see Williams (1993).
4. Murdoch does sometimes mention Kant's categorical imperative (e.g. *MGM*, 406, 412) and this might be taken as adverting to his stern sense of duty, and thus to the moral necessities I have stressed. But in fact she tends to treat the categorical imperative as Kant's substitute for the Good. It is to occupy the same distant and ideal place.

REFERENCES

Antonaccio, M. 2007. Reconsidering Iris Murdoch's moral philosophy and theology. In *Iris Murdoch: A reassessment*, ed. Anne Rowe, 15–22. Houndmills and Basingstoke: Palgrave Macmillan.

Legend, J., and T. Gadd. 2013. All of me [song]. Online. YouTube https://www.youtube.com/watch?v=450p7goxZqg.

Malcolm, N. 1960. Anselm's ontological arguments. *Philosophical Review* 69 (1): 41–62.

Mulhall, S. 2007. 'All the world must be "religious"': Iris Murdoch's ontological arguments. In *Iris Murdoch: A reassessment*, ed. Anne Rowe, 23–34. Houndmills and Basingstoke: Palgrave Macmillan.

Murdoch, I. 1992. *Metaphysics as a guide to morals* (Abbreviated *MGM*). London: Chatto & Windus.

Murdoch, I. 1996. *The sovereignty of good*. London: Routledge.

St. Anselm. 1968. St. Anselm's ontological argument. In *The ontological argument: From St. Anselm to contemporary philosophers*, ed. Alvin Plantinga, 3–30. London: Macmillan.

Williams, B. 1993. Moral incapacity. *Proceedings of the Aristotelian Society*. New Series, 93: 59–70.

CHAPTER 14

Vision and Encounter in Moral Thinking (*MGM* Chapter 15)

Christopher Cordner

The relation of religion and God to morals was a recurring concern of Iris Murdoch's. In an early essay she wrote:

> I shall suggest that God was (or is) a *single transcendent perfect non-representable and necessarily real object of attention*; and I shall go on to suggest that moral philosophy should attempt to retain a central concept which has all these characteristics. (Murdoch 1997, 344, italics hers)

This 'central concept' is indebted to Plato's Form of the Good. In *Metaphysics as a Guide to Morals* (henceforth *MGM*) Murdoch remained committed to replacing a traditional idea of God with a roughly Platonic idea of Good:

> Morality and demythologised religion are concerned with what is absolute, with unconditioned structure, with what cannot be 'thought away' out of human life, what Plato expressed in the concept of the Form of the Good, and Kant in the categorical imperative. What is in question

C. Cordner (✉)
University of Melbourne, Melbourne, VIC, Australia

© The Author(s) 2019
N. Hämäläinen and G. Dooley (eds.),
Reading Iris Murdoch's Metaphysics as a Guide to Morals,
https://doi.org/10.1007/978-3-030-18967-9_14

here is something unique, of which the traditional idea of God was an image or metaphor, and to which it has certainly been an effective pointer. (*MGM*, 412)

As she also puts it a little later: 'This "Good" is not the old God in disguise, but rather what the old God symbolized' (*MGM*, 428).

In Chapter 15 of *MGM*, Murdoch's concern with how god and religion relate to morals is brought to bear on Buber's conception of God. (That concern also brings into play a second theme of the chapter, which I will indicate in a moment.) Murdoch sees Buber as presaging a revival of what she calls a traditional idea of God. She says that his conception of God as the eternal Thou is just 'the old father God in disguise'. So, in critiquing this conception she is helping to spell out her reasons for rejecting 'the old God'.[1] Does Murdoch think *anything* of God might survive this rejection? She briefly ponders what 'the demythologisation of religion'—'something absolutely necessary in this age' (*MGM*, 460)— might have to offer here. She moots various ways in which demythologised religion might take shape. One would be 'the transformation of Christianity into a religion *like* Buddhism, with no God and no literally divine Christ, but with a mystical Christ', though she adds that this 'may be, if possible at all, a long task' (*MGM*, 458). But she does not develop this hint, or any other suggestion along these lines. Her view seems to be that anything offered by demythologised religion could amount to little more than an imaginative spur to our acknowledging and responding to the unconditional authority of morals.

Buber's key idea is that the fundamental moral relation is an I-Thou[2] relation (Buber 1970). He contrasts the two 'word pairs' I-Thou and I-It, holding these to constitute the two fundamental human orientations to reality. Buber says: 'When I confront a human being as my Thou and speak the basic word I-Thou to him, then he is no thing among things nor does he consist of things' (Buber 1970, 59). The I-Thou relation is enacted between human beings, but it is also ultimately realised in the meeting between a human being and God, where God is the Person whose loving presence we can encounter with certainty in meditation and prayer. Buber speaks of God as 'the eternal Thou' and says that 'in religious reality ... unlimited Being becomes, as absolute person my partner' (Buber 1953, 45). One theme of Murdoch's chapter on Buber is her explanation of why 'I do not believe in Buber's I-Thou God, or in his fundamental key idea of dialogue' (*MGM*, 464).

Before sketching that explanation, let me identify the second theme of Murdoch's chapter. It is introduced at the chapter's start, even before any mention of God:

> Like Heidegger, [Buber] thinks of Plato as having made a mistake, the substitution of *eidos* for *phusis* as the basis of metaphysics, of visible form for natural growth, of vision for movement or flow. I quote here a passage where Buber tells us that, influenced by Plato, European philosophy has tended to picture spirituality as looking upward, rather than as a movement or making of contact here below. 'The Greeks established the hegemony of sight over the other senses, making the optical world into *the* world, into which the data of the other senses are now to be entered.' They also gave an optical character to philosophy, 'the character of the contemplation of particular objects ... The object of this visual thought is the universal as existence or as a reality higher than existence. Philosophy is grounded on the presupposition that one sees the absolute in universals' (Buber 1953, 56). As I have argued in other contexts, the view expressed in the last two sentences represents a misunderstanding of Plato's doctrine.[3] (*MGM*, 461)

Murdoch's second theme concerns her reasons for rejecting Buber's critique of the 'hegemony of sight over the other senses' first in Greek thinking and then in western philosophy and thought thereafter. Murdoch ascribes to Buber the view that this 'hegemony' mistakenly makes 'the optical world into *the* world'. While she thinks Buber mischaracterises 'Plato's doctrine', Murdoch does not dispute its emphasis on vision, an emphasis she herself shares: 'The activity and imagery of vision is at the centre of human consciousness' (*MGM*, 461). Murdoch defends 'visual metaphysics' against Buber's criticisms of it, and rejects his partly Jewish- influenced alternative to such a metaphysics.

Murdoch evidently takes the two themes of her reflections on Buber—her critique of Buber's I-Thou God and her rejection of Buber's alternatives to 'visual' metaphysics—to be intertwined. But their links need some teasing out. We can get clearer about them by first sketching Murdoch's reasons for rejecting Buber's I-Thou God.

She seems to have two reasons. One of them might be called metaphysical. Murdoch refers approvingly to Kant as thinking that 'any God we could meet or see would be a demon, a mere idol' (*MGM*, 441). A God who could be met or seen would *ipso facto* be within our world and so would lack the absolute transcendence of God. Here Murdoch moots a sort of reverse-ontological argument: 'Any existing God would be less than God. An existent God would be an Idol or a Demon ... God does not and cannot exist' (*MGM*, 508). The very idea of God's absolute transcendence makes impossible his real existence. (Why does the same not apply to 'the Good', whose transcendent reality Murdoch, along with Plato, insists upon? Because the reality of the Good is the reality of an Idea not of a Person.)[4]

Murdoch's second reason for rejecting Buber's I-Thou God is a moral one. About Kant she writes, again approvingly: 'Even looking at Christ can be dangerous, Kant tells us. ... The consoling, forgiving figure may weaken the moral fibre and serve as a substitute for moral will ... That way lies weakness and illegitimate consolation' (*MGM*, 441). She says something similar about Buber's God as eternal Thou:

> If in the darkness of prayer I meet a person may this not be myself in some disguise – and why not? I am indeed, to use Buber's terms, constantly a 'thou' to myself as well as an 'it' ... The *tutoiement* between me and myself can be various, and good or bad. (*MGM*, 468)

And again:

> Seen in a Kantian context, the I-Thou concept can seem (by contrast) thrilling and dramatic, readily compromised by various self-regarding consolations. It holds out a promise of experience and ever-available company. (*MGM*, 470)

These are two of several places in *MGM* where Murdoch emphasises the moral dangers of the *consolations* of religion. (She also speaks of the falsifying consolations of all but the very best art.)[5]

So, any conception of a personal God, a God who interacts with us, who can love us and forgive us and to whom we might pray, is necessarily an illusion. Such a God cannot exist. Moreover, by bringing God near to us, so to speak, the very idea of such a personal God carries the serious danger of our immersing ourselves in 'various self-regarding consolations', which will disable us from properly attending and responding to morality's absolute demands upon us.

It is this moral reason Murdoch gives for resisting 'traditional' ideas of God—including Buber's version of the idea—that constitutes the link to the second theme of her reflections on Buber: her defence of Platonic 'vision metaphysics' against Buber's criticisms of it and his alternative to it. The link is indicated in her referring (in two passages I quoted earlier) to

> what Plato expressed in the concept of the Form of the Good, and Kant in the categorical imperative. What is in question here is something unique, of which the traditional idea of God was an image or metaphor, and to which it has certainly been an effective pointer. (*MGM*, 412)

> This 'Good' is not the old God in disguise, but rather what the old God symbolised (*MGM*, 428).

Although 'God does not and cannot exist ... what led us to conceive of him does exist and is *constantly* experienced and pictured' (*MGM*, 508). And what is thus 'constantly experienced and pictured' is the absolute, unshakeable, necessarily compelling reality of the Good, similarly thematised by Plato and Kant.

Our orientation to this reality is for all-too-human everyday reasons constantly assailed. Murdoch thinks that the centrality of 'the activity and imagery of vision' in human existence helps sustain in us an appreciation of the absolute beyondness of the Good, of the Good's being a reality distant and apart from us. By contrast, Buberian imagery of hearing—as also the imagery of touch, of encounter, of dialogue—blurs or compromises that appreciation.

In this context, it is Murdoch's defence of the centrality of vision, along with her criticisms of Buber-type objections to it, that I want to explore from here on.[6] The views Murdoch develops in this connection are articulated in self-conscious emulation of Plato. (In this respect there is direct continuity with her earlier work.) Here is Murdoch near the beginning of her chapter on Buber:

> The activity and imagery of vision is at the centre of human existence, wherein we are conscious of ourselves as both inward and outward, distanced and surrounded ... The visual is an image of distance and non-possession. This idea of space and quietness, thinking, seeing, attending, keeping still, not seizing, is important in all education ... Reflection, reverence, respect ... Seeing is essentially separate from touching, and should enlighten and inspire appropriate movement. There are proper times for looking, and, after looking, for touching. Speaking of morality in terms of cognition, the imagery of vision, which is everywhere in our speech, seems natural. Sight is the dominant sense, our world, source of deep imagery,

is a visual world ... We speak of the veil of appearance. We know when we are being satisfied with superficial, illusory, lying pictures which distort and conceal reality ... By looking at something, by *stopping* to look at it, we do not selfishly appropriate it, we understand it and let it be ... Looking can be a kind of intelligent reverence. Moral thinking, serious thinking, is clarification (visual image). The good, just, man is lucid. (*MGM*, 461–462)

This Murdochian *credo* about the visual is my main text for commentary in what follows. We can begin by agreeing with Murdoch that 'in terms of cognition' the 'imagery of vision ... is everywhere in our speech'. We say 'I see', meaning 'I understand, I get it'; we 'look into' something we want to know about; we 'get a better perspective' on some situation, or a 'clearer view' of it; we are 'blinded' by anger or selfishness; we 'focus' our attention on the matter; we 'overlook' an important detail; and so on and so on.

But not only is such vision imagery pervasive in our speech and life. Murdoch believes it is also profoundly *morally* important. In the passage above, she describes various ways in which she sees this imagery helping sustain our orientation to the (absolute and transcendent) Good: 'The visual is an image of distance and non-possession ... By looking at something, by *stopping* to look at it, we do not selfishly appropriate it, we understand it and let it be'; and so on.

Relatedly, the visual imports ideas of continual improvement, even perfectibility: clarity, lucidity, refinement, sharpness, increased detail and 'resolution' of vision, the possibility of ever-renewed attention and effort in our continuing attempts to understand the world, ourselves, and other people. The 'dominant metaphor' of vision in western cultural history is thus linked with the cultural emergence of a highly refined conception of truth as at once difficult, elusive and inescapably important.

Another related point—only hinted at here, but made explicitly in Murdoch's earlier work—is that we often see more than we can articulate: 'Where virtue is concerned we often apprehend more than we clearly understand and *grow by looking*' (Murdoch 1997, 324). That very gap between vision and articulation can then itself press us towards further and better articulation. This thought is compatible with holding, as indeed was held by Plato from whom Murdoch draws these ideas, that the 'highest' *cannot* be articulated but only 'seen', with the eye of the soul.

Let these merits and fruits of visual imagery be granted. Still I think they do not justify Murdoch's privileging of the visual. First of all, they do not show that images drawing on other sensory modes are either misleading or unnecessary. Perhaps we can also greatly benefit from, and perhaps we *need*, images from various such modes. Perhaps confining ourselves to vision imagery seriously limits us 'in terms of cognition', leading us to miss other important ways of making sense of our world and ourselves. I shall come back to suggest that this is indeed so.

Secondly, some of the terms in which Murdoch characterises those merits and fruits of visual imagery are already tendentious. She says that the visual *is* an image of distance and non-possession, and so of letting things be, and letting us appreciate them in their own right, without our 'reaching out to grasp and appropriate them' (*MGM*, 463). Well, the visual *can* be such an image, and looking *can* be 'a kind of intelligent reverence'. But these things are not necessarily so. Looking ('the visual') can also be lustful, or coldly objectifying, or possessive, or envious, or aggressive and hateful—'if looks could kill!' Moreover, even when the visual *is* an image of distance and non-possession, this need not import or even suggest 'reflection, reverence, respect'. Recognition of distance (from) and non-possession of something or someone can be manifested in attitudes of casual disregard, not caring, inhuman detachment, or even readiness to ride roughshod over it or her.

Within a sense of the possibilities just mentioned, a Judaic concern about *idolatry* of the visual image can find its place. The Judaic prohibition on images reflecting just this concern evidently plays a role in Buber's resistance to the 'hegemony of sight' in Greek thought. Murdoch mentions the prohibition:

> The deep Judaeo-Christian idea that God is essentially invisible is in tension with the natural ubiquity of the visual image. Is vision discredited because of the Second Commandment? 'No images' means no visible or visual images. Looking at something we may turn it to stone – or be turned to stone ourselves. (*MGM*, 463)

But Murdoch seems to mention this possibility only to ignore it. She appears to regard her own question as merely rhetorical: i.e. she takes it that the moral credit of visual images is *not* cancelled by the possibility of their being used idolatrously. If so, I would agree with her. But then why not grant similar licence to images in other sensory modes? Murdoch dwells on the dangers of ideas of (non-visual) encounter with God: 'If in the darkness of prayer I meet a person may this not be myself in some disguise'; 'the I-Thou concept can be seen as (by contrast) thrilling and dramatic, readily compromised by various self-regarding consolations'. These are indeed real dangers attached to the use of images of encounter, 'meeting', speaking and hearing. But why should these dangers of abuse be taken, as Murdoch seems clear to take them, as immediately morally discrediting the images of hearing and encounter themselves in comparison with images of vision, when the danger of idolatry of visual images is not taken to discredit visual imagery itself? Why is the danger of (say) mistaking for God's voice what is only a projection of my own voice (or of my society's) inherently more problematic than the danger of idolatrous worship of visual images? It is not easy to see what is meant to warrant Murdoch's different responses here.

It is instructive here to ponder this passage from Murdoch's chapter:

> acting rightly toward another person does not necessarily, in fact more often does not, involve face-to-face encounters. There is here a contrast of styles which can be comprehensively illustrated in everyday terms. One man does good by stealth, attends carefully to the situation of others, sees their needs, helps them without close involvement, even anonymously, admonishes indirectly, by implication and example, shuns close encounter. Only in rare situations would it be a duty, or indeed possible, to achieve complete mutual understanding. Another man prefers to draw people close to him, to have confessions, frank meetings, warmth and friendship, to give support by voice and presence. No doubt the afflicted human race needs both of these philanthropists. There is an essential area of coldness in morality, as there is an essential area of warmth. Seen in a Kantian context, the I-Thou concept can seem (by contrast) thrilling and dramatic, readily compromised by various self-regarding consolations. It holds out a promise of experience and ever-available company. (*MGM*, 470)

On the face of it this passage seems aimed at doing justice to the 'contrast of styles' between a Kantian/Platonic conception of ethics and a Buberian conception. But the appearance is deceptive, in several ways. First, the suggestion that it is always optional, a matter merely of moral 'style', whether one does good anonymously or not, is surely mistaken. *Sometimes* it may be optional, but very often the moral requirements of the situation will settle the matter: 'She needs to know that it was *Bill* who helped her!'; 'I can't help him properly without finding out from him how he sees the situation.' Secondly, Murdoch writes as if the only alternative to doing good anonymously is to prefer to 'draw people close to' oneself, to 'have confessions' and 'warmth'. But why should recognition of the importance, sometimes, of speaking face-to-face, or of 'being there' for someone, require the sticky *schwärmerei* suggested by these terms of Murdoch's? One can recognise and act on the need to 'be there' for someone, or the need to listen and respond to someone, without seeking to draw them close, or to have confessions, or even to be 'warm'. What is needed may instead be dispassionate candour, or vigorous firmness, or a cool, respectful steadiness of response. In these and many other possible ways, appreciation of the kind of presence to another that is morally needed can require one precisely to *avoid* going for warmth, or doing what is naturally suggested by the phrase 'drawing the other close' to one. Even if encounter necessarily involves *some* kind of closeness, this might avoid 'coldness' not by being warm but instead by being (say) gentle but firm.

Why, also, should it be supposed that responding non-anonymously to another on some occasion is morally permissible only if 'complete mutual understanding' can be achieved? Why not just a *serious attempt* to understand, in the respect relevant to what is at issue, by speaking honestly with another?

Moreover, no doubt the 'I-Thou concept'—which seems to be what Murdoch takes herself to be illustrating with these references—*is* *sometimes* 'applied' or enacted in a 'thrilling and dramatic' way, and/or 'compromised by various self-regarding consolations' and/or regarded as 'holding out a promise of experience and ever-available company'. But I see no reason to suppose that someone who recognises and responds to the moral need for an encounter with another *must thereby* embroil himself in such cosily self-regarding delusions.

There may be specific moral dangers attendant on 'encounter' that are absent from anonymous helping—and different specific dangers for different sorts of encounter and with different people. But so there will be specific moral dangers attendant on helping people by stealth or anonymously too—to mention just one example, the danger of a self-congratulatory pleasure at the very thought of one's moral purity in doing the thing anonymously! *Any* mode of response carries attendant dangers and risks; and the risks have to be faced and negotiated in the course of enacting the response the situation calls for.

Here it is worth noting a shift in the context of Murdoch's reflections on vision, between her earlier philosophy and *MGM*. In several of those justly celebrated early essays, the contrast was between vision, on the one hand, and 'movement of the will' on the other. There the point of invoking vision was to emphasise moral insight, knowledge, understanding, registering of the reality of the Good, by contrast with movement of the will—deciding, choosing, acting. There was no need, in the context of *that* contrast, to emphasise vision over (say) hearing or indeed various other possible ways or modes of 'morally knowing'. And there was no attempt there to privilege images of vision over those of hearing or touch or encounter by reference to formal qualities of visual images—for example that they were uniquely well-fitted for enshrining 'distance' and 'non-possession'. 'Looking' was used as a neutral term while 'attention' was reserved for 'just and loving' looking. Moreover, in that connection neither looking nor attending needed to be distinctly visual.

In the context of that governing contrast between vision and choice/will, 'looking' was being used in the already-extended everyday sense which *also* ranges over understanding via hearing, touch, encounter and so on. Attention can just as readily be manifested in someone's being 'all ears', for example—in her *listening* well—as in her looking better or more closely. Nothing in the context of Murdoch's invoking of vision, by contrast with movement of the will, was at odds with her recognising this.[7] In the strand of *MGM* we are here concerned with, though, the emphasis on vision is no longer contrasted with an emphasis on movement (choosing, deciding, acting). The contrast now is of the visual, on the one hand, with hearing, encounter, dialogue, touch (and so on), on the other.[8] (So criticisms of Murdoch's privileging of vision in the present connection do not undermine her earlier critique of 'the movement picture'.)

Here are some reflections aimed at bringing out something of what is missed by side-lining imagery of touch and holding, specifically, or even by just *subordinating* these to the visual. About touching and its relation to seeing, Murdoch writes: 'Seeing is essentially separate from touching, and should enlighten and inspire appropriate movement. There are proper times for looking, and, after looking, for touching.' I wonder what any mother of an infant would make of these remarks? Should her touching and holding her child really *always* be 'enlightened and inspired' by a prior seeing that will make her touching and holding 'appropriate'? Well, sometimes a 'looking' might play that role—perhaps her baby looks pale and she picks it up. But as a perfectly general claim what Murdoch says is surely off-beam. Mother *hears* the baby cry, perhaps in hunger or discomfort; she *smells* the dirty nappy; she *feels* the baby is hot, or restless. More generally, touching—and more importantly *holding*—is the most fundamental way she relates to her baby, and is utterly crucial to any infant's normal and healthy development. A blind woman who can 'hold' (and smell and feel and hear) can mother, care for and love her child perfectly well. By contrast, a mother who can see but not touch or hold *cannot* do this. The child never touched or held would be very seriously deprived, and likely to become depraved.

But even if Murdoch's view does implicitly relegate touch and holding behind 'looking' in the context of maternal care of infants, this might be thought not to matter very much. 'Isn't that just one context after all?' I think that would be a mistaken response. Tenderness and gentleness have a much broader significance in expressions of love which can be fully recognised only if touching and holding are given their proper due. From her earliest work, Murdoch emphasised the importance of love in morals. She did so in self-conscious imitation of Plato, who himself spoke about love with no reference to tenderness or gentleness. The ascent of love in Plato's *Symposium* is an entirely visual business, from the merely *seen* beauty of individual bodies all the way up to the vision of the Forms. And in the *Phaedrus*, where *bodily* sensations and effects of loving are indeed spoken of, what is described is only the *perturbations* of the lover's body— its prickings, its giddiness and its agitations at the sight of the beloved. There is nothing at all about tender and gentle inflections of the body as modes of one person's lovingly attending to another, and about the giving and receiving of these as elemental in the living of many forms of loving human interaction. This large absence from Plato's reflections on love seems to be closely linked to the pre-eminence of the visual in his philosophical orientation. And that absence, along with its link to the emphasis on vision, is I think replicated in Murdoch's own work.[9]

Tenderness can take various forms, and be manifest in various ways. As well as maternal tenderness, there is tenderness to those who are ill, or in particular need of comfort or of holding, or to the elderly; and there is the distinctive tenderness—which can be vigorous and even rough—of sexual love. To be sure, tenderness does not always involve actual touch or physical holding. There can be tenderness in a tone of voice, and also in *written* language where we hear and *feel* it in what we read. And there can also be a tender looking, recognisable as such both by the one looked upon and also by a witness to the look. But still, the tenderness of a looking is revealed as a kind of visual caressing of its object, experienceable in just that way. The tenderness even of a look thus sustains a crucial link to 'touch' and holding, effecting a connection across the very 'distance' on which it depends. (There can be *gentleness* in these modes too.)

But, granting this extending of tenderness into look and voice, tenderness of *actual* physical touch and holding remains a crucial dimension of human loving responsiveness. As such it is a mode of encounter, of one person's immediate presentness to another, a kind of active receptiveness to another. Murdoch's championing of the visual as acknowledgement of distance, non-contact, non-possession, letting-be, I think fails to engage with, or to make any conceptual-moral space for, the kinds of encounter realised through such tenderness. And with what warrant? Apparently nothing better than that when people touch there is a risk they might seize and appropriate what they touch, or perhaps indulge sentimentally in the contact. Again, that *might* happen, but as noted earlier this says no more than that *any* form of human acknowledgement and response has correlative risks and dangers attendant upon it. And when tenderness is actually manifest, that specific danger has *in fact* not materialised.

To recapitulate: tenderness of loving responsive touch informs the very ways in which we are brought into the human world, and helped to become fully human denizens of that world through being touched and held as infants. But tenderness then also continues to be important in our further living and loving relations with others, along the lines I've just been sketching. To the extent that this is so, Murdoch's emphasis on vision as capturing what is most important in our orientation as moral beings already seems flawed.[10] For tenderness brings into play touch, holding, encounter, and contact effected through receptiveness. 'Non-possession'?, yes; 'non-appropriation'?, yes; but spatial distance drops out as irrelevant to those things in this context (except perhaps in the specific case of a tender look).

My critical comments so far have mainly aimed to bring out some ways in which Murdoch's privileging of vision distracts from appreciation of the moral importance of hearing, touch, holding and encounter. I move now to a thought in a rather different register. I noted earlier that Murdoch moves from the visual as an image of distance and non-possession to the visual as the site, of 'reflection, reverence, respect', apparently without appreciating the size of this step. I think the visual *can* be a site of reflection, reverence, respect, but that we cannot make sense of its being so if we conceive of the visual *in opposition* to the other senses, and more broadly to our embodied encounter with the world, as Murdoch seems to do. Let me explain.

Murdoch quotes Buber approvingly: 'without the truth of the encounter all images are illusion', and 'Faith is not a feeling in the soul of man but an entrance into reality, an entrance into the *whole* of reality' (*MGM*, 463–464). But her own invoking of the visual, specifically, as enabling that 'entrance', arguably fails by abstracting the visual from 'the truth of the encounter' in something very like the way Buber is here critiquing. A passage from R. G. Collingwood's *The Principles of Art* can help to bring out more clearly what I mean by this. Having discussed how the common assumption that painting is a visual art was manifested, indeed celebrated, in nineteenth-century impressionism, Collingwood continues:

> Then came Cézanne and began to paint like a blind man ... His landscapes have lost almost every trace of visuality. Trees never looked like that. That is how they feel to a man who encounters them with his eyes shut, blundering against them blindly. A bridge is a perplexing mixture of projections and recessions, over and round which we find ourselves feeling our way as one can imagine an infant feeling its way, when it has barely begin to crawl, among the nursery furniture. (Collingwood 1938, 144)[11]

Those paintings, Collingwood suggests, recapitulate the coming-to-be for us in early childhood of a coherently robust world, through the manifold inflexive interactions of our moving bodies with what we encounter. Though immediately addressed to our eyes, the paintings 're-mind' us that only against a background of our mobile, embodied encounter with a variously resistant world is there such a thing as *seeing* at all. To really see even rocks and trees, to see them as they really are, we have to see them as having their actual heft, density, solidity, their robust and impenetrable *thereness*. And to really see *that*, we have to be able to (so to speak) take it into our embodied selves through the imaginative bodily anticipations Collingwood describes. Only then is what we see given to us in its reality through our visual experience. Only then is the distance and separateness of what is seen, a distance and separateness of something genuinely and really existing—'standing out' or 'standing forth' in its own being.[12] The 'standing out' of a thing in its own reality in our seeing of it depends on that seeing of it being the imaginative re-enactment of that whole-of our-embodied-being encounter with it that

Collingwood describes. Putting it just slightly differently: the very reality of that which is given as 'at a distance' from us in visual experience, is realised by us only as a result of the embodied encounter that is imaginatively recapitulated in that visual experience.

And that the seeing of something is constituted *that* way is very inadequately reflected in Murdoch's talk of the visual as 'an image of distance and non-possession'. It is only against the background Collingwood describes that we can we make sense of images of vision as portending reverence and respect for things in their 'otherness'. Then their otherness as 'at a distance' is an otherness of things as existing—'ex-isting', 'standing forth'—in world-ordered co-dwelling with us as in-relation with them, in just those ways Collingwood describes Cézanne as reminding us of. But if this is so, then Murdoch's *opposing* of images of vision to those of encounter, on which her privileging of the former depends, is the result of a falsifying abstraction—the substitution of an image-that-is-illusion for 'the truth of the encounter'. For it is only as exemplifying the truth of the encounter that the visual image is indeed 'an entrance into reality'. One thing Collingwood helps us appreciate, I suggest, is that we can accept Buber's emphasis on the spiritual importance of encounter without having to dismiss the spiritual significance of vision. The visual *can* be a site of reflection, reverence, respect, but it can be so only because of the rootedness of seeing in our humanly embodied encounter with the world, and only so far as our own experience of seeing remains nourished by those roots.

Now I must be explicit about something I have so far not fully clarified. Grant that every I-Thou relation is one of reciprocity and dialogue, and therefore of *encounter* between I and Thou. The converse, though, does not hold. There are forms of encounter—forms of our genuine 'entrance into reality'—that do not involve reciprocity, or at least the reciprocity of *dialogue*. Murdoch points out that 'our relation with a foreign language which we are learning is not reciprocal' (*MGM*, 478): the language does not *address* me, enter into dialogue with me. It does not and cannot *attend to* me as I can attend to it. If I-Thou is a form of encounter involving reciprocity and dialogue, there are also forms that do *not* involve reciprocity and dialogue.[13] The learning of a language is of the latter kind.

This point both clarifies and strengthens resistance to Murdoch's critique of Buber. It helps bring out that there are so to speak two levels of critical response to Murdoch's defence of vision. There are broad objections to the exclusive privileging of vision-imagery, even in relation to forms of encounter that involve no I-Thou reciprocity and dialogue. And then along with those objections, there are *additional* objections to thinking visual imagery adequate to reflecting the moral character of I-Thou encounters as involving such reciprocity and dialogue. My discussion has developed objections at both levels. In now explicitly marking the two levels, I also note the importance of the fact, not made explicit in my discussion so far, that I-Thou encounters are always potentially sites of moral challenge by those who encounter one another, and of their being summoned to respond to, and to be ready to be changed by, such challenges. This (potentially deeply unsettling) character of I-Thou encounters—also a basic Levinasian theme—is utterly fundamental in our moral relations with others.[14] This is something which Murdoch—with her emphasis on the sustaining of 'distance and non-possession' as the key to due respect and reverence for reality, including the reality of other people—does not really engage with at all. Maintaining distance from another can per se just as well be a way of avoiding a morally important challenge of encounter with her as it can be morally commendable.

As I hope is clear, I have not said that visual imagery is itself inherently unsuited to orienting us to duly respectful responsiveness to reality's transcendence of us. That is not so. I have, though, opposed Murdoch's exclusive privileging of visual imagery in that connection; and I have also tried to bring out some aspects of what, along with Buber, I believe does lie beyond its reach. Perhaps one general lesson of my discussion is that we should beware placing 'theoretical' limits or restrictions on the kinds of image that can illuminate the variety of our ways of coming to make sense of, to understand and to relate truthfully and respectfully to the world wherein we dwell.

Acknowledgements   My thanks to Hugo Strandberg for helpful comments on an earlier draft.

Notes

1. Murdoch's talk of 'the old God', 'the old father God', a 'traditional' idea of God, is left unclarified.
2. The archaic 'Thou' translates Buber's 'Du', the 'intimate' German form of 'you'.

3. For some reason, Murdoch here omits the following sentence from the middle of the Buber passage she quotes: 'The history of Greek philosophy is that of an opticising of thought, fully clarified in Plato and perfected in Plotinus'.

4. I think Murdoch's line of thought here has problems; but as they are not my present concern I pass them by.

5. She says that 'the classical Greeks seem to have been incapable of romanticism and *a fortiori* of sentimentality' (*MGM*, 499); and she seems to take this fact to be connected with the absence of a personal God from their outlook.

6. The specific implications her criticisms have for Buber's conception of God as the eternal Thou I will not consider. Neither, for reasons of space, will I consider her critique of Buber's 'take' on Plato's *Timaeus*.

7. All the same, it is worth noting that the most celebrated example of looking and attending in Murdoch's early work—the example of M and D—has M 'looking again' at D in explicit abstraction from actual *encounter* with her. Even in that early work, Murdoch's emphasis on vision perhaps reflected some unease with the morally complicating effects of interaction and encounter between people. But the unease there remained mostly philosophically submerged.

8. What explains this shift to problematising the other senses? My speculative answer is that confrontation with Buber (and perhaps other philosophers of dialogue) challenged her either to acknowledge that her accent on vision simply bypassed too much that mattered, or to purify her privileging of vision. I also think that her opting for the latter path answered to tendencies already immanent in the earlier work—consider, for example, the isolating of M's reflections on D from any actual encounter with D that I mentioned in the preceding note.

9. This is more evident in *MGM* than in the earlier work, but—see the preceding two notes—it can also be glimpsed there.

10. As already noted, the flaw is not Murdoch's alone. Plato has a share in it, as I think Simone Weil—another strong influence on Murdoch—also does.

11. Collingwood here draws on, while he also extends, Bernard Berenson's celebrated discussion of 'tactile values' in Renaissance painting (Berenson 1896). Merleau-Ponty's brilliant essay, 'Cézanne's doubt' develops a similar theme, without reference to Collingwood (Merleau-Ponty 1964).

12. Henry Bugbee speaks in similar terms in likewise querying what he calls 'the dogma of the ultimacy of a merely *optical* mode of thought in the conception of manifest reality. What needs to be accommodated seems to be a kind of feeling of emergent definiteness, of the standing forth of the distinct thing. The thing that does not *touch us*, the merely "looked

at", the mere object, cannot be manifest reality basically understood. In the ancient Hebrew sense of the word—that with which there is not the intimacy of touch is not truly *"known"*. No intimacy: no revelation. No revelation: no true *givenness* of reality' (Bugbee 1999, 130).

13. Buber himself seems to blur this very contrast, when he says that even in our 'life with nature' the I-Thou relation can arise. He gives the example of real encounter with a tree: in that case, he says, 'the [I-Thou] relation vibrates in the dark and remains below language' (Buber 1970, 56–58). It is hard to know what to make philosophically of this poetic image. Moreover, if we ask *why* Buber insists on assimilating all forms of encounter to I-Thou, an answer is not easy to find.

14. This is not for a moment to deny that relations of love and tenderness with others are also thus fundamental.

References

Berenson, B. 1896. *The Florentine painters of the Renaissance*. New York and London: G.P. Putnam's Sons.

Buber, M. 1953. *Eclipse of God*. London: Victor Gollancz.

Buber, M. 1970. *I and Thou*. New York: Charles Scribner's Sons.

Bugbee, H. 1999. *The inward morning*. Athens, GA: University of Georgia Press.

Collingwood, R.G. 1938. *The principles of art*. London: Oxford University Press.

Merleau-Ponty, M. 1964. Cézanne's doubt. In *Sense and nonsense*. Evanston: Northwestern.

Murdoch, I. 1992. *Metaphysics as a guide to morals* (Abbreviated *MGM*). London: Chatto & Windus.

Murdoch, I. 1997. *Existentialists and mystics*. London: Chatto & Windus.

The Urge to Write: Of Murdoch on Plato's Demiurge

David Robjant

Murdoch first invokes the *Timaeus* Demiurge in *The fire and the sun: Why Plato banished the artists*, where he is 'Plato's portrait of the artist' (Murdoch 1997, 430). The *Timaeus* is also much returned to in *Metaphysics as a Guide to Morals* (henceforth *MGM*). There she offers that:

> Goodness is an idea, an ideal, *yet it is also evidently and actively incarnate all around us, charged with the love which the Demiurge feels for the eternal Forms as he creates the cosmos.* (*MGM*, 478, my italics)

Omitting the italicised, I once dodged a discussion of Murdoch on the *Timaeus* that is overdue. The debt is difficult because the *Timaeus* is difficult, but also because, as intimated, Murdoch has two strands of thought about it. On the one hand she thinks it a defence of Forms, and on the other hand she thinks it is an allegory on the inspiration and limitations of the artist, or creative literary writer. Arguing that the two strands get in each other's way, and that one is mistaken, I will defend and expand on 'Plato's portrait of the artist'.

D. Robjant (✉)
London, UK

© The Author(s) 2019
N. Hämäläinen and G. Dooley (eds.),
Reading Iris Murdoch's Metaphysics as a Guide to Morals,
https://doi.org/10.1007/978-3-030-18967-9_15

Bête Noire

Murdoch is mistaken to insert the Forms into the *Timaeus* in precisely the way she does. The context is disagreement with Gilbert Ryle, for whom Plato is 'an Odysseus rather than a Nestor' (Murdoch 1997, 448). Ryle's Odyssean *Plato's Progress* (1966) treats Plato as stuck on a rickety 'middle period' theory of forms exemplified by the *Republic*, but then escaping from this nonsense in a 'late period' journey to reasonableness, crucially represented by the *Parmenides*, but encompassing also, among other texts, the *Timaeus*. Murdoch's irritation with this reading may surprise no one, and is seen in her copy of Ryle's book, where, beside one characteristic bit of Rylean interpretative charity, she has scrawled, exasperatedly, 'Oh God!'.[1] Not sharing Ryle's antipathy to the Forms, Murdoch is keen to dispute his suggestion that Plato later abandoned them:

> The discovery of truth and reality, the conversion to virtue, is through the unimpeded vision of the transcendent Forms. At the same time, in his more logical metaphysical contexts, Plato criticizes and even attacks this picture, without however abandoning it; it reappears in a splendid mythological guise in the *Timaeus*, and evidently expresses something for which Plato cannot find any other formulation. (Murdoch 1997, 408)

Murdoch's suggestion that criticism could accompany continued commitment is fair. (Much would hang on how one fleshes that out—I have my guess.[2]) The trouble is that Murdoch hangs her argument with Ryle on a reading of the *Timaeus*, and perhaps motivates her reading of the *Timaeus* out of that argument.

Murdoch so emphasises the forms in her discussion of the *Timaeus* that she invites the innocent complaint: the forms are not named in this dialogue! Allusion however is made, and citing *Timaeus* 51 she is right to observe suggestive evidence of continued authorial interest in the forms: 'an argument for their existence is given in the most curtailed but essential version at 51d-e' (Murdoch 1997, 434). Timaeus observes that knowledge 'is always accompanied by a true account' (Plato 2008, 51e) and that 'if knowledge and true belief are two distinct kinds of thing, then these entities', the objects of knowledge 'absolutely do exist in themselves' (Plato 2008, 51d). But admitting this strength to her case, there are two drawbacks to Murdoch's general reliance on *Timaeus* 51–52. In preview: (1) 51–52 does not yield a conception congenial to Murdoch's project with Plato, and (2) given the role Murdoch wishes the forms to play in the work of the Demiurge it is not adequate textual support for her reading merely to show that Timaeus alluded to them. On the first trouble, recall that for Murdoch, the Good is

> not something obscure. We experience both the reality of perfection and its distance away … If we read [Plato's] images aright they are not only enlightening and profound but amount to a statement of a belief which most people unreflectively hold. (*MGM*, 508)

This 'not something obscure' has the flavour of the *Meno*, and 'experience' the smell of G. E. Moore intuiting the good, but those are not the affiliations of Timaeus:

> Is there such a thing as fire which is just itself? […] if knowledge and true opinion are two distinct kinds of thing, then these entities absolutely do exist in themselves, even though they are accessible only to our minds, not to our senses […] the former is the property of gods, but of scarcely any human beings, while the latter is something every man has. (Plato 2008, 51b–52b)[3]

Relocating the forms away from their home contexts in morals and geometry to this new pseudo-scientific context of the four elements, we are left with an idea of fire-by-itself which could never be elicited from a slave-boy. Fire *by itself* would be an oddity and Timaeus himself raises doubts at 49b. Here 'scarcely' anyone has access to the objects of knowledge. Indeed no-one. Murdoch, recognising the departure from the *Meno*, attributes the 'scarcely' to 'Plato's increasing pessimism about politics and human possibility' (*MGM*, 476). This does not much help. Murdoch's project with the form of the Good is at home with Socrates, not Timaeus. 'Plato's increasing pessimism', if that is what it is, hardly helps the thought that the Good is 'not something obscure', and here Murdoch's *anti-Ryle* Plato is scarcely coincident with Murdoch's *pro-Murdoch* Plato. 'It is always a significant question to ask about any philosopher what is he afraid of?' (*MGM*, 359). Murdoch is afraid of

Ryle's story about Plato rejecting the theory of forms, as well as irritated by it. 'Oh God!' indeed—but her reaction against this *bête noire* compromises her own preferred treatment of the Forms, and also her sensitivity to the *Timaeus*.

While we might perhaps conclude from 51 that the *Timaeus* does not take part in any *general repudiation of* 'middle period' epistemology, this is not in itself evidence that the forms play, in the myth of the Demiurge from 27 onward, precisely the role Murdoch attributes to them. Yes, the evidence of 51d–e might be used to support, if inconclusively, a view that Plato remained interested in *Republic* themes. What that evidence will not support, even inconclusively, are Murdoch's specific claims:

> The Demiurge in the *Timaeus*, creating the world, looks at and (in so far as his alien material will allow) copies the Forms. (*MGM*, 400)
> (Creation is) charged with the love which the Demiurge feels for the eternal Forms as he creates the cosmos. (*MGM*, 478)

This Murdoch gloss is not something that Timaeus himself offers about the Demiurge and his creation. Worse, it is not compatible with what he does say.

Timaeus says that the gods created us, and were in their turn created by another sort of god or craftsman, for which the Greek is δημιουργός or *dēmiourgos*, whence Demiurge (Plato 2008, 41a–c, 31a). The Demiurge in making the cosmos was copying a perfect 'eternal model' (Plato 2008, 29a, 37d, 38c) of the cosmos. Said model or 'exemplar' (Plato 2008, 39e) is then treated by Murdoch as a place-holder for 'the Forms'.

Of the stages of this identification, the most attractive is the idea that the forms and the model are alike in 'eternity'. But even this is difficult. What do we mean by 'eternity'? The forms are eternal in the sense that they exist now and yesterday and for *all time*—thus it is that things in time can participate in the good. For Timaeus however 'eternity' is sharply distinguished from 'all time' (Plato 2008, 38c), the distinction being that to be in time and in all time means persistence in a world where other things move, whereas 'eternity' is entirely elsewhere. The movements of the planets and stars in our universe together constitute time, because their movements are countable. This creates the problem of how moving time in the heavens can be supposed to be a 'moving likeness of eternity' (Plato 2008, 37d), given that the essence of eternity on Timaeus' conception is that it is separated from moving time (Plato 2008, 38c). What Timaeus says here is either confusing or confused or both, but the least we can say is that identification of the 'eternity' of the model with the 'eternity' of the forms is not straightforward. Resolve eternity as we may, a 'model' that is a complete solar system visible only to the Demiurge is still not the same sort of thing as a collection of universals or qualities or essences or, in the sense explored in the *Republic* and *Meno*, forms. It is rather a particular world of particular objects like our own, except available only to the Demiurge. The movements of our universe are not explained by appeal to impersonal reason but to the will of the Demiurge to faithfully copy what only he can see. The exact movements of *our* heavenly bodies 'exist in order that this universe of ours might, by imitating the eternity of the perfect (model) ... be as similar to it as possible' (Plato 2008, 39e). This is of course not explanation as such. It is just relocation of a mystery in our skies to mystery in the skies of the craftsman's eternal 'model'. Timaeus indeed breaks off the pretence of explanation:

> As for the other three planets, a thorough account of where and why he located them as he did would make this supposedly subordinate discussion longer and more troublesome than the main discussion it's meant to be serving. (Plato 2008, 38d)

But what main discussion is all this 'meant to be serving'?

As previewed, Murdoch has two thoughts here, and one is that the cosmology serves a mythological setting of the theory of forms (*MGM*, 408). I have so far put obstacles in the way of this story: (a) if Timaeus is talking about the forms he is not doing so in a way helpful to Murdoch, (b) citation of *Timaeus* 51 is not adequate support for 'The Demiurge ... looks at and (in so far as his alien material will allow) copies the Forms' (*MGM*, 400), (c) the supposed common point that the model and the forms are both 'eternal' is not as easy as it looks, and (d) it doesn't look as if the Demiurge's model is a quality or a universal. I want now to add (e), the grammar problem. What Murdoch is proposing (*MGM*, 400; 478) is to treat 'the Forms', plural, and the Demiurge's 'model', singular, as essentially two names for the same thing(s)—and in the dislocation of that bracketed plural is the rub. The forms are plural, and each is simple. The Demiurge's eternal model is explicitly singular, and its components are also complex particulars.

To go along with Murdoch's idea that the Demiurge copying the model, singular, *just is* his copying 'the Forms', plural, one would need to hear some story about how the Forms plural can together constitute a model cosmos, singular. A parallel story is alluded to by Timaeus, but only in order to dismiss it:

> People talk as if it were clear what fire and so on are and take them to be principles and letters, so to speak, of the universe, when in fact they shouldn't even be compared to syllables. Only someone of slight intelligence is likely to make such a comparison. (Plato 2008, 48b)

This might be an allusion to the 'dream' theory rejected at *Theaetetus* 201–202. There the 'elements' were unknowable and only the complexes knowable, which is an inversion of what Timaeus is tempted to say, at 51, about Fire as an object of knowledge. *How* to reconcile the model with the forms is not directly confronted in Murdoch's account. Murdoch instead treats the trouble as already surmounted by her invocation of the mythological 'as if'. It is for her *as if* the model were the forms, and *as if* the Demiurge in 'creating the world, looks at and ... copies the Forms' (*MGM*, 400). Indeed Plato's stories are mythological as-ifs, but this is not of itself licence to gloss them as suits struggle with Ryle.

REMEMBER THE *REPUBLIC*?

Socrates, silent for the most of the dialogue, opens the *Timaeus* with a wry pretended summary of the 'main points' (Plato 2008, 19a) covered in last night's conversation, the *Republic*. 'And what about procreation? Not that we could easily forget what was said on this topic, since it was so unusual'. 'Yes', says Timaeus. 'There's no difficulty remembering *that*'. Socrates then asks if he has left anything out, 'anything missing, anything we still need to recall?' Well, yes. There is nothing in the summary of Socrates' central and ambiguous confrontation with Thrasymachus; nothing of the complications of Socratic commitment around Glaucon's much teased demand for luxury; nothing of the myth of the cave; nothing whatsoever of the copious extended reflections on literature and art; nothing on the place of 'poetry'; in short, not a whit of Murdoch's main topics in the *Republic*. Have we forgotten something from our summary of the *Republic*? Timaeus, ludicrously: 'No, that was *exactly* how the conversation went, Socrates' (Plato 2008, 18c–19b, *my italics*). To which absurdity Socrates reacts with a proposal that takes us straight back to the most prominent unsummarised theme of the *Republic*: the uses and dangers of literature.

What would be fun would be to hear some sort of epic story of this tripartite city 'contending against others in typical inter-city contests' (Plato 2008, 19c), he says. On his conceit, the yearning for such a story is intensified by the fact that he, Socrates, wouldn't be able to offer such a fiction, and, moreover, neither would the poets be capable of such a thing, because 'none of them finds it easy to reproduce on stage anything that falls outside his experience' (Plato 2008, 19d). Socrates is recalling *Republic* 604e:

> Now, although the petulant part of us is rich in a variety of representable possibilities, the intelligent and calm side of our characters is pretty well constant and unchanging. This makes it not only difficult to represent, but also difficult to understand when represented, particularly when the audience is the kind of motley crowd you find crammed into a theatre, because they are simply not acquainted with the experience that's being represented to them. (Plato 1998, 604e)

Murdoch comments: 'Goodness, being lucid and quiet and calm, cannot be expressed or represented in art' (*MGM*, 12). Which is as much as to suggest that if the tripartite city of the Republic could be successfully represented in epic narrative, this would serve as a proof that it was not, in fact, good.

Socrates' ironic allusions to the literary concerns of the *Republic* at *Timaeus* 19 are as lost on Timaeus as they are on Critias, who suggests that by offering up the Republic in narrative epic he is about to help Socrates secure and illustrate the nobility of the tripartite state (Plato 2008, 20c), rather than, as *Republic* 604 would tend to suggest, undermine it. The speech he then gives is *funny*. I will paraphrase for effect— the effect of condensing and exhibiting what Critias actually says—but the original is no less amusing. *Well Socrates, you may think that you were describing something fanciful in last night's conversation (The Republic) (Plato 2008, 25e, 26c), but Athens was once exactly like the tripartite city you were talking about (Plato 2008, 25e, 26d), 9000 years ago (Plato 2008, 23e), when we went to war with an empire from the west which was based on a big island in the Atlantic (Plato 2008, 24e), which sank*

(Plato 2008, *25d). I have all this on the best authority because the story was told to the great Solon by some Egyptian priests (Plato* 2008, *22a), according to my grandfather, who got it from his dad, who was a friend of Solon – as everyone knows (Plato* 2008, *20e). I admit I didn't remember too well what my grandfather actually said about all this (Plato* 2008, *26a), but thinking of entertaining you I spent the whole of yesterday perfecting my tale about it (Plato* 2008, *26b, 26c), because speeches are the important thing at festivals, like my grandfather's recitation contests (Plato* 2008, *21b). It's all true as well (Plato* 2008, *20d), and I hope you like it.* He then adds: *But maybe the best place to start this whole story would be with the origin of the universe (Plato* 2008, *27a). So first we have an expert in astronomy, Timaeus – he's going to go first tonight, and explain for your pleasure everything that happened before Athens fighting Atlantis. After all that the panel can judge our two stories together, at the end, if that's OK (Plato* 2008, *27b).* Critias' riotous ramble makes a unity of texts until recently presented as separate: the *Timaeus,* dominated by Timaeus' speech, and the *Critias,* dominated by Critias' tale of Atlantis, previewed here at *Timaeus* 20e–27b. The two speeches are set up in dialogue, as the sort of story-telling inspired in Socrates' audience by their defective reception and selective memory of the *Republic.* Both pick up from themes of the *Republic* as they have remembered them, and both see themselves as helping Socrates' *Republic* discussion along in their own stories, despite both generally failing to spot his irony about their memory of that conversation. The evening is advertised as a double bill festival extravaganza, and with perfect continuity between the two (the opening to the *Critias* is Timaeus announcing his relief at finishing his speech in the *Timaeus*) there would be no difficulty in presenting them as a single dialogue, the *Timaeus-Critias* (as Robin Waterfield's OUP translation all but does).

Focus on the dramatic unity of a creation myth with a quixotically introduced tale about a sinking island, as told to great-grandfather's friend, as far as one can remember. Are we, in fact, so far from Cervantes? Exhibition of Critias having raised a smile, Timaeus then gives his history of creation from the planets to the intestine by way of the Gods and the four elements, Earth, Air, Fire and Water. Lest we think that in such expert cosmology we have left behind the playful teasing of the audience evident in Plato's characterisation of Critias, Timaeus confides along the way various homely absurdities. He says that exercise is the best medicine, that the creator god considered giving the universe legs and arms but decided not to for lack of anything for it to stand on, that for similar reasons the universe does not eat anything except its own waste, and that the reason we aren't just heads is that we would roll into dips in the ground (Plato 2008, 93c, 33d, 33c, 44e). A case might be made that this stuff would seem a lot less amusing to Athenians, but one might ask whether this is not a way of manifesting our own conceit of ourselves as sophisticates. If there's a problem with legs and arms being attributed to the universe why isn't there a problem with 'waste'? Continuing the scatological theme, Timaeus later describes how our intestines slow down the passage of our food in order to extract sustenance from it (Plato 2008, 73a), so his straight-faced suggestion that the body as a whole was created *as a method of transport for the head* could not be entertained in all seriousness even by himself. There is moreover authorial distance, and the allusion to Critias' silly claim to authority evident in what Timaeus is made to say about the Olympian gods. Much as Critias invited us to believe his story of Atlantis on the basis of what his grandfather said although he doesn't quite remember, we are now invited to believe in the gods because our elders, supposedly, claimed to be descended from them, and, well, they ought to know (Plato 2008, 40d–e).

Timaeus' contrary contention at 51e that there is 'scarcely' a human capable of knowledge is a striking thing for him to say. His reasoning out the 'likely' (Plato 2008, 30b) construction of the universe, is after all *reasoning*. Offering reasons hardly fits with suggesting to your audience that they are incapable of anything but belief under persuasion. Otherwise odd, the 'scarcely' might make sense as authorial tease. Are *you*, dear reader, one for fairy stories? In that case 'scarcely' is not so much ordinary 'pessimism' about the intellectual capacities of the audience, as a sort of probing irony about them, in the same vein of irony probingly mined in the opening conversation gambit, where they pretend to sum up the *Republic*:

SOCRATES: Is there anything missing, anything we still need to recall?

TIMAEUS: No, that was exactly how the conversation went. (Plato 2008, 19a)

It was not, but the summation seems to work in this company—it is *plausible*, much as Timaeus announces an aspiration to be 'plausible' (Plato 2008, 29c). Plausibility is a theme uniting the opening interventions from Socrates and Critias with the entirety of Timaeus' speech, and plausibility depends on the audience. What is the good in being plausible, if you are plausible among the kind of people who can't remember what Socrates said about literature?

As noted, the *Republic* topics that Timaeus and Critias conspicuously fail to remember are precisely the ones that most interest Iris Murdoch: the fire and the sun, the cave, the merits and dangers of literary art. In discussion of the *Timaeus* in *The fire and the sun*, she interweaves discussion of the *Timaeus* with consideration of Freud on the soul's corrupting uses of the art-object (Murdoch 1997, 422–423). She returns to this in *MGM*:

> In spite of their different aims, it is arguable that Plato and Freud mistrust art for the same reason, because it caricatures their own therapeutic activity and could interfere with it. Art is pleasure-seeking self-satisfied pseudo-analysis and pseudo-enlightenment. (*MGM*, 423)

Can we speak of good artists? One excellence of Murdoch's treatment of the Demiurge is her emphasis on his status as an ideal artist, and an idealised one. 'He is such because his art is animated not by pleasure but by love: The artist, ideally ... should imitate the calm unenvious Demiurge who sees the recalcitrant jumble of his material with just eyes' (Murdoch 1997, 452). Recalling: '"attention", which I borrow from Simone Weil, to express the idea of a just and loving gaze directed upon an individual reality' (Murdoch 1997, 327). As 'ideal' artist the Demiurge is perfectly good, and moved in his creation by love of something outside himself. These two attributes are one:

> Plato's mythical God is a restless imaginative creative artist, Eros, seen in the *Timaeus* as the Demiurge, the spirit who, looking with love toward a higher reality, creates an imperfect world as his best image of a perfection which he sees but cannot express. (*MGM*, 320)

This seems to better convey what had been meant at *MGM* 478, without direct invocation of the forms. In these passages, Murdoch's grasp of Eros-Demiurge might conjure Plato writing the task of his love for Socrates, copying him lovingly into 'another material' (*MGM*, 477). But Socrates is not a form, and the same holds of the Demiurge's 'model'. Where Murdoch understands the Demiurge as Plato's allegory on his own creative process, the forms will not serve as the thing copied by the craftsman-god. Certainly, the Good is loved. This is essential to

Murdoch's Plato. But the *immediate* love-object of the creator of the dialogues is Socrates, and it is likewise Socrates that is *directly* portrayed; it is Socrates who Plato imitates; Socrates imitated, discoursing in imitation in art. Yes, a story can be told that in being in love with Socrates one may be in love with Wisdom itself and the Good itself, and yes, Plato might offer up a story of this kind. But what, in all this, is the creative-artist-in-love actually producing an image of? He writes us Socrates, Glaucon, Timaeus, Critias. Only through them and in their conversations is the Good itself glimpsed, hinted at, on occasion allegorised. Here Plato is the bereaved admirer of Socrates and creative artist, both:

> The energy of the attentive scholar or artist is spiritual energy. The energy of the bereaved person trying to survive in the best way, or of the mother thinking about her delinquent son (and so on and so on) is spiritual. [...] Plato calls such energy Eros, love. Zeus became Eros to create the world ... The *Timaeus* Demiurge is inspired to create by love of the Good. (*MGM*, 505)

Yes, the *Timaeus* Demiurge is inspired to create by love of the Good. But his creations are not mere copies of the forms. Every one of his creations is described as a 'living being'—and applying this to planets and stars and the universe itself this is perhaps the most over-used colocation in the whole of the *Timaeus*, ad nauseam and *passim*. Nor is the point a verbal tic.

Consider the attribution to the cosmos of a 'world soul', an attribution which Murdoch finds suggestive and attractive but also 'mysterious' (Murdoch 1997, 431) and baffling. Many might share the bafflement—Timaeus' speech is much odder than any tale that could be told of it. But one effect of the general banishment of inanimate being is to emphasise that this particular creation story was never really bothered about matter in the first place. In the beginning, Jehovah created the heaven and the earth. It is not until verse 11 that He makes grass, 14 before the stars, and 20 before there is 'life'. But for the literary craftsman-god there is never anything *but* life:

> So the god took thought and concluded that, *generally speaking*, nothing he made that lacked intelligence could ever be more beautiful than an intelligent product, and that nothing can have intelligence unless it has a soul. And the upshot of this thinking was that he constructed the universe by endowing soul with intelligence and body with soul, so that it was in the very nature of the universe to surpass all other products in beauty and perfection. (Plato 2008, 30a–b; italics mine)

It is charmingly nonsensical to speak of 'other products' besides the universe, and I have italicised *'generally speaking'* to emphasise the possibility of another platonic leg-pull. *Generally speaking*, things that are alive are more beautiful than things that aren't? What is an empirical qualification like 'generally speaking' doing here, in pre-creation ruminations, where *ex-hypothesi* the craftsman-god has no 'generally' to speak of? I accused Murdoch of granting herself too much slack with the 'as if' of the myth, and now you will say that I am not granting enough. But staying tight to it, this weird creation myth beginning in banishment of the inanimate might perhaps be helped along if we insist that the Demiurge is the allegory not merely of a *literary* craftsman, but of that specific kind of literary craftsman who depicts the interactions of intelligent 'living beings', because he finds them more beautiful. In other words, a playwright, or the author of ironic philosophical dialogues. Plato lets in other characters, other amusements, and fair dollops of inanimate beauty from time to time, but *'generally speaking'* he's in love with Socrates. Nothing that lacked intelligence could ever be more beautiful than an intelligent creature.

I connect also the bizarre process where the qualities of the cosmos are continually precisiled in relation to certain attributes of human beings, which it doesn't have. Why do these comparisons even arise? The cosmos is 'alive', because *generally speaking* only living beings are beautiful enough to be the sort of thing a perfectly good craftsman-god would create (Plato 2008, 30a). So does it have hands or legs? Does it eat and excrete? Does it have eyes and ears? (Plato 2008, 33b–34a). One might well conclude from this line of questioning that the 'living beings' Plato is more interested in are the walking talking and eating sort of living being, rather than spherical bodies in circular motion. The universe (fictional or cosmological) exists only because its 'model' is *beloved*, and as only souls can be so beautiful as to be so beloved, so the heavenly bodies, if created by the craftsman, must themselves have souls on the 'model' of something with a soul.

DIVINE MADNESS

To produce an idealised image of a good artist motivated by selfless love to render their muse as perfectly as possible is not, of course, to show that any such good artists exist on earth—and the suspicion that Plato might have been reflecting on his *own* creative activity when he set himself to model the ideal does not entirely help. 'Art is pleasure-seeking self-satisfied pseudo-analysis and pseudo-enlightenment' (*MGM*, 423). Storytelling can give the dangerous pleasure of bringing form out of disorder, irrespective of faithfulness to any model, and there are more corrupting satisfactions. And yet ... outside motivation by pleasure, perhaps there are those 'possessed' by 'the visions and the voices' of their model? (Plato 2008, 72b; 71e).

Timaeus' discussion of oracular madness at 71e–72b is presented in character as an explanation for the liver, and is introduced in the course of Timaeus' similarly anatomical reworking of tripartite soul imagery from the *Republic*. Throughout, Critias and Timaeus are trying to outdo each other in 'return for' Socrates' 'feast of words' (Plato 2008, 27b) in the *Republic*. Much as Critias claims to offer Athens' war with Atlantis as a living illustration of the tripartite state, it seems inevitable that Timaeus will try to make our bodily organs an illustration of the tripartite soul. The rational part is put in the head, that hungry for esteem is put in the chest, and the base appetites in the stomach. Then Timaeus thinks of a *fourth* component of the soul, 'divination', and sticks it among the intestines, in the liver. The addition is poetically fecund in ways that would take whole books to make prose. Partly, it is commentary on the psychologies explored in the *Republic*. Much as Critias' wont to illustrate the tripartite analysis of the city in a combat narrative tends to undermine any attribution of goodness to that city, Timaeus' yen to support *Republic* psychology has the effect throwing it into doubt. How many parts do souls have? If these parts have physical locations and we can add 'divination' for the liver, are we going to end up with as many parts of the soul as we have organs in the body? A less absurd question: do we need to posit a new part of the soul every time we discern a new motivating force there, like oracular inspiration? Well, why not? Putting 'divination' in the liver is also a provocation on the (un)clarity and situatedness of oracular insight, and Plato is perhaps engaged in some variant of Murdoch's project: the defence of literature against the Socratic critique. One strand of the defence is that literature, of the oracular sort, is as natural to embodied souls as food or sex. I omit much of the strangeness, but connecting livers with literature we are at last aswim in the oddity of the *Timaeus*, and might need a diversion to come to the point.

Oracular madness in the *Timaeus* should be understood in the light of passages throughout Plato's work (but above all in the *Philebus*, *Phaedrus*, *Ion*), associating the divine madness of oracles with the divine inspiration of artists and lovers. Suggesting the playwright or the philosophical writer, the oracle requires command of his intelligence ... to recall and reflect upon the messages conveyed to him by divination or possession, whether he was asleep or awake at the time, but also to subject to rational analysis all the visions that appear to him. (Plato 2008, 72b)

Not all diviners are equally capable of such two-way transit between inspiration and consideration, as great writers must be. If a diviner remained in divine madness, he would require a second person to interpret:

These interpreters are occasionally called 'diviners', but that just displays utter ignorance of the fact that they're really translators of riddling sayings and seeings, and should properly be thought of not as diviners, but as interpreters of omens. (Plato 2008, 72b)

This recalls the exegete. But to return to our defence of literature: the liver. The created gods who created us knew that the appetitive part of the soul would never pay attention to reason, and that it would be 'more readily bewitched by images and phantasms' (Plato 2008, 71a).

But the gods had planned for exactly this eventuality, and had formed the liver ['for 'divination'] and put it in the place where this [appetitive] part of the soul lived [namely, the intestines]. *They made the liver dense, smooth, bright, and sweet (but with some bitterness), so that it could act as a mirror for thoughts stemming from intellect, just as a mirror receives impressions and gives back images to look at.* (Plato 2008, 71a–b; italics mine)

Compare: 'the representational arts ... hold the mirror up to nature' (Murdoch 1997, 370). By hiding the 'mirror' somewhat un-optimally in the intestines alongside the appetites and waste, Plato on the literary liver might be summarised: 'we are all in the gutter, but some of us are looking at the stars'.[4] What sight we can have of them reflected in blood and shit amid our baser appetites is left open to doubt by Plato's imagery, and a project to construct the mirrors of refracting telescopes out of 'smooth' livers is perhaps inadvisable. Nevertheless, while Dionysian and drunk on something, the liver of divination imagery defends literary art as a way of reflecting, confusedly, certain omens of otherly perfection, and of making them digestible to parts of the soul that consume nothing else. Liverish literature is a mirror, and also part of our guts. These aspects are not simply contradictory, but they are in tension in the image.

Might there also be a response to Freud's worry to be found in Plato's association of art's bloody mirror with divine madness, rather than self-seeking pleasure? Any status of Plato's readers as 'interpreters of omens' is in fruitful contrast with Critias' earlier talk of the audience for this evening's entertainment as a 'panel of judges', who are to evaluate his own speech against Timaeus'rather as befits a 'recitation contest' (Plato 2008, 27a; 21b). Amusement is the second-rate prize. Plato's riddling is certainly a kind of fun, but the defence of this potentially corrupt and corrupting fun is that it is also divine madness, possession by a 'model' you love and wish to recreate as best you can. This sense in which the craftsman-god (and Plato) are 'artists' is not the sense in which 'we are all artists': 'We are all poets. Well, surely one will empty the concept by such treatment! If we are all poets, what about real poets?' (*MGM*, 505). What about real poets, indeed? It is only with real poets that talk of 'divination' and 'possession' is in place, and here the ideal artist and the real artist present the same demand. If there is good art and if there is any good reflected liverishly in his dialogues, Plato is telling us, this is only in virtue of his being possessed by Socrates.

CONCLUSION

Murdoch tells us that in the *Timaeus* Demiurge Plato's 'splendidly complex mythical image of the creative process' presents 'interesting analogies with art of the mortal variety' (Murdoch 1997, 435). Indeed so, and far more than Murdoch's discussion itself allows. Murdoch, far along the right path, does not go to the ends of these 'interesting analogies' because she comes to the *Timaeus* in a quarrel with Ryle. She wants to press this 'late' dialogue as an example of Plato still mythologising the forms. The forms are there, perhaps. Yet what the Demiurge is possessed by and trying to copy is not 'the forms'. It is rather his 'model', and it is possible to gloss this 'model', as Murdoch herself sometimes does, as an allegory on the 'living beings' right in front of us, seen as the ideal artist could see them, and judged justly as the ideal artist could love them, had he no word limit, and were missing nothing of his guts.

NOTES

1. Murdoch's London and Oxford libraries are held in the Kingston University Archives and Special Collections, London.
2. See Robjant (2012).
3. In this chapter, ellipses included in brackets indicate the omission of a complete sentence, while ellipses without brackets indicate the omission of a few words.
4. Not Oscar Wilde, but Lord Darlington in Oscar Wilde's *Lady Windermere's fan*, Wilde (2008).

REFERENCES

Murdoch, I. 1992. *Metaphysics as a guide to morals* (Abbreviated *MGM*). London: Chatto & Windus.

Murdoch, I. 1997. *Existentialists and mystics*, ed. Peter Conradi. London: Chatto & Windus.

Plato. 1998. *Republic*, trans. Robin Waterfield. Oxford: Oxford University Press.

Plato. 2008. *Timaeus and Critias*, trans. Robin Waterfield. Oxford: Oxford University Press.

Robjant, D. 2012. The earthy realism of Plato's metaphysics, or: What shall we do with Iris Murdoch? *Philosophical Investigations* 35 (1): 43–67.

Ryle, G. 1966. *Plato's progress*. Cambridge: Cambridge University Press.

Wilde, O. 2008. *The importance of being Earnest and other plays*. Oxford: Oxford University Press.

CHAPTER 16

Fields of Force: Murdoch on Axioms, Duties, and Eros (*MGM* Chapter 17)

Mark Hopwood

INTRODUCTION

In writing about Iris Murdoch, it is difficult to resist the urge to try to *place* her somewhere in the contemporary debate in moral philosophy. To the extent that one feels that Murdoch's work deserves to be taken seriously, it is natural to want to find some kind of identifiable position that can be attributed to her and defended against its rivals.[1] The problem is that it is not always entirely clear what that position would be. She is obviously not a utilitarian, although she does at various points say quite positive things about utilitarianism. It is equally obvious that she does not mean to identify herself as a Kantian, although she often acknowledges the profound influence of Kant on her own views.[2] Those who have attempted to categorise Murdoch according to the standard taxonomy of available positions have generally placed her within the 'virtue ethics' tradition, but despite some obvious points of resonance between Murdoch's work and the writings of her friends and contemporaries Philippa Foot and Elizabeth Anscombe (to whom *Metaphysics as a Guide to Morals* [henceforth *MGM*] is dedicated), sensitive readers have

M. Hopwood (✉)
The University of the South, Sewanee, TN, USA

© The Author(s) 2019
N. Hämäläinen and G. Dooley (eds.),
Reading Iris Murdoch's Metaphysics as a Guide to Morals,
https://doi.org/10.1007/978-3-030-18967-9_16

generally noted that Murdoch seems to be trying to do something quite different from standard virtue theorists.[3] Aside from the fact that her primary inspiration is drawn not from Aristotle but from Plato, Murdoch does not seem to be putting forward a systematic theory of virtue, or indeed any kind of systematic theory at all. Indeed, the most tempting strategy of all might be to classify Murdoch as a kind of particularist who believes that the solution to the central questions of morality is to be found not through the application of general principles but through 'loving attention' to particular individuals and situations.[4]

In this chapter, I want to argue—through a reading of chapter 17 of *MGM* ('Axioms, duties, Eros')—that none of these interpretations gets Murdoch quite right. The problem with all of them is that they take Murdoch to be committed to a methodological approach to moral philosophy—foundationalism—that she specifically rejects both in that chapter and elsewhere in her work. A foundationalist theory, according to Linda Zagzebski, is one that 'is constructed out of a single point of origin' (Zagzebski 2017, 9). Utilitarianism, for example, is constructed out of the principle of utility. A utilitarian may be prepared to allow a role for virtue, rights, duty, and other moral concepts, but each of these concepts will be explained in terms of the principle of utility. (A virtue is a character trait that tends to facilitate bringing about the greatest happiness for the greatest number, etc.) Foundationalist theories do not have to be based upon rules or principles, however. Aristotelian particularism (of the kind often attributed to John McDowell) is based upon *phronesis* or practical wisdom.[5] An Aristotelian particularist might be prepared to allow that some moral problems are best addressed by employing the principle of utility, but only in those circumstances in which the practically wise person would employ it. A version of Murdochian particularism could be constructed along similar lines, with loving attention taking the place of practical wisdom as the foundational concept of the theory.

As I hope to show, even a relatively cursory reading of chapter 17 of *MGM* makes any foundationalist interpretation of Murdoch untenable. Not only is Murdoch not proposing a single point of origin for morality; she makes it clear that she does not think that there can be one. The more difficult question is what kind of interpretation of Murdoch's project *would* be tenable. The best way to read Murdoch, I will suggest, is as a methodological descriptivist.[6] In order to clarify what it means to label Murdoch as a 'descriptivist', I will take a brief detour into her earlier work. There, we see Murdoch setting out a philosophical methodology that remains remarkably consistent throughout her career. Although this methodology is descriptivist in the sense that it seeks to establish (as Murdoch puts it) what our moral concepts *are* as opposed to what they *must be*, it should not be construed as a form of 'neutral analysis'. Description, for Murdoch, is never neutral: it is always at least in part an attempt at persuasion. In the final section of the chapter, I will try to say something about what Murdoch is trying to persuade us of in *Metaphysics* by looking in more detail at the central (but underexplored) metaphor of the 'field of force'. Once we understand what Murdoch is trying to do with this metaphor, we will be in a better position to see how we might attempt to 'place' her within the contemporary debate. Murdoch is not the proponent of another form of foundationalism, even one based on the concept of loving attention or 'the Good'. She is the proponent of an entirely different approach to moral philosophy that presents a radical alternative to the foundationalist project.[7]

Murdoch and Foundationalism

The decisive blow against foundationalist readings of Murdoch comes in the very first sentences of chapter 17, 'Philosophers have sought for a single principle on which morality may be seen to depend. I do not think that the moral life can be in this sense reduced to a unity' (*MGM*, 492). These two sentences very clearly rule out any Kantian or utilitarian interpretation of Murdoch, but they might be thought to leave room for the particularist reading. When Murdoch says that she does not think that, 'the moral life can be in this sense reduced to a unity', it might be thought that Murdoch is rejecting the idea of basing morality on a single principle (like the principle of utility or the categorical imperative), but not necessarily the idea of basing it on a single capacity (like practical reason or loving attention). Only a few lines later, however, Murdoch makes it clear that she is using the term 'principle' in a broader sense to encompass any kind of single foundation, including the capacity for loving attention:

> I used earlier the image of a field of force, a field of tension, between modes of ethical being, divided under the headings of axioms, duties, and Eros. There is a necessary fourth mode which I name Void, which I have mentioned earlier and will return to. This picture is of course awkward since the entities, besides being of different types, are internally divided against themselves. (*MGM*, 492)

When Murdoch uses the term 'Eros' in chapter 17, she intends it to denote a 'mode of ethical being' that includes the concepts of loving attention, consciousness, 'moral vision', etc. There is no doubt that this mode of ethical being is absolutely central to Murdoch's account of morality. As she writes later in the chapter, 'a large part of what I have been concerned with comes under the heading of Eros' (*MGM*, 494). Nevertheless, Eros is still only *one* mode of ethical being, alongside axioms, duties, and void. Murdoch had actually made this point quite explicitly a number of years previously, towards the end of the essay 'The idea of perfection':

> I have several times indicated that the image which I am offering should be thought of as a general metaphysical background to morals and not as a formula which can be illuminatingly introduced into any and every moral act. There exists, so far as I know, no formula of the latter kind. We are not always the individual in pursuit of the individual, we are not always responding to the magnetic pull of perfection. Often, for instance when we pay our bills or perform other small everyday acts, we are just 'anybody' doing what is proper or making simple choices for ordinary public reasons; and this is the situation which some philosophers have chosen exclusively to analyse. (Murdoch 1999, 334)

Since Murdoch herself postpones any further discussion of 'void' for the following chapter of *MGM*, I will follow her in leaving it to one side for the purposes of my argument here.[8] It might be worth, however, reviewing the basic points that she makes in her analysis of axioms and duties.

In chapter 17 Murdoch is to a great extent (as she acknowledges) repeating things that she has said in previous chapters. In particular, her discussion of axioms draws on chapter 12 ('Morals and politics') and her discussion of duties on chapter 10 ('Notes on will and duty'). Axioms, according to Murdoch, are 'isolated unsystematic moral insights which arise out of and refer to a general conception of human nature such as civilized societies have gradually generated' (*MGM*, 365). In chapter 17, Murdoch gives the example of the three 'unalienable rights' of the American Declaration of Independence (life, liberty, and the pursuit of happiness), as well as the 'general command "Be kind"' (*MGM*, 493). In chapter 12, she provides a range of other examples, including the principle that torture is wrong (*MGM*, 367) and that violence is not a justifiable means to achieve political ends (*MGM*, 357).

Murdoch defines duties in chapter 10 as 'moral rules of a certain degree of generality' (*MGM*, 302), for example 'don't lie'. Murdoch takes duties, unlike axioms, to be primarily private and individual. As she puts it: 'duty recedes into the most private part of personal morality, whereas axioms are instruments of the public scene' (*MGM*, 381). In describing duties as 'private', Murdoch does not mean to suggest that one's sense of duty cannot be communicated in public. Someone with a strong sense of civic duty, for example, might express that sense of duty by turning out to vote and exhorting others to do likewise. The point is rather that duties are a matter of personal commitment, whereas axioms are taken to express the shared values of a whole society or political community.[9] It is essential to the character of duty that it should be encountered as an absolute and rigid limit on one's behaviour:

> Duty can appear when moral instinct and habit fail, when we lack any clarifying mode of reflection, and seek for a rule felt as external. Most often perhaps we become aware of duty when it collides head-on with inclination. (A place for the concept of will-power.) Anyone may suddenly find himself, in an unforeseen situation, confronted in his stream of consciousness by the notice DON'T DO IT. (Socrates's daemon told him only what not to do.) (*MGM*, 302)

Murdoch's discussion of axioms and duties makes it clear that she is not (as she has sometimes been interpreted) hostile to the very idea of rules and principles playing a role in moral life. Nevertheless, it might be thought that it is still possible to accommodate what Murdoch says about axioms and duties within a foundationalist interpretation of her view. One of the most subtle and interesting attempts to develop this kind of reading is Bridget Clarke's. She presents Murdoch as a virtue ethicist for whom virtue is 'a capacity for a kind of moral perception' (Clarke 2012, 228). Clarke acknowledges that Murdoch regards rules and principles as a significant part of moral life, but argues that such rules and principles take a secondary role to moral perception.

> The agent's critical resources consist in habits of thought, attention, and communication which depend on some normative commitments even as they call others into question. Virtue is the perfection of these habits. And while virtue understood in this way involves principles of conduct, these principles ultimately originate and operate from within the agent's evaluative outlook. (Clarke 2012, 228–229)

On Clarke's reading of Murdoch, principles of conduct are 'character-dependent' in the sense that they 'depend upon the agent's character for their proper application' (Clarke 2012, 230). To illustrate the notion of character dependence, Clarke gives the example of John Dashwood in Jane Austen's novel *Sense and Sensibility.* John is instructed in his father's will to 'look after' his sisters, but is not told precisely what this entails. After initially considering the possibility of sharing his money with his sisters, John eventually convinces himself (with the help of his wife Fanny) that it would be 'absolutely unnecessary, if not highly indecorous' to offer them anything more than 'neighbourly assistance' (such as helping them move into a new house). In this case, Clarke argues, John is committed to the right principle—i.e. that he should look after his sisters—but his cold-heartedness and selfishness prevent him from applying this principle in the right way. If we think about axioms and duties as being character-dependent in this way, then we can allow them to play a role in Murdoch's account whilst still preserving moral perception—i.e. Eros—as the foundational concept.

I think there is a great deal about Murdoch's view that Clarke's reading gets right. Murdoch would agree that principles of conduct are often character-dependent in the sense Clarke suggests, and there is certainly good textual support for giving Eros a privileged place among Murdoch's modes of moral being. A morality of axioms, Murdoch writes, 'needs the intuitive control of a more widely reflective and general morality' (*MGM*, 362). The case of duty is similar:

> If thought of without the enclosing background of general and changing quality of consciousness, of moral experience, of acquired moral fabric, [the idea of duty] may seem stark, inexplicable except as arbitrary orders given by God, or be considered as mere historically determined social rules. It may also suggest that morality is an occasional part-time activity of switching on the ethical faculty on separate occasions of moral choice. But to return to an earlier metaphor, we can only move properly in a world that we can see, and what must be sought for is vision. (*MGM*, 303)

Murdoch is well aware that axioms and duties may lead us astray and thus need to be 'enclosed' and 'controlled' by loving attention. In another passage, she makes the priority of Eros even more explicit:

> Someone may say, so you want to distinguish rough general rules of morality, such as constitute important inspirations and barriers in politics and public life, from a private progressive spirituality, connected with a total

change of consciousness? Yes, but the situation is more complicated, since (political) axioms must also be distinguished from imperatives of duty. I certainly want to suggest that the spiritual pilgrimage (transformation-renewal-salvation) is the centre and essence of morality, upon whose success and well-being the health of other kinds of moral reaction and thinking is likely to depend. (*MGM*, 367)

These passages make it clear that Eros does indeed have an important kind of priority for Murdoch. Murdoch uses the metaphor of health to describe the role of Eros, and I think it is helpful to extend this metaphor as a way of interpreting the claim that Eros is the 'centre and essence' of morality. For Murdoch, Eros is the heart of morality, pumping blood to the other organs. Without consciousness and loving attention, axioms and duties may come to seem 'stark and inexplicable', and may even lead us down morally dangerous paths. As Hannah Arendt's study of Adolf Eichmann makes clear, a commitment to 'doing one's duty'detached from a sense of the reality of other individuals can lead to horrifying consequences (Arendt 2006). In the case of axioms, Murdoch is quite clear that a liberal state needs both the stability provided by widely accepted axioms and the occasional destabilisation brought about by 'conscientious law-breakers'. To that extent, something like Clarke's reading—i.e. that axioms and duties 'operate within' the agent's evaluative outlook, with loving attention providing the corrective principle for both—seems about right.

For all that Clarke gets right about Murdoch's view, however, there are other moments in the text that sit less comfortably with her reading. As we have seen, in chapter 17 Murdoch writes that the picture she has presented is 'awkward' since the four different modes of moral being, 'besides being of different types, are internally divided against themselves'. We can get a better understanding of these internal divisions by looking more closely at what Murdoch says about axioms and duties. The role of duty is to 'confront' us in our stream of consciousness; it is what appears 'when moral instinct and habit fail'. Murdoch is insistent that duty is not to be 'reduced away' to anything else. Indeed, she could not be much clearer on this point: 'Duty is not to be absorbed into, or dissolved in, the vast complexities of moral feeling and sensibility' (*MGM*, 302). In order for duty to play the role that Murdoch envisages, it must be able to *interrupt* the stream of consciousness. We need to be able to recognise the moral demand as 'external, contrary to instinct and habit, contrary to usual modes of thought' (*MGM*, 303). To respond to the call of duty is, at least in some cases, to ignore or even actively go against the current of one's moral vision. As Murdoch writes in 'The idea of perfection': 'We may sometimes decide to act abstractly by rule, to ignore vision and the compulsive energy derived from it; and we may find that as a result both energy and vision are unexpectedly given' (Murdoch 1999, 334–335). When Murdoch says that we may sometimes decide to act 'abstractly' by rule, she seems to have in mind a kind of act that is divorced from one's usual evaluative outlook—one that comes about as a result of ignoring vision. Murdoch often talks about duties as 'moral taboos' learned in childhood, and notes that duties framed as negatives ('don't lie'; 'don't steal') are useful precisely because of their clarity—i.e. because their correct application does not depend to any great extent upon moral character. (It is no accident that Murdoch takes Socrates' *daimon*—which only tells him what not to do, without offering any explanation or argument—as a paradigmatic example of the call of duty.)

If Murdoch's account of duty sits awkwardly with Clarke's reading, then something similar could also be said of her account of axioms. Axioms, Murdoch writes, 'are public banners flown for complex reasons which may be partly, even grossly pragmatic'. Of course, politicians and statesmen are ordinary moral agents too, and sometimes 'we are moved to claim the rights of others by our own general moral understanding and sensibility', but ultimately 'we do not "live" the world of politics in the way we "live" our private lives' (*MGM*, 386). Although Murdoch is quite clear that morality cannot be reduced to axioms, she is also at pains to point out the tensions between the public world of axioms and the private world of Eros. Axiomatic morality is designed to be 'inflexible'—i.e. not open to interpretation. As Murdoch puts it: 'we "cut off the road to an explanation" in order to safeguard the purity of the value' (*MGM*, 386). The point of formulating simple and axiomatic statements of human rights, for example, is to reduce as much as possible the role of moral character in determining the application of those rights. Murdoch recognises, of course, that even the simplest principle requires interpretation, so axioms can never entirely be separated from vision and consciousness, but the whole point of introducing the category of axioms is to emphasise the existence of areas of morality in which the role of individual moral character is reduced to the smallest possible extent.

Clarke's account of the character dependence of rules and principles, though plausible in its own right, thus seems to obscure an important feature of Murdoch's account—i.e. the inherent *tensions* between axioms, duties, and Eros. These three modes of moral being do not form a seamlessly integrated whole; in fact, they seem to pull us in different directions. Axioms and duties, while less fundamental than consciousness and vision, lay claim to a kind of independent authority that cannot fully be brought under the authority of Eros. In fairness to Clarke, it ought to be said that she recognises this point, at least to some extent. She acknowledges that for Murdoch, axioms and duties offer guidance that 'does not depend upon the deliverances of [the agent's] sensibility' (Clarke 2012, 243). For Clarke, however, the apparent independence of axioms and duties presents a problem for Murdoch's view:

> [Duties] and axioms themselves may stand in need of revision (or rejection). They are, for Murdoch, historically and socially conditioned norms, not infallible edicts from a metaphysical beyond (*MGM*, 493). So while duties and axioms can, and doubtless do, check the agent's impulses, perceptions, and reflections, the question is how the virtuous person can ever check *them*. (Clarke 2012, 244)

Clarke's concern here seems like a reasonable one. As she points out, Huck Finn's duty by the received standards of the antebellum south is to return the runaway slave Jim to his master. In order to do the right thing, Huck has to go against his sense of duty, no matter how powerfully it calls to him. With such examples in mind, Clarke is sceptical about the usefulness of axioms and duties for Murdoch's account. Indeed, she almost seems to be somewhat puzzled about what they are doing there. Why introduce the idea of axioms and duties as an external check on moral perception if such principles are just as likely—if not *more* likely—to lead us astray?

It is at this point that we need to come back to the question of Murdoch's philosophical methodology. The problem for Clarke, I want to suggest, is that she is reading Murdoch in the wrong way—i.e. as a foundationalist. She is (on her own account) trying to find a place for Murdoch in the contemporary debate as the proponent of an original form of virtue ethics based on moral perception as a foundational concept. Although this reading captures much of what is important about Murdoch's view, it leaves other aspects looking somewhat mysterious— specifically, Murdoch's account of axioms and duties. What I want to suggest is that we will only understand what Murdoch is trying to do with these concepts if we read her in the way that she presents herself—not as a foundationalist, but as a descriptivist. On this reading, the goal of Murdoch's moral philosophy is not to *resolve* the tensions between different modes of moral being, but simply to *describe* those tensions in an accurate way. In order to explain precisely what Murdoch's descriptivism amounts to, however, we need to take a brief detour into some of her earlier essays before returning to look at the role it plays in her later work.

MAKING PICTURES

Murdoch's philosophical methodology, although it developed in various ways over time, remained remarkably consistent over the course of her career, and the early essays help to illuminate what she takes herself to be doing in *MGM*. In one of her very earliest published pieces, 'Thinking and language', Murdoch argues for a view to which she would remain committed throughout her writings—i.e. the fundamentally metaphorical nature of much of our thought and language:

> [Metaphor] is not a peripheral excrescence upon the linguistic structure, it is its living centre. And the metaphors which we encounter, and which illuminate us, in conversation and in poetry, are offered and are found illuminating because language also occurs in thinking in the way that it does. We do not 'suddenly' have to adopt the figurative mode; we are using it all the time. (Murdoch 1999, 40)

For Murdoch, metaphor is not merely useful for describing our experience; it is to some extent *constitutive* of our experience. As Murdoch writes:

> If we think of conceptualizing ... as the activity of grasping, or reducing to order, our situations with the help of a language which is fundamentally metaphorical, this will operate against the world-language dualism which haunts us because we are afraid of the idealists. Seen from this point of view, thinking is not the using of *symbols* which designate absent *objects*, symbolizing and sensing being divided strictly from each other. Thinking is not designating at all, but rather understanding, grasping, 'possessing'. (Murdoch 1999, 41)

This account of the nature of thought is crucial to understanding Murdoch's view of moral philosophy. As a mode of thought, moral philosophy can be understood as the attempt to 'grasp' or 'possess' our moral experience. For example: thinking of morality in terms of a system of laws helps us to grasp and 'reduce to order' our sometimes confused sense of duty. Similarly, the principle of utility—morality as cost/benefit analysis—offers a way of simplifying, ordering, and prioritising what might otherwise be a bewildering array of moral demands. What makes moral philosophy so difficult is that such metaphors are already part of moral life, playing a central role in shaping the phenomena that the moral philosopher is called upon to analyse. In her essay 'Metaphysics and ethics', Murdoch begins to lay out a positive conception of a philosophical methodology that would take this difficulty into account:

> Philosophers have usually tended to seek for universal formulae. But the linguistic method, if we take it seriously, is by its nature opposed to this search. Logic, whatever that may be determined to be, has its own universality; but when we leave the domain of the purely logical we come into the cloudy and shifting domain of the concepts which men live by – and these are subject to historical change. This is especially true of moral concepts. Here we shall have done something if we can establish with tolerable clarity what these concepts *are*. We should, I think, resist the temptation to unify the picture by trying to establish, guided by our own conception of the ethical in general, what these concepts *must be*. All that is made clear by this method is: our own conception of the ethical in general – and in the process important differences of moral concept may be blurred or neglected. (Murdoch 1999, 75)

Murdoch once again denies that moral philosophy can hope to establish anything 'which has a sort of logical universality' and attempts to explain why she thinks this is impossible:

> The difficulty is, and here we are after all not so very far from the philosophers of the past, that the subject of the investigation is the nature of man – and we are studying this nature at a point of great conceptual sensibility. Man is a creature who makes pictures of himself and then comes to resemble the picture. This is the process which moral philosophy must attempt to describe and analyse. (Murdoch 1999, 75)

Although the statement that 'man is a creature who makes pictures of himself and then comes to resemble the picture' has become well known, Murdoch's reasons for making it are not always fully understood.

When Murdoch says that we come to resemble the pictures we create, that is another way of articulating the point made earlier in 'Thinking and language'—i.e. that the pictures and metaphors we use play a central role in constituting our experience. When the moral philosopher sits down to attempt to grasp and reduce to order the moral domain, she is faced with a set of human subjects who are already being shaped by the metaphors and pictures they use to grasp their own experience for themselves. Consequently, any attempt to impose a single picture or universal formula—in other words, any attempt to say what our moral concepts *must be*—risks obscuring the complexity and differences of our moral concepts as they *are*.

There is a good example of the kind of problem that Murdoch is concerned with in the essay 'Vision and choice in morality', published around the same time as 'Metaphysics and ethics'. In that piece, Murdoch discusses the 'current view' of morality, according to which 'a moral judgment, as opposed to a whim or taste preference, is one which is held by the agent to be valid for all others placed as he is' (Murdoch 1999, 77). As Murdoch points out, a problem for the current view is that some people seem to regard themselves as being 'set apart from others, by a superiority which brings special responsibilities, or by a curse, or some other unique destiny' (Murdoch 1999, 86). Such agents would *not* necessarily say that what is morally required for them is necessarily valid for everyone else. Of course, the proponent of the current view can attempt to 'force the situation into the model' by arguing that even someone who takes themselves to be subject to a unique destiny is committed to the claim that what is morally required of them would hold universally for anyone subject to precisely the same destiny, even if that turns out to be no-one but them. Murdoch's question at this point is simply: 'whatever is the point of doing [this]?' (Murdoch 1999, 86). If we insist, we can find a way to reinterpret all the various and diverse forms of moral experience we encounter to fit them within the constraints of a single picture. In doing so, however, we may find that we 'have won a similarity, but we have lost a much more important and interesting difference' (Murdoch 1999, 88). Moral philosophy, Murdoch argues, 'should remain at the level of the differences, taking the moral forms of life as given, and not try to *get behind them* to a single form' (Murdoch 1999, 97).

This is the core of Murdoch's descriptivism. The first task of moral philosophy, as Murdoch sees it, is to give an accurate account of our moral concepts as they are. It would be misleading, however, to suggest that in seeking to provide an accurate description of our concepts the moral philosopher is able to remain neutral. We need to remember that the moral philosopher is no less human than the subjects of her analysis. She too is a picturing creature. Consequently, any moral theory is likely to be 'half a description and half a persuasion' (Murdoch 1999, 75). In Murdoch's own work, persuasion does not take the form of trying to establish what our moral concepts must be, but rather of trying to remind us of a set of concepts we are in danger of losing altogether: consciousness, attention, love, truth, the Good, etc. The loss of these concepts would not merely represent the loss of a way of describing the world; it would represent the loss of a way of being in the world. Murdoch's concern about the potential loss of this way of being is a *moral* concern. As we have already seen, she thinks that a morality of axioms or duties detached from the concepts of vision and loving attention would carry distinctive moral dangers. In reintroducing these concepts, Murdoch is aiming to give us the resources to avoid such dangers.

Force Fields

I think that we are now in a position to return to *MGM* to reassess Murdoch's account of the relation between axioms, duties, and Eros. I suggested above that if we take Murdoch to be committed to foundationalism, her theory is likely to appear unsatisfyingly incomplete. If we understand her in the way that she understands herself, however—i.e. as a descriptivist—then her willingness to accommodate a certain degree of 'awkwardness' in the picture makes perfect sense. If there is a tension in moral life between different modes of moral being, then her job is simply to describe this tension as accurately as possible in order to help us to confront it when it arises. The specific metaphor that Murdoch uses to describe the tensions between different modes of moral being— the 'field of force'—is worth dwelling on. It is borrowed from Theodor Adorno, a debt that Murdoch acknowledges in the course of a relatively lengthy discussion of his work in chapter 12. As Martin Jay writes in his book *Force Fields*, Adorno uses the force field metaphor 'to suggest a nontotalized juxtaposition of changing elements, a dynamic interplay of attractions and aversions, without a generative first principle, common denominator, or inherent essence' (Jay 1993, 2). The first appearance of the phrase in *MGM* comes in a paragraph in chapter 10 that begins with another metaphor that Murdoch uses more than once in the book:

> Simone Weil uses an image of the human situation as being like that of
> a mountain walker who is aware of what is very distant, what is less dis-
> tant, what is near, as well as of the uneven ground beneath her feet. Our
> confused conscious being is both here and elsewhere, living at different
> levels and in different modes of cognition. We are 'distracted' creatures,
> extended, layered, pulled apart. (*MGM*, 296)

I think that it is illuminating to read this passage in the light of our
earlier discussion of the constitutive role of metaphor in language and
thought. In 'Metaphysics and ethics' and 'Vision and choice in morality',
Murdoch sets up different positions against each other—the 'Liberal
view' and the 'Natural Law view'—in order to bring out the contrast
between different sets of moral concepts. As she is well aware, however,
no actual human being is ever completely identified with a single set
of moral concepts. Although she often makes use of stylised characters
('Kantian man', etc.) in her work, Murdoch makes it clear that real individuals are capable of thinking in terms of multiple different pictures or
metaphors at different times. In 'Vision and choice' she notes that, 'there
are fundamentally different moral pictures which different individuals
use *or which the same individual may use at different times*' (Murdoch
1999, 97, my emphasis). What she is trying to bring out in chapter 17 is
that each of us is not only capable of thinking in terms of axioms, duties,
and Eros; our experience itself is partly *constituted* by these concepts. We
are capable of feeling the pull of duty or the weight of political commitments and the tension between these different modes. When Murdoch
describes us as 'distracted creatures, extended, layered, pulled apart', she
is trying to describe what it is like to live within a set of different pictures
and metaphors that are internally divided against each other.

The force field metaphor, then, is intended to give us a way of doing
justice to the tensions between different modes of moral being that
characterise our lived moral experience. These tensions, however, are
only one half of the picture. In chapter 17, Murdoch acknowledges that
although it may not be possible to reduce moral life to a single principle,
there is nevertheless a kind of unity to it:

> When assessing others and ourselves, we may discriminate between differ-
> ent 'aspects'. But a human being is a whole entity, there is also something
> essentially one-making about morals, and we may seek to exonerate or
> accuse on the basis of a seen or felt unity. ... The image of good here takes
> the place of God in its connection with a whole being. (*MGM*, 492)

It is tempting in reading this passage to think that Murdoch must be committing herself to a kind of foundationalism after all. Surely there is a single principle upon which morality may be seen to depend—i.e. the principle of the Good?[10] Although an analysis of Murdoch's account of the Good would take us well beyond the scope of this chapter, I think that it is important to see why Murdoch does not take it to play the role of a foundational principle. In fact, I think that for Murdoch the Good is not a *principle* at all. It is encountered in and through our experience, in our intuitions of a 'seen or felt unity' underlying the tensions and conflicts between different modes of moral being. This unity is transcendent, however, in the sense that it cannot be captured in any single philosophical principle or concept. It is in a sense the inspiration for all of our moral principles and concepts, but for precisely that reason it cannot be brought fully within any of our conceptual schemes. To put the point in another way: the Good is responsible for a sense of *lived* unity that can never adequately be translated into a *theoretical* unity.

Understood in this way, the deepest tension in Murdoch's 'field of force' is not the tension between the four different modes of moral being; it is the tension between 'the imperfect soul and the magnetic perfection which is conceived of as lying beyond it' (Murdoch 1999, 384). This, of course, is where Murdoch's Platonism comes to the fore. At the end of chapter 17, she returns to Plato's *Phaedrus*:

> The myth in the *Phaedrus* tells us that every human soul has seen, in their pure being, the Forms (Ideas) as justice, temperance, beauty, and all the great moral qualities which we 'hold in honour', when dwelling with the gods in a previous existence; and when on Earth we are moved toward what is good it is by a faint memory of those pure things, simple and calm and blessed, which we saw then in a pure light, being pure ourselves. This seems to me an excellent image of our apprehension of morality and goodness. (*MGM*, 497)

What Murdoch does not mention (or at least, not here) is that in the *Phaedrus* myth the sight of beauty is initially a source of pain and irritation as the lover's wings begin to sprout again from their stumps. This part of the myth seems to be an excellent image of what it is like to experience the field of force between axioms, duties, and Eros. We are 'distracted creatures, extended, layered, pulled apart'. Our lives are illuminated by a sense of unity that we find ourselves unable fully to express in thought and language. While we still retain our human form, philosophy cannot resolve these tensions for us, but it can describe them in a way that helps us re-orient ourselves towards the good that lies beyond description.

NOTES

1. Maria Antonaccio's *Picturing the Human* (2000) is probably still the best and most comprehensive attempt to undertake this task, although Antonaccio's interpretation of Murdoch as a 'reflexive realist' has recently come under criticism (Robjant 2011).
2. Some interpreters have attempted to read Murdoch as a kind of Kantian (Velleman 1999). For criticism of this approach, see Millgram (2004) and Hopwood (2018).
3. See Nussbaum (1999), Brewer (2011), and Banicki (2017) for discussion of Murdoch's relation to the category of 'virtue ethics'.
4. Denham (2001) is a good example of this line of interpretation. The particularist reading is criticised in Hopwood (2017) and also discussed in Millgram (2005) and Driver (2012).
5. See McDowell (1979, 1995) for classic statements of this position.
6. In a recent article, Nora Hämäläinen (2018) argues for a similar reading of Murdoch's approach. See also Hämäläinen (2016).
7. In contrasting descriptivism with foundationalism, I do not mean to suggest that these two approaches exhaust all the methodological options open to moral philosophers. One might, for example, adopt a kind of theoretical pluralism grounded in multiple different 'points of origin'. (Martha Nussbaum [2000] might be read as proposing such a methodology.) Although I do not have the space to explore this issue in any depth here, the main difference between theoretical pluralism and the kind of descriptivism I want to attribute to Murdoch is that the theoretical pluralist retains the aspiration to 'pin down the exact relations between the different registers of moral thought', as Nora Hämäläinen has helpfully put it to me. As I hope to show, Murdoch's descriptivism does not seek to achieve (and indeed, might be seen as actively trying to avoid) this kind of systematic unity. See chapter 4 of Hämäläinen (2016) for a helpful discussion of Nussbaum's relationship to foundationalism.
8. See Hämäläinen's chapter on 'Void' in this volume.
9. I am grateful to Nora Hämäläinen for pressing me to clarify this point.
10. This, I think, is Clarke's way of reading her.

References

Antonaccio, M. 2000. *Picturing the human: The moral thought of Iris Murdoch.* Oxford: Oxford University Press.

Arendt, H. 2006. *Eichmann in Jerusalem: A report on the banality of evil.* New York: Penguin Classics.

Banicki, K. 2017. Iris Murdoch and the varieties of virtue ethics. In *Varieties of virtue ethics,* ed. David Carr, James Arthur, and Kristján Kristjánsson, 89–104. London: Palgrave Macmillan.

Brewer, T. 2011. *The retrieval of ethics.* Oxford: Oxford University Press.

Clarke, B. 2012. Iris Murdoch and the prospects for critical moral perception. In *Iris Murdoch, philosopher,* ed. Justin Broackes, 227–254. Oxford: Oxford University Press.

Denham, A.E. 2001. Envisioning the Good: Iris Murdoch's moral psychology. *Modern Fiction Studies* 47 (3): 602–629.

Driver, J. 2012. 'For every foot its own shoe': Method and moral theory in the philosophy of Iris Murdoch. In *Iris Murdoch, philosopher,* ed. Justin Broackes, 275–292. Oxford: Oxford University Press.

Hämäläinen, N. 2016. *Descriptive ethics: What does moral philosophy know about morality?* New York: Palgrave Macmillan.

Hämäläinen, N. 2018. Iris Murdoch and the descriptive aspect of moral philosophy. *Iris Murdoch Review* 9: 23–30.

Hopwood, M. 2017. Murdoch, moral concepts, and the universalizability of moral reasons. *Philosophical Papers* 46 (2): 245–271.

Hopwood, M. 2018. 'The extremely difficult realization that something other than oneself is real': Iris Murdoch on love and moral agency. *European Journal of Philosophy* 26 (1): 477–501.

Jay, Martin. 1993. *Force fields: Between intellectual history and cultural critique.* New York: Routledge.

McDowell, J. 1979. Virtue and reason. *The Monist* 62 (3): 331–350.

McDowell, J. 1995. Eudaimonism and realism in Aristotle's Ethics. In *Aristotle and moral realism,* ed. Robert Heinaman, 201–218. Boulder, CO: Westview Press.

Millgram, E. 2004. Kantian crystallization. *Ethics* 114 (3): 511–513.

Millgram, E. 2005. Murdoch, practical reasoning, and particularism. In *Ethics done right: Practical reasoning as a foundation for moral theory.* Cambridge: Cambridge University Press.

Murdoch, I. 1993. *Metaphysics as a guide to morals* (Abbreviated *MGM*). New York: Viking.

Murdoch, I. 1999. *Existentialists and mystics: Writings on philosophy and literature.* New York: Penguin Books.

Nussbaum, M. 1999. Virtue ethics: A misleading category? *Journal of Ethics* 3 (3): 163–201.

Nussbaum, M. 2000. Why practice needs ethical theory: Particularism, principle, and bad behavior. In *Moral particularism*, ed. Brad Hooker and Margaret Olivia Little, 227–255. Oxford: Oxford University Press.

Robjant, D. 2011. As a Buddhist Christian: The misappropriation of Iris Murdoch. *Heythrop Journal* 52 (6): 993–1008.

Velleman, J.D. 1999. Love as a moral emotion. *Ethics* 109 (2): 338–374.

Zagzebski, L. 2017. *Exemplarist moral theory*. New York: Oxford University Press.

CHAPTER 17

Which Void? (*MGM* Chapter 18)

Nora Hämäläinen

THE NEED FOR VOID

Readers of *Metaphysics as a Guide to Morals* (hereafter *MGM*) often tend to go straight for the chapters and topics that interest them and bother less with the book as a whole.[1] This at least is what I did initially. After having read it through, with poor concentration, not really knowing what I was confronted with, I went for the passages that I had earmarked, treating them as aphoristic evidence of whatever view I was attempting to attribute to Murdoch. Something like this is perhaps often unavoidable, given the plurality of topics in the book.

There is, however a frame to the book, constituted by the first and two last substantial Chapters (17 and 18),[2] which is necessary to appreciate if one wants to understand the nature and role of the chapter on void. The first chapter sets the agenda: to speak about the predicament of thinking in our time, of our moral and metaphysical present, its guiding metaphors, its emotional cadences, and especially its take on the images of *unity and disunity* that guide so much of thinking. The chapters on 'Axioms, duties and Eros', and 'Void' order and qualify what has been said in the book. Murdoch has in much of the book explored a take on moral experience that is distinctly unifying: that of our longing

N. Hämäläinen (✉)
University of Pardubice, Pardubice, Czech Republic

© The Author(s) 2019
N. Hämäläinen and G. Dooley (eds.),
Reading Iris Murdoch's Metaphysics as a Guide to Morals,
https://doi.org/10.1007/978-3-030-18967-9_17

for and attempts at ascendance towards what is good. We could perhaps think of this as a secular theology. But she does not want to leave the reader with the impression that unification is her last word. Our moral life does not fit into any one unifying vocabulary or style of thinking, and no improvement can be hoped for from a procedure which seeks illumination through reduction.

Axioms, duties and Eros are her names for three different but equally important ways of approaching ethical issues: a political domain of axioms, a personal (and interpersonal) domain of duties, and a perfectionist ethics of Eros. These are not alternative theories, but rather different conceptualisations and vocabularies that are equally available to us and at play in different areas of our moral lives. The tripartition should be seen as a heuristic one: there are no watertight boundaries between these, considerations pertaining to these three dimensions often intermingle in our moral thinking.

The chapter on void comes as a postscript, a tail, an *aber* to that disunifying chapter. It is presented by Murdoch as a fourth dimension to be added to the three previous ones, but she also emphasises that it is different, a 'tract of experience' rather than a dimension of moral thought. This manner of linking void to the other three and yet giving it a chapter of its own indicates two different things. On the one hand she wants to emphasise that the tripartite list of dimensions of moral thought is not meant to be complete: there are indeed aspects of moral thought that escape these categories, and we should want to talk about those too. Maybe more dimensions need to be added? On the other hand, the function of void is not here primarily to extend the taxonomy, but to check misleading interpretations of her philosophy of Eros.

She puts words in the mouth of an imaginary opponent to formulate a specific risk with her morality of Eros and spiritual ascent: 'Your view of spiritual refreshment as everywhere available is ridiculously optimistic, even sentimental. It seems to neglect how miserable we are, and also how wicked we are' (*MGM*, 498). It may seem curious to think of the ethics of Eros as particularly optimistic, the way the imaginary opponent does. Hasn't Murdoch emphasised how difficult it is to do good, to see clearly, to purify one's vision of selfish fantasies? Isn't this a substantially less cheerful morality than the standard idea of morality as doing the right thing in circumscribed moral situations and then minding your own business the rest of the time?

The optimism that the imaginary opponent points out lies not so much in the idea that an ethics of Eros would be easy to live by, but in the promise of a guiding light in human life, a good or a God, that structures our experience as meaningful and directed. No matter how difficult the ascent, we can always start to climb, there is always a direction that will come clear to us if we attend properly, if we wait. But this isn't quite true. The *always* here involves a lazy oversight. There are extraordinary places in human life where the sun of the good does not shine, where we are beaten into indifference through severe suffering, where we are metaphorically forsaken by God. Void, in Murdoch's vocabulary, becomes the name for the 'black misery' and 'wickedness' that may seem to make the idea of moral ascent a romantic fantasy.

Thus, where the penultimate chapter is a critique of the idea that she would want to present an all-encompassing ethics of Eros, for all areas of life, the last chapter is a critique of the idea that the light of the good would always be available to us. The fact that both mistaken ideas have been attributed to Murdoch by very capable scholars shows that both of these chapters were necessary.[3] The same fact indicates, however, that she did perhaps not quite succeed in articulating the importance of these themes at the end of the book.

THE STRUCTURE OF THE CHAPTER

The chapter on void, like many other chapters of the book, is far from a model case of pedagogical structuring. But there is much to learn from the actual sequence of thought in it.

It begins with Murdoch introducing an experiential region of 'despair' or 'affliction' that moral philosophy needs to take into account. Her expressions here are very tentative, 'might seem to have been left out', 'might be thought of', indicating that she is unsure about something or saying only what someone else might say.

> It might be thought of as an opposing companion piece to happiness. It might also, in a different way, be placed in opposition to 'transcendence', a word that I have used to mean a good 'going beyond' one's egoistic self, as in the Platonic pilgrimage or innumerable ordinary experiences. What I refer to here is something extreme: the pain, and the evil, which occasion conditions of desolation such as many or most human beings have met with. (*MGM*, 498)

The indirectness here is, however, not due to a desire to distance herself from the ideas she is presenting. It is rather that she does not quite know which words or images she should use to assemble the topic or area of concern. We could also say that as an experienced writer she achieves a specific kind of precision by candidly confessing her difficulties.

Then she assumes the voice of someone deeply concerned by the state of the world: it is a terrible thing to be human, there is so much suffering and 'even in "sheltered" lives there is black misery, bereavement, remorse, frustrated talent, loneliness, humiliation, depression, secret woe' (*MGM*, 498–499). In such a situation, shouldn't one 'think statistically', bring relief to the greatest possible number, instead of talking about individuals and spiritual sources?

The imagined opponent here both is and is not Murdoch herself: in the voice of a progressive, reform-oriented utilitarian (who obviously is someone else), she formulates worries that she finds perfectly valid, at least *as worries*. Then she recommences in a voice that is completely her own. Having thus tuned into the topic she wants to talk about, she points at the particular difficulty of bringing it properly into view. 'It is not easy to discuss such a matter or take it as a single subject' (*MGM*, 499).

Our difficulties with this area are not due to any simple negligence of it as a philosophically interesting one. The problem is more fundamental: it is difficult for people to access this region of thought without distorting it. When people suffer severely, when they are in the void, they cannot do philosophy or art, and when and if they recover they are to a certain extent protected by forgetfulness. Art often romanticises despair. 'Christ on the cross is an image so familiar and beautified that we have difficulty in connecting it with real awful human suffering' (*MGM*, 499). It is, in Murdoch's view difficult to find true pain in art, although there are a few exceptions: Greek tragedy and poetry, some great novels.

Philosophers, too, have relatively little to say about it, although their reasons may be somewhat different. 'Philosophers, even while consigning whole areas of human existence to blindness and suffering, do not feel moved to exhibit distress' (*MGM*, 499). That is, while acknowledging the reality of suffering, philosophers are unlikely to express it, explore it, make it vivid. This is due to the human difficulties that they share with artists (forgetfulness etc.), but also because they do not see it as part of their job. The 'existentialist tradition' has done its share to correct this, but Murdoch sees something of an aestheticising of despair in both Kierkegaard and Sartre. Simone Weil is mentioned as a 'fine writer on the subject'. Then Murdoch notes that 'perhaps art does it best after all' (*MGM*, 499–500).

The charge is that most philosophers and artists do not quite know suffering, affliction, void. Yet they should at least try to know it better, because without a grasp of this region of experience our understanding of morality is severely limited. Murdoch doesn't purport to know it any better and is consciously tentative. She uses the remaining pages to hover over the question of what kinds of suffering there may be, and to what extent they can be of moral use.

First, she considers the idea of suffering as a form of education: the idea that suffering of guilt and remorse can purify and bring the wrong-doer closer to god. Then she considers the pain of bereavement, mixed or unmixed with feelings of guilt. In all such cases human beings mostly seem capable of recovering: '"nature" reasserts itself' (MGM, 500). There are worse things: 'The more terrible pictures are of solitary prisoners with no term of release.' In such a situation even religious faith may fade away and 'the idea of death and non-being are made real' (*MGM*, 501).

Then she goes back to the question of learning. Shouldn't the emptiness of severe suffering be used as a *memento mori*? When we see that 'anyone can be destroyed', that all can be taken from us, even our personality: is there not a spiritual possibility in this? She notes that 'Buddhism teaches the unreality of the world of appearance' and St John of the Cross talks about the dark night and the 'abyss of faith into which one *falls*'. She clearly sees the charm in these ideas, yet doesn't quite buy into the idea of suffering as something to be used for enlightenment. 'Yes, it is possible, but very often it is just too difficult, to "learn" from deep despair' (*MGM*, 501–502). This is the voice of ordinary, sanguine, compassionate Murdoch, cautious of spiritual excess. She does not spell it out, but she seems to think that those who claim that we should use our despair for our moral edification do not quite know what real despair is.

Then she turns to Simone Weil, and introduces her concept of *malheur*, which she translates as 'affliction', noting that Weil means something more than ordinary unhappiness or sorrow. She provides three quotes from Weil's notebooks, talking about three experiences of suffering: bereavement, the inability to forgive, and the experience of painful thought felt as a burn. Elaborating on these, Murdoch emphasises that we must not, when experiencing such things, deflect from the pain and fill the void with fantasies of 'bouncing back'. 'Void makes loss a reality. Do not think about righting the balance, but live close to the painful reality and try to relate it to what is good. What is needed here, and is so difficult to achieve, a new orientation of our desires, a re-education of our instinctive feelings' (*MGM*, 503).

It is not easy to tell whether Murdoch is speaking in her own voice or if she is recounting the perspective of Weil. The use of 'fantasy' here does not have a counterpart in Weil. But in the next paragraph she describes what she has just said as 'a partly metaphorical description of *malheur*' using the French word rather than the translation that she has just provided. So, where are we?

Murdoch's style of moving between different voices and perspectives evokes literary free indirect discourse. She is, herself, *in* all the voices because she has made them, out of the thought stuff that is in circulation: things we are expected to or feel inclined to take seriously. But she is not equally in agreement with all of them, as we saw with the utilitarian voice above. With Weil the relation is to some extent unclear, because she has borrowed so much from her, and is so impressed.

In the last long paragraph, she talks about ways out of affliction, looking at the matter from different angles. Friends can help, starting a new life, a moral or spiritual effort, love, some 'pure or innocent thing which could attract love or revive hope'. 'The inhibition of unworthy fantasies is perhaps the most accessible discipline' (*MGM*, 503). She suggests that there might be an element of this kind of discipline in our day to day lives and relations to other people. And here we may be surprised to find a void that isn't the negative counterpart of Eros after all. It was supposed to be the pit into which we fall in great suffering, when we have lost our natural striving for whatever we find good, when the world has lost its allure. But this place outside the Erotic striving is now strangely incorporated in Murdoch's ethics of Eros in the very last paragraph. She notes that 'we have (gravity, necessity) a natural impulse to derealise our world and surround ourselves with fantasy. Simply stopping this … is progress. Equally in the more obscure labyrinths of personal relations it may be necessary to make the move which makes the void appear' (*MGM*, 503).

This last paragraph is so 'typical Murdoch' that we may not notice how odd it is. It seems that she is just returning to her safe bravura, talking about the overcoming of selfish fantasy. But we need to think about this more carefully. After having shrugged off the idea of void (severe affliction?) as a path to edification, she makes a small place for a necessary void (painful/difficult emptiness?) in the middle of everyday activities and relations. It turns out that void might be a central component of Erotic ascent and edification after all. But which void?

Is she aware of what happens here? If she is, why didn't she spell it out more clearly? The chapter seems unfinished: It says interesting things, but probably the wrong things to pin down what she thinks of the importance of void. Maybe the work was completed before she quite knew what to say. Nevertheless, I will try out the possibility that the strangeness of this ending is due to a certain lack of transparency in her relationship to Weil. There is a systematic metaphysical difference that she doesn't spell out, perhaps because she does not see it clearly. Yet it causes the two aspects of void borrowed from Weil's thought to fall apart in her own.

MURDOCH AND WEIL

Murdoch's discovery of Weil in the 1950s was a turning point in her philosophical thought.[4] At the time of discovering Weil's work, Murdoch was growing weary of the thin conception of moral life and consciousness in Sartre's work, which in many other respects a few years earlier had greatly impressed her. In Weil she found several ideas that would provide a basis for her new orientation in moral thought. One of them was Weil's non-dualist and moral reading of Plato. In this line of reading, Plato's central concerns are not to be understood in purely epistemological and metaphysical terms, and he does not postulate a transcendent world beyond this one. He is rather interpreted as a thinker concerned with the moral task of accurately seeing the common world that is right in front of him. He also provides, through his notion of Eros, a dynamic picture of our strivings towards the good, which places love at the centre of the moral life. Another theme that Murdoch picked up is the Weilian notion of 'attention', with its emphasis on the active, attentive, self-forgetful waiting, which is required in order to overcome selfish and distorted conceptions of other people and social situations (Larson 2009, 2014; Conradi 2001).

Focusing on these influences, it may seem as if Murdoch took the whole of her moral philosophy from Weil, adding little to it. As Kate Larson (2009) observes, one of Murdoch's critical contrasts with Weil has to do with the role of the imagination. Weil has little regard for the imagination, seeing it mainly as a source of projections and an obstacle to accurate vision. Murdoch in her turn, as we know, gives great importance to our imaginative capacities in moral life. Hence the distinction between perceptive imagination and selfish fantasy, by which she seeks to save what she finds valuable in the imagination, while acknowledging what she thinks of as sound caution on the part of both Plato and Weil.

A second central point of disagreement is the role and nature of Eros. Where Weil wants to see our erotic energy, our desire, purified from selfish and earthly concerns, and turned towards God, Murdoch persists in the belief that personal, physical and romantic love participate in the good, and are great teachers of goodness. For Weil, as Larson puts it, 'there is to be no touching, no fantasy, no projections' (Larson 2009, 154). Personal love of the kind that requires the lover's company and presence, is represented as devouring the beloved. Self-negation and purification of love from the selfish component is, on the other hand, seen as a lever, which lifts the lover to a higher spiritual level. Murdoch, to the contrary, sees much of value in personal and erotic relationships, and distrusts them mainly in their potential for excess and self-indulgence.

In these points of disagreement, we find intimations of a fundamental difference between Weil and Murdoch, which, though duly noted, is not fully appreciated by Larson. What seems to me left out in her account is the disturbing sternness and strangeness of some of Weil's thought. As Murdoch puts it in her review of the English translation of Weil's notebooks in 1956, 'The personality which emerges from these writings is not always attractive, but it compels respect. She is sometimes unbalanced and scarcely accurate' (Murdoch 1997, 160).

Unless we pay proper heed to this dissonance between them, we run the risk of domesticating Weil into a context of secular moral philosophy where she does not quite fit. A possible consequence is that Murdoch's contribution stands out as less original than it is, just a pale copy of Weil's central ideas. Another potential risk is that a reader who experiences a rebarbative quality in Weil's writings will be more likely to project her spiritual 'extremism' on Murdoch.

One reader of the latter kind is Sabina Lovibond (2011), who has argued that Murdoch, under the influence of Weil, developed a philosophy which elevates feminine masochistic forms of self-denigration, and thus is deeply anti-feminist and anti-egalitarian. This reading is based, among other things, on a certain way of understanding the self-forgetfulness of 'attention' in contrast to the self-assertiveness that is an essential part of social movements and social critique. Murdoch's image of the self-forgetful aunt is on this reading a dubious moral ideal, since it seems to give consent to social oppression and fundamental hierarchy. I have criticised this reading elsewhere (Hämäläinen 2015) and it seems to me that the negative assessment could in part have been avoided if the contrasts between Weil and Murdoch were better understood.

THE CONCEPT OF VOID

The concept of void is a central place where the difference between Murdoch and Weil can be perceived. Weil's discussion of void is the product of a metaphorical rendering of a human being's spiritual life. In this picture, the self, with its desires and imaginings, fills the whole space it can enter, like a gas. We must struggle against this tendency, we must not fill the void. This is excruciatingly painful because it goes against our natural impulse, but only through the void can divine grace enter our lives. Through suffering the void, we achieve detachment and are able to reach a higher spiritual level. 'A time has to be gone through without any reward, natural or supernatural' (Weil 2002, 11).

In this metaphorical metaphysics of self, suffering gains a positive valence, not perhaps of means to an end, but as an *indispensable passage*. In an explication that recalls the book of Job, Weil sings the praise of affliction.

> Affliction in itself is not enough for the attainment of total detachment. Unconsoled affliction is necessary. There must be no consolation—no apparent consolation. Ineffable consolation then comes down.
>
> To forgive debts. To accept the past without asking for future compensation. To stop time at the present instant. This is also the acceptance of death.
>
> 'He emptied himself of his divinity.' To empty ourselves of the world. To take the form of a slave. To reduce ourselves to the point we occupy in space and time—that is, to nothing.
>
> To strip ourselves of the imaginary royalty of the world. Absolute solitude. Then we possess the truth of the world. (Weil 2002, 12)

A similar drive to nothingness is present in Weil's reflections on Zen. In *MGM* Murdoch quotes Weil who writes that: 'The primitive Zen method seems to consist of a gratuitous search of such intensity that it takes the place of all attachments. But, because it is gratuitous, it cannot become an object of attachment except in so far as it is actively pursued, and the activity involved in this fruitless search becomes exhausted. When exhaustion point has been almost reached, some shock or other brings about detachment' (*MGM*, 247).

Murdoch comments that: 'The imageless austerity of Zen is impressive and attractive. It represents to us "the real thing", what it is like to be stripped of the ego, and how difficult this is. (Plato's *distance* from the sun.)' She notes approvingly that Weil 'felt a natural affinity with this "extremism" which indeed she practiced in her own life' (*MGM*, 247). But such religious 'extremism', a spiritual striving to self-effacement, does not follow into Murdoch's own philosophical account.

In the theme of void, we see the merging of eastern influences with Christianity, distinctive of Weil's work. Murdoch finds this combination attractive, for a variety of reasons that have little to do with her supposed love for the ascetic extreme. Anscombe, to whom *MGM* is dedicated, addressed the disappearance of the Christian moral framework and the necessity of formulating a viable moral psychology and philosophy of action. In a sense, Murdoch finds all of these missing things in Weil: 'we are presented with a psychology whose sources are in Plato, in Eastern Philosophy, and in the disciplines of Christian mysticism, and yet which bears upon contemporary problems of faith and action' (Murdoch 1997, 158).

The account is, much to Murdoch's taste, profoundly metaphorical and 'platonic', as she summarises it in her distinctive style:

> The soul is composed of parts, and justice, and also faith, consist in each part performing its own role. 'The baser parts of myself should love God, but not too much. It would not be God.' We do not know what we are – (the lesson of psychoanalysis). Until we become good we are at the mercy of mechanical forces, of which 'gravity' is the general image. (Murdoch 1997, 158)

This account of the human condition is defined by 'gravity', a force that pulls us down to act upon and perceive with the 'lower parts of the soul'. This is what we need to struggle against (as Murdoch's famous M struggles against jealousy and prejudice). Making sense of this struggle is difficult since we do not necessarily recognise the good, or see it as something to strive for, from the perspective of our lower impulses. This is why goodness is so difficult. 'We make advances by resisting the mechanism: but there is no reward. Energy and imagination are on the side of the low motives. To resist gravity is to suffer the void' (Murdoch 1997, 158).

For Weil void is the painful and necessary nothingness of *not striving to and desiring various good things*. She wants to empty our desire of its objects and preserve its energy. Thus, void is a transitory nothingness that we suffer from because we cannot see its point. As Murdoch puts it: 'During our apprenticeship good appears negative and empty' (Murdoch 1997, 158).

Here Murdoch is paraphrasing and explicating Weil, but when she later puts the idea of void to use in *MGM* it has, as we saw, assumed a different form and function. Murdoch's void here is, as mentioned, a 'tract of experience' quite like Weil's, but a different one. It is constituted by a sense of ordinary experiences of severe suffering, and loss of meaning and orientation. The importance of void at the end of *MGM* derives from the philosophical need for a well-rounded descriptive account of moral and spiritual life. These terrible things exist, they sometimes need to be endured, and they have implications for morality, for our conceptions of good and evil, for what kind of moral theory we can take seriously.

For Murdoch suffering, despair or nothingness do not take the role of a necessary means to spiritual ascent that they do for Weil. There is natural goodness, and we can learn through love, compassion, friendship, art and imagination. We need of course to practise our attention and learn to forget about ourselves. But only in certain situations do we need to 'endure the void' in Weil's painful manner: in grief, or when we need to let go of a loved one, or of a cherished ambition that has oriented our life this far, for example. In such cases it does matter how we proceed: whether we indulge ourselves with comforting fantasies or endure with composure, for example. Here Weil's reflections, as paraphrased by Murdoch, are helpful: 'Void makes loss a reality. Do not think about righting the balance, but live close to the painful reality and try to relate it to what is good' (*MGM*, 503).

But this is for Murdoch a recipe for the afflicted, not for everyone. In Murdoch's normative ethics of self-formation, the imperative of 'enduring the void' is checked by various other considerations and spiritual possibilities, which may render renunciation and suffering superfluous. The Weilian spiritual necessity of void is only comprehensible if we seek God. Her theology also motivates the link between deep suffering and the compulsory void to be observed in our relation to other people. They are two aspects of the same necessarily painful path to God. Their painfulness is in a sense defining rather than empirical. If it does not hurt, you are not doing the right thing.

For Murdoch the ordinary attention, the holding back that is characteristic of a good relation to people and situations, is not necessarily painful. Whether it is, is an empirical matter: it might come easily to some people. It is thus not comprehensible as a small token of affliction; it is not an aspect of the severe suffering of opening up for grace. This connection only makes sense within Weil's spiritual anthropology. For Murdoch it is something else, an *askesis*, a small moral exercise. Thus, the two meanings of void in the last paragraph of the chapter on void in *MGM* fall apart. Thinking 'with' Weil causes Murdoch to give a characterisation of void which does not really have a place in her own thought: a change of topic occurs. From the tract of experience which resists a reduction to the erotic ethics of spiritual ascent, she moves to the *askesis* of holding oneself back, which is internal to the ethics of Eros.

Thus, part of the difficulty with the chapter on Void is that Murdoch at the end, enticed by Weil, fails to stick to the topic: to keep affliction properly in view and explore its significance for moral life. This is a small thing and forgivable, but it may indicate that Murdoch is not the best guide to what she herself is doing with Weil's work, how it transforms in the absence of God and in the light of Murdoch's emphasis on the plurality of human experiences.

It may also have the consequence that the reader of the chapter fails to take seriously the idea of affliction/void as a place beyond the erotic order of ascent towards the Good. If void can be turned into a necessary aspect of erotic edification, then perhaps there is no valley of death in life? Perhaps the good can always be accessed if we just try hard enough? But Murdoch contradicts this clearly: there are places where trying doesn't help. This should be a check on our eagerness to embrace the potentially naïve optimism of Eros.

THE CHRISTIAN AND THE SECULAR REVISITED

One way to parse the contrast between Murdoch and Weil here would be to emphasise the fact that one is a secular and the other is a religious thinker. This is central, but it needs to be qualified. In an interview Cora Diamond notes that she, although deeply influenced by Murdoch, has avoided the religious stuff in her work. Diamond expresses her discomfort with this aspect by referring to Stanley Hauerwas who 'once remarked that the problem with Murdoch is not that she is not religious but that she is *too* religious, where "religious" is used in a very Barthian kind of way, as a term of criticism' (Bronzo 2013, 274).

Murdoch surely is more 'religious' in her work than most broadly analytic moral philosophers, but it is easy to exaggerate the religious aspect of her thinking, especially if one fails to appreciate the fundamental friction between her and Weil. For Murdoch 'god does not and cannot exist'. For her this also means that the possibility of Christian faith has been lost for us. Our challenge is to figure out how to save the moral insight that is stored in religious understanding, and to find new non-Christian or post-Christian ways of attending to our souls.

From Weil's point of view the alleged impossibility of faith is a mistake: faith is the central thing for her, not morality. But her idea of God is not in every respect too different from Murdoch's idea of perfection. For Weil God is a paradox, in him we love that which cannot exist.

> Nothing which exists is absolutely worthy of love.
> We must therefore love that which does not exist.
> This non-existent object of love is not a fiction, however, for our fictions cannot be any more worthy of love than we are ourselves, and we are not worthy of it. (Weil 2002, 110)

The difference thus is not that one believes in an otherworldly being and the other has realised that this faith is no longer tenable. Both conceptualise a necessary and at the same time impossible something, that orients our spiritual life, though under different names. The shape of their thought about god/good is similar: this is perhaps one of Murdoch's debts to Weil.

We should also not mistake Weil as elevating suffering to an end. Weil (like Nietzsche) emphasises that ascetic self-denial should never be an end in itself, but rather a means that is very carefully used.[5] As Weil observes, self-denial, when indiscriminately applied, will only make itself useless as a tool for any educative purpose (Weil 2002, 125). But the need for its application in her theology is so extensive that it is very difficult to accommodate it into a secular world view, without lapsing precisely into pointless masochism. The purpose of Weil's *askesis* is not connected to any ordinary sense of earthly human flourishing, but to the love of and striving towards God. This implies a different metaphysics of the soul, a different hierarchy of value.

In Murdoch's work, in contrast, the striving to selflessness, and the idea of a spiritual ascent, are meaningful precisely as parts of a distinctive conception of quite ordinary human flourishing. The significance of learning to attend without selfish concern, and to endure pain and the void, is directly connected to both one's own happiness and the happiness of others. It is one of the lifeboats by means of which we steer clear of quite ordinary misery, degradation and despair.[6]

NOTES

1. One notable exception is Stephen Mulhall's essay (1997), where he addresses the architecture of the book.
2. There is a Chapter 19 after these, which contains many memorable formulations, but it is intended as a summary and does not take up new substantial themes.
3. For the former view and a critique of it, see Bridget Clarke (2012) and Hopwood's chapter on Axioms, duties and Eros in this volume. For the latter view and a critique of it see Antonaccio (2012), Mulhall (2007), and Robjant (2013). Both Robjant and Hopwood share my reading of Murdoch as an 'earthy' philosopher, seeking to describe our complex lived experience and moral life.
4. In an attempt at dating Murdoch's encounter with Weil Peter Conradi notes that 'IM's copy, in French, of Weil's *The Need for Roots* bears the publication date 1949' (Conradi 2002, 633, Note 122).
5. Concerning Nietzsche, see his discussion on the philosophers' ascetism (in the 'Third essay: What do ascetic ideals mean?') in Nietzsche (1994, e.g. 84).
6. My thanks to Gillian Dooley and Niklas Forsberg for helpful comments on a previous draft of this paper.

REFERENCES

Antonaccio, M. 2012. *A philosophy to live by*. Oxford: Oxford University Press.

Bronzo, S., and Diamond, C. 2013. Philosophy in a realistic spirit: An interview. *Iride: Filosofia e discussione pubblica* 26 (2): 239–282.

Clarke, B. 2012. Iris Murdoch and the prospects for critical moral perception. In *Iris Murdoch: Philosopher*, ed. Justin Broackes, 227–253. Oxford: Oxford University Press.

Conradi, P. 2001. *The saint and the artist*. London: HarperCollins.

Conradi, P. 2002. *Iris Murdoch: A life*. London: HarperCollins.

Hämäläinen, N. 2015. Reduce ourselves to zero?: Sabina Lovibond, Iris Murdoch, and feminism. *Hypatia* 30 (4): 743–759.

Larson, K. 2009. *Everything important is to do with passion*. Dissertation, Uppsala University, Uppsala.

Larson, K. 2014. The most intimate bond: Metaxological thinking in Iris Murdoch and Simone Weil. In *Iris Murdoch connected: Critical essays on her fiction and philosophy*, ed. Mark Luprech, 153–168. Knoxville: University of Tennessee Press.

Lovibond, S. 2011. *Iris Murdoch, gender and philosophy*. London: Routledge.

Mulhall, S. 1997. Constructing a hall of reflection: Perfectionist edification in Iris Murdoch's *Metaphysics as a guide to morals*. *Philosophy* 72 (280): 219–239.

Mulhall, S. 2007. 'All the world must be "religious"': Iris Murdoch's ontological arguments. In *Iris Murdoch: A reassessment*, ed. Anne Rowe, 23–34. Houndmills, Basingstoke: Palgrave Macmillan.

Murdoch, I. 1992. *Metaphysics as a guide to morals* (Abbreviated *MGM*). London: Chatto & Windus.

Murdoch, I. 1997. *Existentialists and mystics*. London: Chatto & Windus.

Nietzsche, F. 1994. *On the genealogy of morality*. Cambridge: Cambridge University Press.

Robjant, D. 2013. Symposium on Iris Murdoch: How miserable we are, how wicked; into the 'Void' with Murdoch, Mulhall, and Antonaccio. *Heythrop Journal* 54: 999–1006.

Weil, S. 2002. *Gravity and Grace*. London: Routledge.

INDEX

N. Hämäläinen and G. Dooley (eds.), *Reading Iris Murdoch's Metaphysics
as a Guide to Morals*, https://doi.org/10.1007/978-3-030-18967-9

Printed in the USA
CPSIA information can be obtained
at www.ICGtesting.com
LVHW021114231023
761793LV00008B/683